Dedicated to the Memory
of My Son

YOSEFI
Who Fell in the Yom-Kippur War

THE CLAIM OF DISPOSSESSION

Jewish Land-Settlement and the Arabs

1878–1948

ARIEH L. AVNERI

Translated by the
Kfar-Blum Translation Group

Transaction Books
New Brunswick (USA) and London (UK)

Library of Congress Catalog Number: 84-40085
ISBN: 0-87855-964-7
Printed in the United States of America

The Yad Tabenkin Institute is the Research and Documentation Center of the United Kibbutz Movement in Ramat Efal, Israel. Its main activities are research, publishing, the organization of symposia, the study of history and current events, education, and archival work.

CONTENTS

PREFACE

Jewish agricultural settlement in the Land of Israel has been the primary practical expression of the idea of national rebirth and the aspiration to establish there a territorial, political and spiritual center for the Jewish people. The Zionist movement defined its political aims at the First Zionist Congress in careful and moderate language, mainly in order not to arouse the opposition of the Turkish regime. There was no fear of opposition on the part of the national Arab movement, even though there were early signs of its rise: Its activities were hardly noticeable in the repressive atmosphere of the Turkish Empire, and its influence was insignificant.

In the early days of settlement the conflicts between the Jewish settlers and their Arab neighbors assumed a purely local character. The national element in the opposition to Jewish land acquisition and settlement kept growing in significance, as the national-political aims of Zionism became more pronounced, and as the early buds of the Arab national movement kept developing.

After the Turkish Empire fell apart, with the assumption of the British Mandate over Palestine, the right of the Jewish people to establish its National Home in Palestine gained international recognition. At about the same time the Arab national movement in Palestine, at a Convention in 1920, established the Arab Executive as its political leadership, demanded the abrogation of the Balfour Declaration and the British Mandate and called for the establishment in Palestine of a political entity which would express the will of its present inhabitants, namely Arab rule. The struggle against Zionism and against the articles in the Mandate which recognized the Jewish claim to Palestine was conducted by the Arab leadership by political action, by attacks on Jewish settlements, sporadically by rebellions against British rule and by seeking the aid of the Arab states.

At the center of Arab activity, both political and by direct action, was the struggle against Jewish immigration (*Aliya*), land acquisitions and settlement. The main Arab claim was that the Jewish land acquisitions dispossessed the Arab fellah and tenant farmer of his land, that the new immigrants were flooding the country and that eventually the Arab population would get expelled from the country altogether. These claims were the subject of investigation committees appointed by the British Government and the basis for a policy which went counter to Britain's obligations toward the Zionist program.

The Arab political leadership rejected any solution that would not forbid outright all Jewish immigration and land acquisition. On the other hand the Zionist movement was not prepared to accept any compromise plan that would involve even partial restriction of immigration and land sale, since such a solution would in effect spell the doom of the Zionist endeavor. The United Nations decision on partition and the establishment of two states – a Jewish and an Arab one – was rejected by the Arabs. The war which the Arabs initiated toward the end of 1947 against the establishment of a Jewish State ended in headlong flight of over 600,000 Arabs. In the years following, the Arabs argued that the refugee problem arose directly out of the dispossession of the Palestinian Arabs from their lands. They claimed that the uprooting of one-half of the Arab population of the country was the inevitable consequence of a long process that began in the early days of the Zionist movement, which aimed at the dispossession of the Arabs and their ultimate expulsion.

The writers of the history of the Jewish-Arab conflict are faced with the problem how to relate the decisive years 1947–1949 to the tendencies and the events which preceded them: Is the refugee problem a direct continuation of a process of expropriation which began with the early Jewish settlement in the country? Was a basic aim of Zionism the removal of the Arab population? Was Zionism guilty of leading astray the Arabs, world opinion and its own followers, when it claimed that the Land of Israel was destined to be the home of the Jews who were returning to it *and* of the Arabs living there?

Many books have been written on the Arab-Jewish conflict and its hundred-year history. Most of them deal with the political issues, with analyzing the Arab and the Jewish political moves, and with offering political solutions. The aim of the present volume is to trace step by step the spread of Jewish settlement in the course of the seventy years until the rise of the State of Israel, and to describe how it affected the existing Arab community: What was the extent of land disputes? How widespread was the tenant farmer problem? What was the influence of Jewish immigration, land acquisition and settlement, including urban settlement, on the position of the Arab community as a whole? Did they bring about the destruction of the Arab economy and of the Arab social and cultural institutions? What was the condition of the Arab community after seventy years of Jewish settlement, i.e. in 1947–1949 – was it worse than before, or perhaps otherwise? These are the questions we will deal with and try to answer.

An examination of the Arab condition in the years of decision, 1947–1949, throws a backward light on the past aims and the policies of the Zionist movement in an attempt to answer the question: Did it aim at expropriating the Arabs, or did it seek to establish a base for the existence of the two peoples side by side? This examination also throws light on the motives of the Arabs in declaring war on the Partition plan – did they go to war out of desperation because they were on the brink of annihilation, or because they refused to forgo their rights over any part of the country?

★ ★ ★

My heartfelt thanks are due to Professor Gabriel Cohen, who accompanied my work with important suggestions and comments. I also wish to thank Professor Roberto Bacchi, Professor Joshua Ben-Arye, Professor Joshua Porath, Joshua Palmon, Zeev Zur, and Yosef Rabinowich, who read the manuscript, in whole or in part, and made valuable comments.

Likewise thanks are due to the workers of the Central Zionist Archives, of the Archives of the Jewish National Fund and of the Israel State Archive, who spared no effort in trying to help me in uncovering the pertinent documents. I was also helped by the workers of the "Beit Hashomer" Archive in the Zahal Museum at

Kefar Gil'adi, the "Beit Sturman" Archive at Ein-Harod, the Labor Archive in Tel-Aviv, the Syrkin Library at "Beit Liessin" in Tel-Aviv and various local archives.

I wish to thank the people who granted me interviews (they are listed under the sources), all of them well versed in the problems of land acquisition and settlement. These interviews helped me a great deal in understanding the historical background of the various periods.

I owe special thanks to the Tabenkin Institute, within whose framework and with whose assistance the book is being published. I wish to mention in appreciation and in sorrow the assistance and encouragement I received from the late Moshe Klieger, one of the founders of the Tabenkin Institute.

My thanks also to the Kibbutz Hameuhad Publishing House, and especially to the late Avital Dafna, who saw the book through the press and passed away in the course of this work.

Finally my thanks to my home kibbutz, Hagoshrim, which placed at my disposal all the time I needed to write the book.

A.L.A.

CHAPTER ONE

THE ARAB CLAIM OF 1300 YEARS OF UNINTERRUPTED POSSESSION

> "Is it in any way just, that the Arabs, who have
> lived on this land uninterruptedly for 1300 years,
> and whose lives are rooted in its soil – should be
> dispossessed by force, should be pushed aside, and
> should be blackmailed to enable the Zionist Jews
> to fashion a Jewish National Home on this land.
> That's the problem..."
> *(Jamal Husseini at the Round Table Conference,*
> *London, February 9, 1939)*

Palestine, the land which lies between three continents and borders on the desert, was throughout the ages an arena of conflict between empires and a magnet for invaders and nomads. After the nation of Israel lost its independence, there were many expeditions of conquest, each of which introduced a layer of new settlers into the country's population. The Arab conquest, too, brought new settlers, who imposed the religion of Islam and the Arab language on all the inhabitants.

Throughout history there are many instances of conquests which led, through a process of absorption and assimilation, to the formation of new national entities. Had the Arab conquest led to the formation of a crystallized Arab nation – no matter how small in number – it would have been difficult to contradict the claim of Arab historical continuity in Palestine. But such was not the case.

The few Arabs who lived in Palestine a hundred years ago, when Jewish settlement began, were a tiny remnant of a volatile population, which had been in constant flux, as a result of unending conflicts between local tribes and local despots. Malaria and disease had taken a heavy toll of the inhabitants. The numerous factors responsible for the dire state of the Arab community a century ago will be discussed in the course of this investigation. Social paroxysms, wars and destruction prevented the Arab population in

11

Palestine from striking root and from handing down a tradition of permanent settlement from generation to generation.

Since the breakdown of the Crusader Kingdom and the subsequent conquest by the Mamelukes, the population of Palestine kept dwindling and reached its nadir after the Black Plague. Western Palestine at that time had a total population of between 140,000 and 150,000: Moslems, Christians and Jews. After the Ottoman conquest, the authorities took a census for tax purposes, and tabulated 49,181 heads of families and single men liable to tax.

Professor Roberto Bacchi calculated that in the years 1553–1554 there were 205,000 Moslems, Christians and Jews in Palestine.[1] During the following 250 years the population growth was minimal. In 1800 the total population was 275,000, of whom 246,300 were Moslems and 21,800 Christians.[2]

In 1890 there were in Palestine 532,000 people: 431,800 Moslems, 57,400 Christians, and 42,900 Jews.[3]

The Christian population was not all Arab. Thus the Christian-Arab population at the time is estimated at 42,000,[4] and so the total Arab population was about 473,000. From this figure the number of Arabs in Palestine in 1880 can be easily calculated: If we take into account a natural increase in population of between 0.7% and 1% *per annum*, we find that in 1880, at the beginning of Jewish colonization, there were about 425,000 to 440,000 Arabs in Palestine. Of these, 40,000 to 45,000 were Bedouin nomads.

Egyptian Colonization

The population in Palestine underwent radical changes in the wake of two destructive wars that swept the country – Napoleon's campaign of 1799, and the invasion by the Egyptian army and the subsequent rule of Ibrahim Pasha between the years 1831–1840. The conquest did establish law and order in the country, but the war, the suppression of rebellions and the subsequent withdrawal caused many old inhabitants to flee and new elements to settle in the land.

As a result of the war, the military draft and heavy taxes imposed by the Government, many fellaheen and urban dwellers fled. In addition, the measures taen by the Government to prevent looting and robbery brought about the flight of many Bedouins. The frequent rebellions and their suppression were accompanied by considerable loss of life and flight of large numbers of inhabitants. It was in this period that the Great Earthquake of 1837 occurred, and in its path pestilence and hunger took their toll. On the other hand, there was a limited influx of some thousands of immigrants whom Ibrahim Pasha brought in to settle the empty stretches of the country. Before them, a goodly number of fellaheen had fled Egypt seeking to evade the military draft imposed by Ibrahim Pasha in preparation for the invasion and settled in Palestine. They sought sanctuary with the governor of Akko, Abdullah, who granted it readily. The French scholar, M. Sabry, whose sources were the archives in Cairo writes: "Abdullah, the Governor of Akko, encouraged the migration of fellaheen from Egypt and gave them shelter. Mohammed Ali, the ruler of Egypt, complained to the Porte (the Sultan), who replied that the immigrants were citizens of the Empire and were entitled to settle anywhere they pleased. In 1831, more than six thousand fellaheen crossed the Egyptian border, and Abdullah, in his bountiful mercy, refused to return them (to Egypt)."[5]

After he conquered Palestine, not only did Mohammed Ali refrain from sending back the draft evaders to Egypt, but he sent new settlers to consolidate his rule. The Egyptian settlers scattered to many urban and rural points, appropriated large tracts of land, and lent variety and numbers to the existing population. Some settled in the Hula Valley. They were the Ghawarna tribes, the most disdained and primitive of Bedouin tribes, who suffered greatly from the malaria endemic to the valley. The death rate among their children was so great that the total population diminished from generation to generation. They replenished their ranks by recruiting criminals and army deserters from time to time.[6] Another Bedouin tribe, Arab ez-Zubeid, (who, in the future, were to sell their lands to the settlers of Yessud-Hama'ala) also came from Egypt, either as refugees or with the encouragement of the Egyptian ruler. In one of the villages of the Hula Valley, Muftahira, the Egyptians established a permanent settlement.[7]

Tristram relates that the inhabitants of one of the villages in the Beit-Shean Valley "are Egyptian immigrants and they are grievously oppressed by the neighbouring Bedouin."[8] The Arab-Hinadi tribe came to the Jordan Valley, and after some years settled in the village of Delhamiya. The village Ubeidiya in the Jordan Valley was settled by Egyptians, as was Kafer-Miser,[9] in the vicinity of Kaukab el-Hawa. Many Egyptians also settled in Akko and its suburbs.[10]

Members of the Arab el-Ufi tribe settled in Wadi Hawarith. They were Egyptian slaves who had been brought by Ibrahim Pasha.[11] The Egyptian ruler also brought the Bedouin slave tribe Arab ed-Damair to the vicinity of Hadera. They settled in the nearby swamps.[12]

According to the British Palestine Exploration Fund regional map of Jaffa, most of the city was made up of Egyptian-populated districts. "Saknet el-Mussariya," "Saknet Abu Kebir," "Saknet Hammad" and "Saknet Abu Derwish" were all setled by Egyptians who had accompanied the conquering army.[13] Another district, "Saknet el-Abid," was settled by freed slaves. The Egyptians settled in the six villages of Fejja, Jaljuliya, Ummlebis, Sumeil, Sheikh-Muwanis and Salame situated on the outskirts of Jaffa, and drove away the indigenous population. A sheikh called Hammed el-Masri occupied a large tract of land by the Yarkon River.[14] Philip Baldensperger states that in 1893 the inhabitants of many villages in the southern part of the country, like Zarnuqa and Kubeiba, were of Egyptian origin; that they were unlike the other Arabs then resident in the country; that the fellaheen used to call them "Masserein"; and that a Palestinian Arab would never give his daughter in marriage to an Egyptian, and would rarely take to wife a woman of Egyptian stock.[15] The dwellers of the village Quttra in the southern part of the country (later the site of Gedera) were originally brought to Palestine from Libya.[16]

In a number of villages in Wadi 'Ara – 'Ara, 'Ar'ara and Kafer-Kara – and south of the triangle in the villages Kafer-Qasim, Taiyiba and Qalansawa, there are hundreds of families of Egyptian origin who accompanied the conquering forces of Ibrahim Pasha. According to the tradition among these people, their ancestors were the camel riders for the army of occupation and when the Khedive's troops left they remained and settled there.[17] Similarly, in the cities of Samaria and Judea there are hundreds of families which, to this day, are named Masri. The origin of all of them is traceable to those who left Egypt at the time of Ibrahim Pasha.[18]

The Egyptians acquired land in various ways. Jews in Haifa and Jerusalem later negotiated for land with Egyptian landowners – not always successfully.[19] Two thousand dunam of land in Kafer-Miser in Upper Galilee were purchased from the heirs of the Egyptian nobleman Shedid.[20]

Egyptian laborers emigrated or were brought to the country by different factors. Before the First World War they worked on the reclamation of the swamp-lands of Hadera. The engineer in charge of the reclamation project writes: "In view of the dearth of local laborers, capable of working in water and mud, I imported 150 Egyptians to do the work of digging. They participated in the laying of the railroad tracks from Jerusalem to Jaffa that a Belgian company executed, and thereafter remained in the country."[21] Many of these Egyptians settled in Hadera and (those who survived the malaria) found work in the citrus groves. Zvi Nadav relates: "In Hadera we worked together with about twenty Arabs, most of them blacks and Egyptians."[22]

The Egyptian laborers were skilled in road-building. In 1904, the Jewish Colonization Association (I.C.A.) built a road from Yavne'el to Kinneret to bypass the hostile village of Lubiya. The road was built by Jewish and Egyptian labor.[23]

The assimilation of the Egyptians with the indigenous Arab population was a drawn-out process. After his visit to Palestine in 1917, Philip Baldensperger relates that the existing population in Jaffa, though essentially Arab, contained at least twenty-five different nationalities, most of them Palestinian and Egyptian Arabs. The blacks, with Sheikh el-Abid as their leader, generally lived among the Egyptians, although they originated from countries just north of the equator. The black population was made up of former slaves who had fled their masters, or had been legally freed, or had come as pilgrims but could not return to their native lands. The Egyptians lived in separate areas called Saknat, and though

15

they had lived in the country for seventy years, they preserved their distinctive native dress.[24] Y. Shimoni writes: "The primary areas of settlement of the Egyptians are in the coastal plain in the south of the country, between Tulkarem and Gaza. The further south one goes, the greater the percentage of Egyptians among the Arab population, both in the villages and the towns. In all the villages in this area, one finds a district, or at the least a family, that is known as el-Musriya, Egyptian. Some villages were actually founded by Egyptian immigrants."[25]

Moslem Refugees Who Found Asylum

In the middle of the nineteenth century, when whole countries began slipping away from Ottoman rule and falling into the hands of Christian states, the Sultan gave asylum to Moslem refugees who fled their homelands for religious or political reasons. After the French conquest of Algeria in 1830, the Algerians rebelled under the leadership of Abd el-Kader el-Hassani. After a prolonged war the rebellion was put down. Abd el-Kader and many of his followers were captured and imprisoned. In 1856, the French permitted Abd el-Kader to leave Algeria, together with some followers. Some of them went to Syria and others to Palestine. The Algerian Arabs settled in several cities and founded about ten villages. These immigrants, who were called by the natives *Mugrabis* (Westerners), founded four villages in Lower Galilee – Shara, Ulam, Ma'ader and Kafer-Sabet. They also founded the village Husha, on the site of ancient Usha, near the present Ramat-Yohanan. They established the villages of Delata, 'Alma and Dishon in Upper Galilee, as well as Teleil and Husseiniya on the banks of Lake Hula. The elders of these villages continued to speak the Berber language up to the end of the nineteenth century.[26]

H.B. Tristram, the devoutly Christian British traveller-scholar, who in 1863/64 travelled up and down the Holy Land in the footsteps of Jesus, found himself at Mais, an Algerian village near Qedesh and he noted in his diary: it is "a colony of Algerian Arabs, refugees, who still wear the Algerian *burnous*, and build the

16

'gourbis' of Mount Atlas. They cordially responded to me when addressed in the patois of North Africa."[27]

Quite a number of Mugrabis settled in Safed, and probably also in Tiberias. We find these facts documented in the reports of the Palestine Exploration Fund. The Mugrabis insulted the members of the Fund delegation, even attacked them, and hindered their work. The delegation sought the intervention of the Emir Abd el-Kader who then resided in Syria. The Emir sent a letter of apology "for the behavior of my people in Safed and Tiberias."[28]

It would seem that the Mugrabis of Safed managed to preserve something of their indentity within the established population. A report by W.J. Masterman, an associate of the Palestine Exploration Fund, dated 1914, describes the Moslem population as being of mixed origin. One of the neighborhoods was called Hareth el-Karad, which denotes a population of Kurdish origin. There were also many families of Algerian origin.[29] In another part of his report Masterman comments that half the Moslem population of Safed were Mugrabis who had accompanied Abd el-Kader when he went into exile. Other Moslem Arabs were immigrants from Damascus, Bedouins from the Jordan Valley, and sundry village dwellers, all of whom had got to Safed, the commercial center of the region.

In the same report to the *Palestine Exploration Fund Quarterly, 1893,* Baldensperger describes the Mugrabis of Jaffa, who had migrated to the country over the years. They tended to live near the mosques and were employed as watchmen in the citrus groves and in the fields. Some established themselves permanently. Most of them had passed through Jaffa on their way to Mecca and some Mugrabis intermarried with the local Moslems, something that the Egyptians and blacks had not succeeded in doing. Asians from all over the world – Persians, Afghans, Hindus and Baluchis – were engaged in commerce.

Baldensperger also tells about North African Arabs in Ramle. There the North Africans lived under the close supervision of their leader and segregated themselves more than in any other place. Whether they were from Tripoli or Morocco, they were known as Mugrabis, and they spoke to one another in the Qebili dialect

17

whenever they did not want strangers to understand them.

In 1878, the Sultan, Abd el-Hamid took under his protection Circassian refugees who had fled the Christian-Russian rule in the Caucasus. Many settled in Trans-Jordan. West of the Jordan they settled in three villages: Kafer-Kamma, Sarona, and Reihaniya. Some Moslems from Bosnia also found refuge in Palestine and settled near Caesarea.[30]

Laurence Oliphant writes about one of the Turkoman tribes that pitched their black tents near a Circassian village. They were new immigrants who had arrived from the mountains of Iraq. They knew no language other than Turkish and had hoped that their fellow-tribesmen in the Sharon Plain would receive them. But a sad disappointment awaited them, for such was not the case, and so they had pitched their tents on the slopes of Mount Carmel.[31]

In the winter of 1908, a group of Arabs arrived in Jaffa from Yemen and settled there.[32] Like the Mugrabis, the Turkomans and the Egyptians before them, they assimilated over the years with the general Arab population.

Just as the Sultan offered asylum to Moslem refugees, so the Christian communities made an effort to help Christians who sought refuge from Moslem and Druse persecutions. On the initiative of Ludwig Schneller, some German Christians established an orphan asylum in Jerusalem to absorb the surviving victims of the murderous attacks on the Christian population in Deir el-Kamer and other places in Lebanon. As these children grew up, they were assimilated into the Arab community in Jerusalem.[33] A few refugee families from the Deir el-Kamer massacre sought safety with the Jews of Safed, who hid them from the Moslems. When the War of Independence was in its early stages in 1947, the elders of the small Christian community in Safed recalled their ancestors' plight, and tried to dissuade the Christian youths from joining in the attack on the Jewish Quarter.[34]

Factors in the Decline of the Arab Population

Despite the massive increase through immigration, the total Arab population in the nineteenth century increased only slightly. One of the chief causes for this slow growth lay in the incessant internal wars between the "Qais" villages and the "Yaman" villages, wars that extended over hundreds of years.

The old conflict between the "Qais" villages, composed of members of the northern tribes, and the "Yaman" villages, composed of members of the southern tribes, no longer had meaning in the nineteenth century. Its roots were in antagonisms harking back to the seventh century, the causes of which had been long forgotten. There was no certainty that the populations were really descended from the southern tribes and the northern tribes, but the hatred existed and fueled wars of conquest, expropriation of lands from weak neighbors, expulsion and even murder. In the Jerusalem area bloody wars were fought for many years between the combative sheikhs of Abu-Ghosh and their neighbors. Every so often a neighboring village would be destroyed, its inhabitants exiled and its lands appropriated.[35]

In Nablus and the surrounding area continuing battles were fought between two groups of tribes, led by the pro-Egyptian Abd el-Hadi and the pro-Turkish Tuqan. These battles involved tens of villages and each side sought the aid of Bedouin tribes from Trans-Jordan. Both sides suffered heavy losses in lives and property. The fellaheen of the Nablus area were especially noted for their cruelty.[36]

Ibrahim Pasha put an end to the internal wars. He gave tracts of land and Government jobs to those loyal to him while disarming and exiling his adversaries. But when his army was defeated, the exiles returned and the wars were renewed.[37] Many Bedouins took part in the fighting – about 5,000 on foot and 1,000 on horseback. The Turkish Army tried to intervene to repress internal strife, and in so doing it acted with great cruelty. In one of the battles the Governor of Jerusalem offered his troops a reward for every decapitated head brought to him. Stewart Macalister relates that at the end of the day's battle, a pile of 350 heads, and a large number of severed hands, ears and limbs were presented to the *Mutissarif* (Governor).[38] In another battle Qasim el-Ahmad, a Qais leader, is reported to have killed 295 Yaman fighting men.[39]

Ramallah and el-Bira belonged to the Qais. The inhabitants of these two towns were dissatisfied with the rule of the Qais sheikhs, and sought the protection of Abu Ghosh which belonged to the Yaman. More than a hundred soldiers were killed in a battle fought by the two sides.[40]

In 1853, as the British Consul James Finn was on his way from Nazareth to Jerusalem, he found himself stranded in the village of Huwara, which at the time was engaged in a battle with the neighboring villages of Quza and Beita. The outcome of the battle was seventeen dead, among them seven women.[41]

Until the Egyptian conquest in the years 1831–1840 there were 19 villages on Mount Carmel. Tristram states that seventeen of them were destroyed during the period of chaos that followed the downfall of Egyptian rule, and by 1863 there were only two Druse villages left, Isfiya and Daliyat el-Carmel.[42] According to Oliphant, who surveyed the region twenty years later, the Druse had founded eight villages, but because of the Egyptian conquest they were compelled to abandon six of them and to leave the mountain. Only two villages remained.[43]

The bloody wars between the villages continued for many years. There were instances when the defeated themselves destroyed their property, uprooted their vineyards and their olive groves, burned and destroyed anything they could not take with them, and went into exile. They left behind scorched earth.[44]

The internal wars had a harmful influence on the growth of population, on the cultivation of the land, and on the degree of rootedness of the fellaheen in their villages. Very often villages passed from hand to hand. There really was not much difference between the fellah who regarded his land as his property and the Bedouin who pitched his tent on it for a brief stay and then moved on to another plot of land.[45]

Concurrent with the internal wars between the villages, an ongoing war was being carried on against Bedouin tribes that had invaded cultivated tracts of land – a war that usually resulted in the abandonment of the area by the permanent residents, and its being taken over by the Bedouins.

H.B. Tristram describes several of these takeovers: "A few years ago the whole Ghor [Jordan Valley] was in the hands of the fellaheen, and much of it cultivated for corn. Now the whole of it is

20

in the hands of the Bedouin, who eschew all agriculture, excepting in a few spots cultivated here and there by their slaves; and with the Bedouin come lawlessness, and the uprooting of all Turkish authority. No government is now acknowledged on the east side; and unless the Porte [Central Government] acts with greater firmness and caution than is its wont, it will lose the last vestige of authority on the right bank also, and a wide strip of the most fertile land in all Palestine will be desolated and given up to the nomads. The same thing is now going on over the plain of Sharon, where, both in the north and south, land is going out of cultivation, and whole villages rapidly disappeared from the face of the earth. Since the year 1838, no less than twenty villages there have been thus erased from the map, and the stationary population extirpated."[46]

Tristram tells the story of the Beni Saher tribe of Bedouins: "When, in 1863, they encamped in the Ghor, just before their raid on the plain of Esdraelon [Jezreel], their tents, like the Midianites', covered the ground for miles, far as the eye could reach from the Mount of Beisan [Beit-Shean], and in a week there was not a green blade to be seen, where before the arrival of these locusts one stood knee-deep in the rank herbage."[47]

T. Drake, who toured the Jezreel Valley in 1870, relates that eight years before his tour the Transjordanian tribes Ghualla and 'Aneize invaded the Jordan Valley. They stole the cattle and crops of the fellaheen and prevented them from cultivating their lands. When Drake visited the region, only a fifth of the area was under cultivation.[48]

C.R. Conder reported in 1878 that the large Jezreel Valley was the refuge of the Bedouins whenever war or famine threatened their existence in Trans-Jordan. From time to time camels filled the valley as the sands fill the shore of the ocean. The Ghualla, the Saher and other large tribes invaded the Valley with their camels, as in ancient times, when the Midianites harassed the Children of Israel, and Gideon went forth to war against them in the Valley of Jezreel. In 1870, only a sixth of the lands were ploughed, because the valley was occupied by the "tents of Kedar." The Turkish authorities brought about a change in the situation when they armed their soldiers with Remington rifles. The Bedouins

21

disappeared miraculously. But, as was to be foreseen, when the governmental reins slackened the Bedouins invaded once again, and in 1877 their sheikh Faiz el-Saher once again ravaged the hapless fellaheen.[49]

H. Kitchener reinforces Conder's description. He reports that the Beni Saher tribe occupied the entire area between Tiberias and Beit-Shean. The Valley was filled with numerous flocks of grazing camels. The fellaheen harvested as much of their still unripened crops as they could. The tribal head, Effendi el-Faiz, commanded 4,500 swordsmen.[50] On patrol he found a Bedouin tribe encamped as far away as Wadi Far'a, an indication of how extensive was the uprooting of the fellaheen.[51]

In the southern part of the country the same phenomenon occurred. Kitchener relates that when his party approached the village of Dura, he found fellaheen watering goats at the well. When they saw his party mounted on horses and riding fr n the direction of the area where the Bedouins were encampea, they gave the alarm that the Bedouins were attacking and hastened to drive their goats into the hills.[52]

James Finn writes in his memoirs that while travelling westward from Hebron he was told that a battle was taking place between the villages of Sanabra and Deir-Nahas and the Tiyaha tribe that had invaded in large numbers from the direction of the desert. The town of Beit-Jibrin was saved, and 35 dead bodies lay strewn on the field of battle.[53]

In 1900 a war broke out between the ed-Dulam tribe and the village of Yatta in the Hebron district. The Bedouin tribe tried to seize 20,000 dunam of land belonging to Tel 'Arad. The dispute and the bloodshed lasted for many years. There were dead and wounded on both sides. In 1912, the Turkish authorities decided to put an end to the unceasing wars. They took control of Tel 'Arad and annexed it to the land holdings of the Turkish Govenment. They then arrested many sheikhs on both sides and threw them into prison in Jerusalem.[54]

Finn describes vividly how wantonly the Bedouins carried out the destruction. They were as numerous as the locusts; their camels ravaged the abundant vegetation; they consumed the fruit of the vines to the very last grape; and they trampled the cultivated fields and the vegetable patches. They left desolation in their wake, after so much labor had been invested in making things grow. On top of the destruction they robbed the fellaheen of their cattle and sheep, and left them no option but to flee.[55]

Much has been written by nineteenth-century scholars and travellers about the bloody wars that took place among the Bedouin tribes. Kitchener records in his diary that in the southern part of the country, near Hebron, a battle took place between the Tarabin and Tiyaha tribes. The latter suffered 101 casualties, the Tarabin only twelve. The Consul Moore wired Kitchener not to take that road.[56]

C.R. Conder writes that the Tiyaha Bedouins were in a state of war with the 'Azazme, who called upon the Tarabin for help. The battles took place about five miles outside of Beer-Sheba and the Turkish Governor did not intervene. After describing the course of the battle, Conder laconically states that because of the battle, in which there were 700 casualties, he decided to make a detour northwards.[57]

The elders among the Bedouin sheikhs told 'Aref el-'Aref, who was governor of the Negev at the time, about the wars, their causes, and their results. 'Aref was engaged in research in the history of the Bedouins of that region, and he writes: "These wars were carried on for hundreds of years." Many legends are told about a war that took place in the middle of the Nineteenth century, the War of Rahma. One of these concludes as follows: "Forty of the finest noble mares were killed, and a large number of riders."[58] Evidently the number of men killed was not worthy of mention.

War broke out again in 1878 between the Tarabin tribe and the 'Azazme, about which both Conder and Kitchener have written. In most of the battles which were spread over a wide area the Tarabin were the victors. The 'Azazme lost 124 men, and large numbers of horses and sheep. In the course of the war the Tiyaha tribe joined forces with the 'Azazme against the Tarabin. "They (the 'Azazme and the Tiyaha tribes) kept getting beaten until they retreated to Dahariya, on the outskirts of Hebron. There a great battle was fought and very many of the 'Azazme tribe were killed."[59]

23

From the writings of Conder, Kitchener, and el-'Aref we learn that the wars and the alliances were not of a permanent nature, but the dispute between the Tarabin and the 'Azazme lasted over many years.

From the Beginning of the Twentieth Century to the First World War

At the end of the nineteenth century and at the beginning of the twentieth, Palestine was a backwater province of the Turkish Empire, in which many political entities sought a foothold. The manifold activities of the Christian churches and the sectarian missions were not only religious in purpose. The German Templars began their colonization project for religious reasons in 1869. At the beginning they were in conflict with the Protestant Church in Germany, but when the Arabs threatened the safety of their new colonies the German Government responded readily. It sent three warships to the shores of Palestine to defend the German citizens and to affirm its presence in the area and its right to intervene in Turkish affairs. In a similar fashion the various societies for the exploration of Palestine and its antiquities were not unaware of their political obligations to their native countries. It was no coincidence that the British Palestine Exploration Fund was established at a time when England was planning to take control of Egypt. Most of the members of the Mission sent by the Fund were army officers of the Engineering Corps.

All these external forces were not sufficient to arouse the country from its torpor. The first real stimulus to economic development came from Zionist settlement. The land purchases, the melioration of the land (despite the limitations imposed by the Turkish authorities), the building boom, the planting of vineyards and citrus groves, the increase in commercial and transportation ties with the outside world – all contributed to the creation of new opportunities for employment and subsistence. In addition the activities of the Turkish authorities, such as building railroads, registering land, establishing telegraphic contact with the outside world, paving roads for carriages and building ports – all helped indirectly in the Jewish settlement effort and in the strengthening of the economy.

24

Palestine attracted not only Jews who came because of national motivation, but also Arab immigrants from neighboring countries, who hoped to find easier ways to earn a living than prevailed in their native lands. On the other hand the immigration wave to the New World, which swept millions of people from Europe to North and South America, did not by-pass the Palestinian Arabs. Thousands of Arabs, mostly Christians, who despaired of bettering themselves economically in Palestine, left the country and went across the seas.

The process of population turnover among the Palestinian Arabs continued but the causes changed: The introduction of a foreign population no longer came in the wake of military conquest, nor was the population any longer diminished as a result of internal strife. Instead, there was migration to and from Palestine usually for economic reasons.

We can learn about the extent of the two-way traffic among the Arabs of Palestine from the population figures for the years 1890 to 1915. In 1915, according to Arthur Ruppin,[60] who received his data from official Turkish sources, there were 689,275 persons in Palestine. Among them were 83,000 Jews and 17,000 non-Arab Christians. (See note 4 above). Thus the Arabs, both Moslem and Christian, numbered 590,000. This figure includes permanent residents and Bedouins. In the twenty-five years between 1890 and 1915 the Arab population increased from 473,000 to 590,000, i.e. by 120,000. This is less than the expected annual increase of 1% through the birth rate. Indeed, the growth was not constant and equal, but as we shall learn further on, it was the result of a simultaneous dwindling of the population within the country and of an infusion from foreign sources.

At the beginning of the century there was a constant Arab emigration. Of this Ruppin writes: "There is emigration from the Christian districts, such as Bethlehem, Beit-Jala and Ramallah to North and South America, even though in smaller numbers than from the Lebanon. In many cities of South America there are colonies of people from Bethlehem who maintain contact with their homeland, and some of them even go back. They are engaged mostly in trade. The American Consul in Jerusalem (*Daily*

Consular Trade Reports 6-6-14) estimates the emigration from the Jerusalem District at 3,000 annually, of whom 30% are Christians, 35% Moslems, and 35% Jews."[61] Thus, from the Jerusalem District alone 2,000 Arabs emigrated annually.

About one town in the Jerusalem area, Bethlehem, there are reliable data on the extent of emigration. In June of 1921 the London *Morning Post* published a denunciatory article against Zionism, entitled *Under the Zionist Yoke*. It stated that the Arabs were weary of the contempt in which they were held by the Jews and the Zionist authorities, and that 7,000 Arabs had emigrated from Bethlehem to South America. The Colonial Office in London made inquiries of the High Commissioner in Jerusalem as to the truth of this report. The High Commissioner replied that the population of Bethlehem was estimated to be about 14,000 to 15,000 people. During the ten-year period between 1910 and 1920, 4,500 people emigrated from the town; 393 returned. In the year 1919/20, 245 emigrated and 35 returned. In 1920/21, 185 emigrated and 65 returned.[62]

Thus the High Commissioner refuted the libellous story of the *Morning Post*'s correspondent, but the fact remains that during a ten-year period, at a time when the Jews had no political standing, a third of the population of Bethlehem emigrated voluntarily.

Masterman reports in 1914 on Jewish and Arab emigration from Safed which, like some other cities, had experienced an exodus of young Jews and Moslems who had emigrated to America, especially to South America.[63] Parenthetically he noted that Safed in those days had the relatively large population of 25,000, of whom 11,000 were Jews. There is no documentation on migration for other Districts. According to Abramowich-Gelfat,[64] Arab emigration ran to about 2,500 to 3,000 annually. The average over a twenty-five year period was undoubtedly lower, but it must have reached 30,000–40,000 for the period under discussion. But, as against the diminution of the population by tens of thousands by way of emigration, there were factors that attracted immigrants from neighboring countries in the tens of thousands, who came intent on settling in Palestine, or who originally regarded Palestine as a way-station to other destinations, but established permanent

26

residence in the country. The new Jewish settlements that were founded at that time grew and developed. They attracted Arab laborers from nearby villages, but there were also Arab workers who came from distant points and settled in the vicinity of these settlements. Laborers of Egyptian extraction settled or the outskirts of Rishon-le-Zion, Ness-Ziona, Rehovot, Gedera, and Ekron, and remained in the country.

The building of the Jerusalem-Jaffa railroad inaugurated in 1892 employed many workers from Palestine and from other coutnries. The Belgian company that built the railroad imported Egyptian laborers to do the digging. They remained in the country.[65] At the start of the century, work on the railway track between Haifa and Edrei was begun. (It was completed in 1905.) At the outbreak of World War I, the Haifa-Nablus railroad was begun. The local fellaheen and urban labor forces did not have the required skills for building and operating railroads. Many workers were imported from neighboring countries, mainly from Syria and Lebanon.[66] In 1880 Haifa was a small town of 6,000 souls, with fewer than two hundred Jews. In 1910 it had 18,000 inhabitants, of whom 15,000 were Moslems and Christians.[67] Many of the newcomers to the city were from Lebanon and Syria, as will be detailed further on.

Jaffa developed as a port city that absorbed Jewish immigrants, and through which passed pilgrims who entrained from Haifa to Edrei, and then went on to Hejaz. Some of them remained in Jaffa, as reported by Baldensperger. The population doubled in the twenty-year period between 1890 and 1910. In the latter year Jaffa numbered 43,000, of whom 30,000 were Moslems and Christians.[68] A large number of pilgrims from North Africa settled in Jerusalem amidst their countrymen, who had established a community in earlier times. The North African group developed a broad-ranged program of communal activities; it had a *Waqf*, mosques, homes for the aged, and residential quarters near the Western Wall.

World War I and the Transition to British Rule

The eight years between 1914 and 1922 were war and post-war years. During this time the country passed from Turkish to British rule. The process of Arab population turnover involved acute change and much suffering.

As mentioned above, the Arab population – Moslems, Christians and Bedouins – numbered 590,000 in 1915. In 1919 there were 515,000 Moslems and about 50,000 Christian Arabs, a total of 565,000.[69] The natural increase of the Arab population for the four years 1915 to 1919 showed an absolute decline of 25,000 people. But the 1922 census showed 643,000 Arabs.* (Moslems, Christians, Druse and Bedouins. As to the errors and distortions of the census, and the rectifications and estimates made by Professor Bacchi more will be said subsequently.) These figures show a sharp decline in the war years, and a quick and unexplained recovery during the ensuing three years.

The harsh regulations imposed by the Turkish rulers, not only on the Jews but on the entire population, during the War years were the prime cause of the steep decline in the numbers of the Arab population. Thousands of Arab young men fled the country to evade the Turkish military draft decree. In 1917, when the British troops were at the gates of Gaza and were on the eve of launching their attack to conquer the country, the Turks banished from the coastal cities not only Jews, but Arabs as well. The expulsion order against the Jaffa Arabs was not carried out with the ruthlessness that marked the the expulsion of the Jews; nevertheless, except for the fellaheen who had sown their fields and the owners of citrus groves, all the other Arabs were required to leave the city.[70] Twenty-eight thousand Arabs were expelled from Gaza and only eighteen thousand returned.[71]

Haifa's population of twenty thousand in 1914 declined to fourteen thousand in 1917. Alex Carmel writes: "The population figures for Haifa dropped by a third for the following causes: the flight or banishment of enemy aliens; the casualties on the various battle fronts; hunger and epidemics; the exodus of numerous military draftees from the city; as well as the exodus of many families because of the economic depression."[72]

The devastating locust attack of 1915 wrought havoc among the

---

* 589,000 Moslem permanent inhabitants and Bedouins, and about 54,000 Christian Arabs.

28

Arabs. Aaron Aharonson wrote in October 1916: "The death toll was especially heavy among the Arabs... Human beings sought sustenance in the fields like animals out to pasture. Needless to say, such a diet furnished ample ground for the spread of epidemics. Many Arab villages were practically deserted, with only a few women and children remaining."[73]

Despite the banishments and the desertions, the famine and the epidemics, the Arab population recovered. In a three-year period it grew to 80,000*. As we shall learn futher on, the factors causing the growth were not only internal. In large portion the growth was due to the influx of many Egyptian laborers, contractors, foremen, and businessmen who accompanied the advance of the British Army. After the British rule was established in the country and in the train of the momentum of renewed Jewish settlement, Haifa and Jaffa grew rapidly, and many Arab workers came from the neighboring countries as well.

The British Army of Occupation brought with it hundreds of Egyptian police who were trained in Ismailia. Many of them were afterwards replaced by local police, but some stayed on.[74]

The building of the railroad to Qantara on the Egyptian border was directed from Haifa. For this project thousands of Egyptians were employed. They began laying the tracks simultaneously from the south and from the north. Many did not return to Egypt, but preferred to settle in Haifa where they found employment with the railroad or other governmental agencies.[75] The head of the Political Department of the Jewish Agency demanded some years later that the railroad employ local rather than foreign labor, but the Chief Secretary of the Palestine Government replied that it would be unfair to discharge veteran employees and hire new ones.[76] In 1922 the population of Haifa grew to a number larger than that which existed before the War.

Jaffa, too, underwent rapid growth. Most of the Jewish immigrants passed through the port of Jaffa. The passage of goods increased as the Jewish population grew. The building of the city of

---

* According to the actual count, after the correction of distortions in the 1922 census.

Tel-Aviv and the development of a Jewish agricultural hinterland brought a concomitant growth in the Arab population of Jaffa. The influx of Arabs who came to share in the prosperity of the city originated not only in neighboring villages, but also in neighboring countries, since the land boundaries of the country were open and uncontrolled.

The officials of the General Federation of Labor, the Histadrut, who were among the pioneers of the *Third Aliya* (1918–1923), were, in their effort to find work for the new immigrants, in constant conflict with the British authorities, who preferred Egyptian, Syrian or other foreign laborers to the Jewish immigrant.

Berl Repetur, a board member of the *Center for Aliya and Labor*, recalls that the case made with the representatives of the British rule was that the Palestine Government employed 15,000 foreigners as against only 500 permanent Jewish residents of the country.[77] At that time the Government was the largest employer in the country. It controlled a variety of types of work, such as building the Haifa-Qantara railway, erecting military bases supplying services to the Army, operating quarries, paving roads, and doing the preparatory work for the construction of the projected Haifa Port.

David Hacohen, writing in his memoirs about the experiences of one of his comrades, relates: "...he worked in a quarry near Tulkarem, together with Egyptian workers..."[78]

The Arab population in the country grew as a result of immigration from neighboring countries, despite the losses incurred during the First World War.

The Period Between the Census of 1922 and the Census of 1931

The 1922 census, taken by the Mandatory Government, showed that among the permanent residents there were 486,177 Moslems, 103,331 Bedouins, 71,464 Christians, 83,790 Jews, and 7,617 Druse. The figures for the Moslem Arabs were the most problematical. It was clear that the number of the Bedouins was exaggerated. There was considerable doubt as to the accuracy of the statistics received from the villages. The Statistical Department of the Mandatory Government found it necessary to revise its estimate of the number of Bedouins to 85,697, because it concluded that the original figure included 17,634 persons who were permanent inhabitants and not Bedouins. But this correction failed to solve the problem as to how many Bedouins were in the country in 1922, since the 1931 census figure set their number at only 66,553.

Professor Bacchi, who made an intensive study of the procedures used in the 1922 census, concludes that there were no more than 62,500 Bedouins.[79] Thus he arrives at a total of 566,311 Moslems in the country in 1922, 503,811 of them permanent residents, and 62,500 Bedouins.

The 1931 census gave the following results: 693,147 Moslem permanent residents and 66,553 Bedouins, an increase for the nine-year period from 1922 of 189,336 permanent Moslem residents and 4,053 Bedouins – a total of 193,389 souls.

The natural increase among the permanent Moslem residents for the years 1922–1931 was 132,211.[80] The difference between the figure for the natural increase during the nine-year period as given by the census and the actual increase was 57,125. What explanation is there for this discrepancy?

One may add to the figures for the natural increase 7,700 Arabs from the Hula Valley who were not counted in the 1922 census – the data for them were furnished by the Mandatory Government only in 1923. One may also add to the figure for the natural increase 7543 births that were not recorded in the 1922 census.[81] That would leave 39,500 souls unaccounted for by the census. In this period the Mandatory Government listed more than 5,000 Arabs who emigrated from the country. Thus, there was a surplus of 44,500 people whose existence was not explicable in terms of the 1922 census.[82]

Professor Bacchi is of the opinion that the big difference between the two sources – the statistics for natural increase and for emigration on the one hand, and the 1931 census on the other – can be explained by surmising that there were about 34,000 Arabs who simply were not counted by the census of 1922.[83] In the 1922 census the Arabs were afraid to furnish true figures, the census takers were untrained, and there were other causes for the lack of accuracy. If this assumption is correct, we are still left without a proper explanation how the Moslem Arab population grew in the years 1919 to 1922 from 515,000 to 590,000. Therefore one must assume that the surplus of 34,000 Arabs includes a large number of illegal Arab immigrants.

From 1931 to the End of the Mandate

No census was taken between 1931 and the end of the Mandate in 1948.

The years 1932 to 1936 were marked by unprecedented economic prosperity. In addition to the increased Jewish immigration there was a considerable influx of illegal Arab immigrants from the neighboring countries.

A memorandum submitted by the Jewish Agency for Palestine to the Peel Royal Commission deals with the ongoing infiltration of Arabs from Trans-Jordan, even though they were legally forbidden to settle without a permit.[84] The memorandum cites the research done by Eliahu Epstein (Eilat) in Trans-Jordan. He sought to elicit the motives for the emigration of the residents of the Hauran Region to Palestine, to estimate their number, and to check the numbers of those who returned to the Hauran. Epstein published his findings in the *Journal of the Royal Asian Society* in October, 1935. He found that between April and November 1934, 20,000 Hauranis entered the country and 30% returned home, but he was unable to establish where the balance had settled.

The above-mentioned memorandum of the Jewish Agency quotes surveys conducted in various places of work in the country. During March 1935, 3,220 Arabs, of whom 1,470 were Hauranis, were employed in the citrus groves of Petah-Tikva. In February 1935 there were 1,654 non-Palestinians employed in the Haifa port on the 25th of the month; 1,854 on the 26th; and 1,892 on the 27th.

Thousands of Arabs from foreign countries worked in the Jaffa port, on constructions projects, and in governmental and municipal jobs. They were mostly Hauranis, who even settled in separate neighborhoods. The riots in Jaffa of April 19, 1936 broke out among the Haurani laborers in port.[85]

The Hauranis in Haifa lived in a special quarter which they called

Hareth el-Tanaq. In the course of time the Government built a housing project for them on the slopes of Mount Carmel, called Howassa. It housed about a thousand souls. In the War of Independence they vigorously attacked Jewish settlements and transportation.

No impediments were placed in the path of illegal Arab immigration. During the Turkish regime before the First World War the Arabs of the neighboring countries, primarily Lebanon, Syria and Trans-Jordan, were all citizens of the Turkish Empire. Passage from one area to another did not require any permit.

Paragraph 40 of the Royal Commission Report of 1937, relating to illegal Arab immigration into the country, states: "Under the Immigration Ordinance persons habitually resident in Trans-Jordan may, unless the High Commissioner otherwise directs, enter Palestine direct from Trans-Jordan although they are not in possession of Passports or other similar documents."[86]

Paragraph 41 goes on to say: "Similarly, in virtue of the order under the same Ordinance, the inhabitants of the adjacent districts of Syria and the Lebanon are free to enter the corresponding districts in Palestine without special formality, except that they must be in possession of border passes issued under the *Bon Voisinage* Agreement between Palestine and Syria made in 1926."

During the Second World War there was a severe labor shortage in the country. Thousands of Arabs infiltrated from the adjacent lands and found work. In 1942, the Mandatory issued Emergency Regulations permitting the British Army to bring laborers from foreign countries, provided the immigration authorities would supervise the process. In effect the borders were open and the private sector of the economy attracted many workers. While the immigration authorities had some supervisory function over the laborers brought by the British Army, such was not the case with the private sector, into which many laborers were absorbed without any kind of permit.

In 1946 in preparation for the coming of the Anglo-American Committee of Inquiry the Mandatory prepared a comprehensive survey of the economic situation in the country and of the political problems involved. A separate chapter was devoted to the subject of illegal Arab immigration. The survey shows that in 1942 the British Army brought into the country 3,800 laborers from Syria and Lebanon. Some fled the country, others were returned home by the Army authorities, and the balance evidently returned of their own free will. After the Emergency Period ended, the data for 1945 were as follows: the Army and the Air Force employed 4,380 workers, 3,300 of whom were from Egypt, and the balance from Syria, Lebanon, Persia, Trans-Jordan, India, Somali, Ethiopia and Hejaz. Private contractors employed 9,687 foreign Arab laborers, of whom about 7,000 were from Syria, Lebanon and the Hauran Region, and about 2,700 from Egypt and Sudan. Whenever the police succeeded in identifying illegal immigrants, their practice was to return them to their countries of origin. During the years 1941–1945, 12,165 such immigrants were repatriated.[87]

The survey prepared for the Anglo-American Committee contained data about the foreign Arab laborers employed by the British Army, but the Mandatory had no information at all about laborers employed in the private sector. Thus it may be deduced that during the time of the Second World War thousands of illegal Arab immigrants settled permanently in the country, and the police authorities did not make any noticeable effort to identify them or to repatriate them.

At the beginning of 1947 elections were held in Syria. The various candidates made strenuous efforts to persuade the voters to support them. The Emir Faghur, who owned lands in the northern part of the Hula Valley and in the Golan, transported Damascus Arabs who were Syrian subjects working in Palestine so that they could be listed in the voting register.[88]

According to Roberto Bacchi's figures, the annual average for Arab immigration – legal and illegal combined – during the years 1935–1945 was as follows:

Legal immigrants	490
Travelers who remained in the country illegally	662
Illegal immigrants who were tried but not deported	902
Annual average for legal and illegal immigrants	2,054

Thus during the ten-year period from 1935 to 1945 more than 20,000 Arab immigrants of the legal and illegal variety came into the country. Since the massive illegal Arab immigration took place during the 1931–1935 period, it would not be excessive to double the annual average for that four-year period.

Illegal Arab immigration continued after 1945, so the total figure for Arab immigration for the years 1931 to 1947 would be between 35,000 and 40,000. It should be emphasized that these figures include the illegal immigration for which there is documented information. There is little doubt that there were many immigrants who escaped the eyes of the authorities and no Government agency had any data on them.

The Mandatory Government gave the figure of 142,289 Christians in the country for June 30, 1946.[90] The 1922 census showed that there were 71,464 Christians. If we subtract 17,000 from the 1922 census figure and 30,000 from the 1946 figure as estimates for the number of non-Arab Christians, it would follow that the Christian-Arab population grew over this 24-year period from 54,000 to 112,000. This represents a growth of more than 100%, the same as among the Moslem Arabs, while it is known that the rate of *natural* increase among the Moslems is considerably greater than among the Christians.

In this period (1922–1946), 18,493 Christians immigrated legally to the country, of whom 25% were Arabs.[91] Just as the growth of the Moslem-Arab population was due in large part to illegal immigration, so was the Christian-Arab population increased by illegal immigration. But there was a difference between the two types of illegal immigration. The former was largely of proletarian background – working people who found work in the country and put down roots; whereas both the legal and illegal Christian-Arab immigration was in a large measure from among the well-to-do class, entrepreneurs and merchants for whom the flourishing Palestinian economy promised profits and good business.

The growth of the Christian-Arab population was particularly marked in the three large cities. In Jerusalem their number more than doubled in the 24-year period, from 15,000 to 32,000. This was primarily due to the increase of the governmental administrative staff, whose Arab employees were mostly Christian.

In the two coastal cities, Jaffa and Haifa, the proportional increase of the Christians was even greater: In Jaffa their number grew by a factor of two-and-half, from 7,000 to 18,000; and in Haifa the growth was more than threefold – from 9,000 to 30,000 at the beginning of 1947.

The outbreak of violence that occurred from time to time, especially between the years 1936 to 1938 and on the eve of the War of Independence, drew thousands of mercenaries from the neighboring countries, both rank-and-file and officers. Az ed-Din el-Q'ssam, a Syrian by birth, was the first to create a halo of heroism and sanctity about his deeds of terror directed against individuals and the murder of Jews from ambush. His deeds preceded the 1936 disturbances.[92] Said el-'A'az, who was one of the leaders of the terrorist bands in 1936 and a lieutenant of Abd el-Kader el-Husseni, was also a Syrian.[93] Kaukji, the "Commander of the Revolt," who headed the Arab mercenaries from the neighboring countries and who suffered defeat twice when he invaded the country in 1936 and in 1948, was born in Tripoli, Syria.[94] Wadiya el-Bustani, a lawyer and a nationalist politician in Haifa, who entered the country shortly before the British conquest and was the secretary of the Governor of Haifa, was a Lebanese Christian.[95]

The blood riots brought about a two-way traffic: from the neighboring countries came the mercenaries, and into those countries – former immigrants returning home. Because of the internal terror that reigned in the Arab community during the years 1936 to 1938, many wealthy Arabs fled to Lebanon, to rejoin their families until such time as peace would return to the country. (See Chapter 13.) A similar situation obtained in 1947–1948.

On the other hand, many mercenaries remained in the country after the 1936–1938 riots. A considerable number of the defeated forces found refuge in the Arab towns and villages, while retaining their military status. When the War of Independence broke out in 1948, they shed their uniforms and joined the fleeing refugees. They, too, were absorbed in the refugee camps and were treated as full-fledged Palestinian refugees. It is to be realized that they had joined the various "Forces of Deliverance" not only for nationalist reasons. Economic factors and love of adventure provided

36

additional motives. These defeated "Foreign Legionnaires" preferred to remain in the refugee camps, there to enjoy the relative economic security that their refugee status afforded them.

CHAPTER TWO

LANDSCAPES AND FACES ON THE EVE OF JEWISH SETTLEMENT

The sparseness of population in Palestine was an indication of the neglected state of the countryside. Ever since the Roman conquest the country was not ruled by its inhabitants. Foreign conquerors came one after another, and each left destruction in his wake. The crusades and conquests by the Arabs, the Mamelukes and the Mongols turned the land into a desolate waste.

A contemporary of the wars between the Crusaders and the Moslems relates in his chronicle that not a single inhabited settlement was to be found between Akko and Jerusalem.[1] Salah ed-Din destroyed the Crusader cities of Ashkelon, Haifa, Arsuf, Jaffa, Ramle and Lydda, and left scorched earth behind him, so as to allow the Crusaders no means of sustenance.

The Mongols who invaded the country from the east (1260) laid waste Trans-Jordan and destroyed the town and villages on the west side of the Jordan, from Nablus to Gaza. The Mameluke invasion under Bibars caused systematic destruction. They laid waste the Crusader domains and whatever remained standing from the previous wars – they filled wells, uprooted trees, destroyed the town of Safed and killed its inhabitants, laid waste to Jaffa, Caesarea, Atlit and Arsuf. On the eve of the Fourteenth century (1299) the Mongols came back and occupied the land, burning towns and villages and plundering as they went along.

On top of all this destruction came earthquakes, attacks of locust, epidemics and periods of starvation.

The Bedouins took advantage of the periodic wars, made peace now with one warring side, now with the other, raided occupied areas, chased off the permanent settlers who had remained behind, laid waste cultivated lands, cut down olive plantations and vineyards, robbed livestock and destroyed irrigation networks.

The Turkish conquest (1516) and the establishment of the Ottoman Empire brought a temporary respite. Beginning with the end of the sixteenth century, as the central government of the Empire got progressively weaker, local overlords assumed control and introduced a government based on extreme forms of corruption, oppression and revenge – for insubordination they would burn down houses and destroy property. Then came the invasions of Napoleon and of Ibrahim Pasha from Egypt. Every invasion brought destruction, every withdrawal – renewed raids by Bedouins and revived internal strife, accompanied by plunder and ruin.

As a result of the prolonged wars fertile lands were abandoned, plantations were uprooted or burned down, water sources were neglected or plugged up, the flatlands turned into marshes and deep-rooted wild vegetation took over. The fertile hillside lands were eroded by rain and wind, natural forests were cut down or allowed to degenerate by turning goats loose upon them. The land was destroyed and laid waste.

In the last century it was thought that the destruction had been caused by a change in the climatic condition. But after a number of scientific expeditions measured the rainfall and the temperature in the various seasons and investigated the quality of the soil and the water resources, they reached the conclusion that the severe damage was caused not by nature, but by the inhabitants. After the first expedition by the British Palestine Exploration Fund (P.E.F.), C.R. Conder (1873) reached the conclusion that there was no significant change in the natural resources of the country – though he admitted that he had scant information on the subject. On the other hand, there was abundant proof that in ancient days the cultivated areas were much more extensive than in recent years. The ancient terraces on the hillsides, now only partly used, testify to the great amount of effort that was put into agriculture in the distant past, unlike anything to be found in recent centuries.[2]

Tourists, pilgrim and scholars were astonished and disappointed by the devastation they found in the parched and largely empty land. The same was true of the early Jewish arrivals, although the sight they saw did not stop them from settling and establishing new communities. An extensive travel literature, produced by scholars who measured, made maps and wrote down data on climate, demography and settlement; memoirs written by early Jewish settlers – all add up to a gloomy picture of the human and natural landscape at the turn of the century.

The total population in 1880 – Arabs, Christians and Jews – is estimated to have been 465,000–480,000. Of these, some 120,000 lived in towns.[3] Jews and non-Arab Christians numbered about 40,000, nearly all of them in towns. This leaves some 80,000 Arabs living in the towns, with the remaining 300,000–320,000 scattered in the villages, and some 40,000–45,000 nomadic Bedouins.

Of the relatively large number of Arabs in the towns only a small minority was engaged in trade and crafts, while the majority worked the soil and raised livestock – the towns were, in fact, enlarged villages. The reason the villages grew into towns was the lack of security in the rural areas, which were open to Bedouin raids, to robbery and plunder. In the town sanitary conditions were much better than in the valleys and plains. The sparse rural population clung mainly to the hills, which offered, due to their topography, better protection against invaders from the desert, and to the hillsides overlooking the swampy, malaria-infested valleys.

The Hula Valley

The land of the Hula Valley is very fertile, and the hills surrounding it contain the richest water resources in the country. It covers an area of 190,000 dunam. One third was once a lake and a swamp next to it; another third had poor drainage and was overgrown with wild deep-rooted vegetation; only the northern third was cultivable and was in fact cultivated by fellaheen.

The Jewish settlers who came into the Hula Valley in the 1940's found a landscape no different from the one described by travellers a hundred years earlier, as if nature had frozen still and no change

39

whatever had occurred, either in the valley's appearance or in its population.

E. Robinson and E. Smith described the southern half of the valley as consisting of a lake and a swamp, eight or ten miles long and four or five miles wide. The southern half of this area – itself about one-half of the whole valley – was a clear lake and the rest a marsh, with streams of water criss-crossing it, two or three streams coming from the north and another one or two from the west, winding their way through the marsh and the reeds, here and there forming small ponds.[4]

II.B. Tristram described the valley some twenty years later: "The western side of the marsh and lake we examined at our leisure, day after day, from our camp at Kedes [Qedesh], as the pestilential character of the plain was too evident to permit us to pitch tents in the lower ground. Riding across the well-cultivated plateau east of Kedes, we descended daily by the steep and perilous path which leads down from Nebi Yusha... The whole marsh is marked in the maps as impassable, and most truly it is so. I never anywhere else have met with a swamp so vast and so utterly impenetrable. First there is an ordinary bog, which takes one up to the knees in water, then, after half a mile, a belt of tall reeds; the open water covered with white water-lily, and beyond again an impenetrable wilderness of papyrus... In fact the whole is simply a floating bog of several miles square – a very thin crust of vegetation over an unknown depth of water, and if the weight of the explorer breaks through this, suffocation is imminent. Some of the Arabs, who were tilling the plain for cotton, assured us that even a wild boar never got through it."[5]

The P.E.F. maps show a total of seven villages in the northern part of the valley. Even these were built on the hillsides near the swamp, since the inhabitants did not dare build their huts down below for fear of malaria.

A chronicler of the early Jewish settlement in the Hula Valley describes the landscape at the time Yessud Hama'ala was founded (1883) as follows: "The entire area bordering on the lake was not suitable for settlement. No village was in sight, and only to the west could be seen a few isolated Bedouins, who would take out their

40

livestock – goats and camels – to pasture for a few days, as long as they were not hit by the fever, and would hurriedly depart as soon as they succumbed to malaria. If one of them would be hit by black-water fever, they would all pick up and flee in a panic. The Arabs called the area 'Zubeid,' after the Bedouin tribe which bravely settled in the dangerous zone at a time of the year when malaria was not at its height. But even they would run away as soon as the Angel of Death began his harvest."[6]

A modern geographer describes the nomads of the area: "The only people who were ready to settle in the area were a motley crowd of deracinated Bedouins, neglected and down-trodden, known to us from the southern end of the Dead Sea – the Ghawarna are so described by Ritter. The new arrivals were drawn to the Hula Valley by the abundance of water, the relative ease of cultivation and the possibility of constructing huts out of reed mats at no cost. Despite the constant influx of new arrivals, the total population did not grow on account of the malaria, which hit hardest at the children and caused in some places a child mortality of 100%... Malaria is... the cause of the repeated abandonment of the valley by the settlers and the repeated destruction of the villages. The same fate would have befallen the new Arab settlement, had it not been for the constant flow of new arrivals."[7]

Kinrot Valley

The Kinrot Valley around Lake Kinneret (the Sea of Galilee) – Betteiha and the Genosar Valley to the north and the Jordan Valley to the south – were in a state of desolation until the arrival of the Jewish settlers. The Genosar Valley is described by Josephus, who goes into raptures over its beauty and the excellent quality of its soil. The climate was suitable for growing all sorts of fruit and so there were many plantations: there were nut-trees, requiring a rather cold climate, right next to date palms, which thrive on heat, and fig and olive trees which require a temperate climate. All grew side by side successfully, yielding fruit almost all year around: The fig and olive trees bore fruit during nine months of the year, and the other fruit trees filled in the remaining months.[8]

Tristram came to the same area some 1800 years later and saw a totally different sight: a green, marshy valley, with a few clay huts at Majdal the only sign of human habitation, where there was once a flourishing garden.[9]

In the early part of the twentieth century the German Templars bought up a stretch of land in the Genosar Valley aiming to settle where Jesus had lived, but because of malaria they were forced to abandon their settlement and the area returned to a state of desolation.[10]

Seventy years after Tristram's visit and thirty years after the failure of the Germans came the Jewish attempt to revive the valley. The founders of kibbutz Genosar relate: "With the destruction of ancient Israel the Genosar Valley turned into a swamp. This can be seen in the mosaic floor in the Church of the Miracle of Loaves and Fishes in nearby Tabha (dating from the Fourth century A.D.), which shows marshland, bushes and birds. The valley was covered with a thick growth of jujube trees, known for their deep roots which despoil the soil. The Arabs eat its poor fruit and use the dried roots for fuel. The jujube forest is the home of many snakes and martens. The Arabs worked the bits of land in between the jujube trees, until their time came to be uprooted by tractor-drawn plows. The new settlers overcame the age-old wilderness... Of all the legends in the Talmud only the jujube trees remained..."[11]

Members of the P.E.F. delegation who mapped the area in 1877 found three permanent settlements: Zemah, Umm-Juni and Ubeidiya.[12] Zemah was a small and wretched town, Ubeidiya had been recently established by immigrants from Egypt, and Umm-Juni was the home of tenant farmers on land owned by a Persian effendi. The Jordan Valley, hot and exposed, with its greyish light soil a mixture of clay, chalk and limestone, was almost totally uninhabited.[13] The Bedouin tribe Arab el-Delaike held sway over the entire area on both sides of the Jordan, and they would periodically bring out their flocks to pasture on the holdings of the tenant farmers whenever pasture was available. Most of the land lay fallow and was considered unsuitable for cultivation.

The first Jewish settlers that came to the land on which Kinneret and Degania were founded (1909) saw "thousands of dunams of bare rock, with some jujube bushes. A small building, half in ruins, stood on top of a hillock, a home for the mare of the wily Sheikh 'Issa... In the spring the waters of the Jordan would overflow the low land near the lake, and would create a swamp, a hospitable home for the malaria-bearing mosquito."[14]

The Beit-Shean Valley

The Beit-Shean Valley, stretching south from the Kinrot Valley along the Jordan River, was in a state of desolation. It was covered with swamps and wild, deep-rooted vegetation. The P.E.F. map shows only one permanent settlement in the entire area – small and sparsely populated Beit-Shean. The valley, covering an area of over 250,000 dunam, was dotted with ruins and *tels*, bearing witness to a developed agriculture in former days.

This neglected valley was populated even less densely than the Hula Valley for the following reason: "While the northern valley could provide some sort of haven for the peasant, or for the Bedouin who decided to setle down, the Beit-Shean Valley lay on the main route between the Jordan Valley and the Valley of Jezreel, and so was open to raids by Bedouins who would swoop down on the farmlands, especially in drought years."[15]

Tristram described what he saw in the valley in the 1860's: "At sunrise we started for Beisan... The ride to Beisan (Beit-Shean of old, and Scythopolis of later antiquity) occupied four hours. We saw not a tree... We came to one inhabited and apparently flourishing village, Kefrah, with some ancient ruins of large stones, bearing the so-called Jewish bevel, one of these ruins having belonged to an edifice of some size... Crossing the third stream... we visited the ruins of a fine Greek church, since perverted into a mosque... Here there is a fourth little stream, and the modern village, a collection of earth and stone-built kennels, circular and flat-roofed, about twelve feet in diameter, and each having one aperture about three feet square. These were the very worst among all the miserable hovels of this wretched land. It is scarsely conceivable how any human beings can inhabit such sties; but such is the contrast, nowhere more startling than here, between ancient civilisation and modern degradation."[16]

Lewis French, the first director of the Mandatory Government's Department of Development, described the area in a report dated 1930. When the British came, he wrote, they found the tracts "inhabited by fellaheen who lived in mud hovels, suffered severely from the prevalent malaria and were of too low intelligence to be receptive of any suggestions for improvement of their housing, water supply or education. Large areas of their lands were uncultivated and covered with weeds."[17]

When the first Jewish settlers came to the Beit-Shean area (1937), they asked themselves: "Will this overheated valley, low on rain, with the sun beating down mercilessly and malaria taking its heavy toll, ever be able to support a settled agricultural population? And this abundance of water – will it forever go to waste? Today this is the home of tent dwellers who live off their herds and camels, by their cudgels and daggers. Is this mode of life forever destined to reign in this spacious valley?"[18]

One of the settlers noted down ten years later: "The place we chose for our settlement hardly fitted the Talmudic saying, 'If the Garden of Eden is in the Land of Israel, Beit-Shean is its gateway.' The Garden of Eden looked too forbidding. From the Beit-Alfa grove – which was then on the outskirts of the Jewish settlement in this zone – all the way to Beit-Shean there were some solitary palm trees, and as we looked up to the mountain of Gilboa we understood well the meaning of the Biblical curse, 'Ye mountains of Gilboa, let there be no dew, neither let there be rain upon you.'"[19]

The Valley of Jezreel

The Jezreel Valley, extending north-westward from the the Beit-Shean Valley to the Akko Valley, is blessed with fertile soil and an abundance of water. From the dawn of history it has served as a route for caravans bearing trade – and for invading armies. It was also an ideal route for nomadic raiders who came from the desert. It had no permanent settled agricultural population, and the fertile land was made use of only partially, sporadically and by primitive methods. Its sparse settlers dwelt on the hills all around, for fear of

44

malaria and the marauders from across the Jordan.

Sir Herbert Samuel, the first High Commissioner for Palestine under the British Mandate, in his first official report on the situation in Palestine in the years 1920–1925, relates that when he first saw the Jezreel Valley in 1921 it was all parched waste land. There were some four or five small and poor Arab villages on the hilltops around, but outside of that there was nothing. Most of the land belonged to Syrian absentee landlords. The Kishon River, which winds its way through the valley, and the numerous springs which feed it from the hillsides created ponds and marshes, as a result of which malaria was rampant. In addition, public safety during the preceding Turkish regime was so poor, that permanent agricultural settlement was not possible.[20]

This description by the first ruler of Palestine in behalf of the British Empire was no different from what Tristram noted in his diary on December 16th and 18th, 1863:

"We were overlooking the sites of the old cities of Jezreel, Megiddo, Shunem, Nain, and many others. The day was clear enough to discern all the positions more or less distinctly, and we had a panorama of three quarters of a circle... For twenty miles the eye could follow the vast expanse, with not a tree and scarcely a village in its whole extent, now a desolate flat, swampy and brown, though said in spring to be a many-coloured carpet with flowers of every hue... From Iksal... we struck straight across the great plain of Esdraelon [Jezreel Valley], to the village of Ender [Ein Dor], perched on the northern slope at the feet of Jebel Duhy [Giv'at Hamore], or Little Hermon. Dreary and desolate looked the plain, though of exuberant fertility. Here and there might be seen a small flock of sheep, or herd of cattle, tended by three or four mounted villagers, armed with their long firelocks, pistols, and swords, on the watch against any small party of marauding cattle lifters."[21]

One of the early Jewish settlers in the Jezreel Valley (in Hebrew often called the *Emek* – the Valley) who years later described his first impressions upon arrival in the area, complements Tristram's observations: "We were few in number as we came to settle in this remote corner, in the heart of the swamps. The few fellaheen who were there were constantly being harassed by the nomadic

45

Bedouins, who would rob them repeatedly of their miserable belongings. The passages across the Jordan were open to them, and their gangs would roam the area back and forth, intent upon plunder."[22]

"The Mameluke regime and the Ottoman conquest brought no benefits to a population harassed by man and nature," writes one of the early settlers of kibbutz Ein-Harod in the Emek. "The land was allowed to lie fallow, the water sources and the irrigation canals were neglected, and the valley turned into a malaria-infested swamp. Some nomadic Bedouins pitched their tents there, living partly off the poor pasture, partly on plunder, and a few tenant farmers, poor and sick with malaria, worked some patches of the impoverished soil."[23]

Of the appearance of the Nuris tract (the Eastern Emek) one of the settlers wrote: "The area is covered with ruts and canals and the flowing waters come to as standstill at every low spot. Near the Tiv'on spring is a forest of common reed and other wild vegetation. There is a big marsh near 'Ayun Ghazalan and a bigger one still between Reihaniya and Tel el-Ferr. There are belts of yellow soil after harvest, and here and there gray belts covered with thistles. This is what 'Ein Jalud (Ein-Harod today) looks like."[24]

The Western Emek looked the same as the Eastern. The agronomist Akiva Ettinger, one of the directors of the Zionist Organization's Agricultural Department and one of the architects of Jewish settlement under the Mandate in the 1920's, describes the lands of Nahalal: "On the land of Nahalal were four swamps: 'Ein Semuniya, 'Ein Mudura, 'Ein el-Sheikh and 'Ein Beida. The swamps, formed from springs whose flow was blocked up, were breeding grounds for malarial mosquitoes. The doctors stated that because of the malaria the area was in no way suitable for settlement. The Arabs, too, thought the area unsuited for human habitation. The name 'Ein Semuniya in Arabic means 'the Poisoned Spring,' and the Arabs believed that whoever drank from it was sure to die of malaria. The ruins found in the area prove that earlier settlements were abandoned. A German colony which was established here some sixty years ago was also abandoned – some of its inhabitants died and the others left."[25]

The German Templars had tried to settle near 'Ein Semuniya, at Ikhnefis (Sarid of today), at Shimron and at Jinjar (Ginegar of today), but malaria forced them to leave. Only in Bethlehem-in-Galilee and in Waldheim, which were far removed from the marshlands, did they succeed in striking root.

The Valley of Zebulun

The P.E.F. map of the Valley of Zebulun shows empty spaces up to 15 km. from the seashore to the east and 15 km. from the city of Haifa to the south-east, along the banks of the Kishon River. Not that this area was inaccessible to the mapmakers, and so they had to leave it blank: there was simply no human habitation in the area covered by swamps and shifting sands. The creeks Na'aman at the northern end of the valley and Kishon at its southern end discharged their waters into lakes and swamps, and the shifting sands covered fertile stretches and turned them into desert.

Laurence Oliphant, who travelled in the area forty years before the Jewish settlers restored it to health, described the Na'aman as coming out of a big swamp at the foot of one of the *tels* in the coastal plain, Tel Kurdani. After some six kilometers it again spread out and covered a wide area.[26]

Tristram was there twenty years before Oliphant, and he wrote in his diary: "...we were off soon after sunrise, intending to spend a few hours at Acre [Akko], and reach Caiffa [Haifa] at the feet of Carmel for the night... Through a rich but neglected plain of alluvial soil, with many decaying remains of old vineyards, and a few straggling palm-trees here and there, we rode on for five hours... Very different must have been this fertile expanse in the days when it was the rich heritage of Asher, who, content to continue on the seashore and to abide in his creeks, left Accho [Akko] and Achzib [Ez-Zib] in the hands of the Phoenicians, but peacefully 'dipped his foot in oil,' for here 'his bread was fat, and he yielded royal dainties'..."[27]

A group of Lovers of Zion from Russia travelled in the area in 1891, planning to purchase the land for settlement. Menahem Ussishkin described what he saw in his memoirs: "...We observed everything carefully and all we saw was centuries-old desolation.

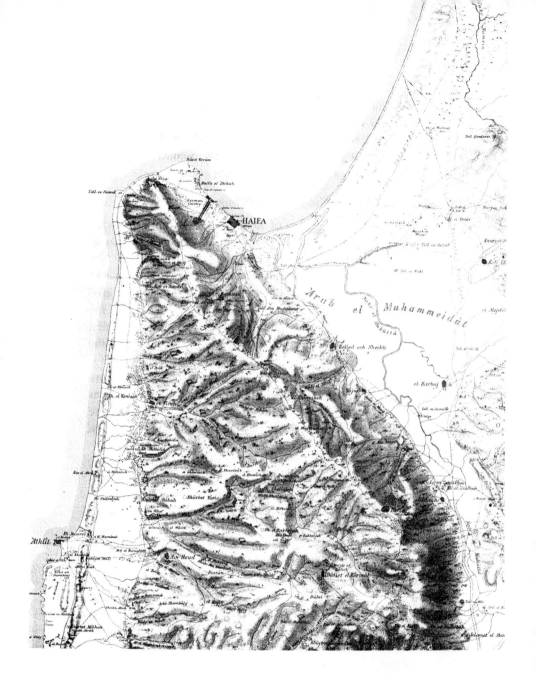

Haifa Bay and the Western Emek Yizre'el. P.E.F., 1878, Sheet V. (This map and the following ones were used by the British Army in 1917, and therefore show telegraph lines)

Hardly anyone lives in this whole wide valley. Here and there we came upon some Bedouin tents. All around were marshes and sands, covered by desert bushes, thorns and thistles. In our mind's eye we saw a brilliant future, but the present was bleak indeed."[28]

When the land was purchased for Jewish settlement 34 years later, its appearance was unchanged. In 1925 Saadia Paz, the assistant of Joshua Hankin, led a delegation that came to investigate the area prior to its purchase by the Zionist agencies. He relates: "We left Haifa for Hartiya (today the site of kibbutz Shaar-Ha'amakim), from there we continued along the foot of the hills up to Harbaj, and then we travelled on foot up to Wadi Milk. We had to hurry so as to cross Wadi Fuara (today the site of the Haifa Bay industrial center) before nightfall, because the area was a large swamp, and anyone unfamiliar with the place could easily get bogged down in it. We crossed the dangerous zone with difficulty at twilight, walking along stepping stones that had been placed along the way by the Bedouins... More than a million cubic meters of sand was later poured into this marsh."[29]

Dr. Sliternik, of the Department of Health of the *Vaad Leumi* (the Jewish National Council) wrote to the Agricultural Center of the Histadrut in 1938: "After visiting the northern part (of the Zebulun Valley), which is intended for agricultural settlement, I have reached the conclusion that these settlements will be affected by the Kurdani (Naaman) creek which runs parallel to them and no more than a kilometer away. This creek causes tens of thousands of anopheles mosquitoes to cover the area, and the Bedouins nearby provide an inexhaustible source of malaria carriers... With all my desire to assist in the projected settlement, I am forced to take a totally negative view of it at this time – not until the problem of drying these swamps has been solved."[30]

The *moshava* Nahariya, to the north of the Zebulun Valley, was also founded about this time, on an area of 2,400 dunam. A marsh covered the center of this tract of land.[31]

Mount Carmel

Mount Carmel, which separates the Jezreel and Zebulun Valleys from the Coastal Plain, was ruined by wars, foreign and local, and its western slopes were laid waste by malaria. A traveller in the area in 1851/52 bemoans the fact that the one-time splendor of its wild nature had all but disappeared. Wasteland and desert were everywhere. Where did the famed Carmel vineyards – for which the mountain was named – "kerem" in Hebrew means vineyard – which once covered its slopes go to? There was nothing but wild vegetation, hardly passable thickets.[32]

The seventeen abandoned villages (according to Tristram; Oliphant speaks of eight) were mentioned in the previous chapter. Jewish settlers arrived in 1882 and found nothing but waste land. The first settlers of Zikhron-Ya'akov relate: "Upon arrival we found 16 Arab families, and we settled in four Arab houses. The soil of Sabbarin (Zikhron-Ya'akov) was covered with stone, which made plowing impossible, and our first job was stone clearing. The Arabs we found were poor and starving. To relieve their hunger they would eat the grass alongside their goats. They were half-naked, with burlap rags covering their loins like fig-leaves..."[33]

The ruins of a Crusader castle stand to this day at the foot of Mount Carmel, at Atlit. Oliphant, who came to visit it, saw about a hundred bedraggled Arabs, who had put up their miserable huts among the ruins and prevented the visitor from making a thorough study of the place.[34]

Thirty years later, Joseph Baratz, one of the founders of Degania, passed through the area on his way to the Jordan Valley. He writes in his memoirs: "The place was neglected, one of the worst malaria nests in the whole country. All the Arabs in the area had malaria, and the women suffered the worst. With nightfall the mosquitoes would come out to attack, and the fever would rise. The only remedy the Arabs knew was blood-letting from the sick person's ear. The women's pitiful screams were heard all around."[35]

The Coast of Samaria (Shomron)

The Mediterranean coast, from the foot of Mount Carmel south as far as the Sharon Plain and beyond, was in a state of desolation for hundreds of years, and was completely ravaged after the campaign of Napoleon and Ibrahim Pasha of Egypt. The creeks which feed on the spring waters and the rains falling in the Hills of Samaria were clogged up and failed to reach the sea. As a result they fed the marshes, which were a breeding ground for malaria-bearing mosquitoes. The shifting sands from the sand dunes on the west covered up more and more of the fertile land.

The P.E.F. maps show only a few settlements, clinging to the hillsides, but they do show remnants of ancient forests, which at the end of the last century came near to total despoliation by coalers, and whatever they left was cut down during the First World War as fuel for the Turkish railroad.

In 1874 C.R. Conder described the shore between the Carmel and Dor (Tantura) as the wildest and least settled part of the whole country, although there is no doubt that in ancient times it was as fertile and as populated as the rest of it. Along the coast there was the main road to Egypt, which here and there showed traces of the ancient road for wheeled vehicles. From it led side-roads to the various settlements, and along these were to be found ruins of hostels for transients. The buildings had broken down long ago, but there were signs of wells, of stone steps and of foundations, pointing to the existence of large buildings and a prospering agriculture.[36]

To the south of Dor were the Kabara swamps, formed by the Zarqa River – the Creek of the Crocodiles, where the last remaining crocodiles were still extant at the end of the last century.[37]

To the south of the Kabara swamps were the dunes and shifting sands of Caesarea as far as the swamps of Hadera. The anopheles mosquitoes to the north and to the south took their heavy toll of those trying to settle in Caesarea. First there were the Circassians, many of whom perished of malaria,[38] then came the German Templars, who left after a short stay. They were followed by refugees from Bosnia, to whom the Sultan gave refuge. For a short time they were successful, and their settlement counted about 300 souls, but in the end only a very few remained.[39] Some Bedouin tribes, several hundred souls in all, were roaming the area between Dor in the north and the Hefer Valley in the south.[40]

Moshe Smilanski, one of the founders of Hadera, wrote in 1891: "The land belonging to Huzera (the Arab name for Hadera) amounted to more than 30,000 dunam... extensive fields bordering on marshes on three sides: the Swamp of Fuqara to the south, the Swamp of Fuqara to the north and the Swamp of Sarcas to the east. The land is fertile, but is all waste, with thorns and thistles high enough to cover a horse and its rider... The land has not been plowed, nor has anything been planted on it, except for narrow strips around the *khan*, where Selim Khuri's tenant farmers are to be found, in the vicinity of the few tents of Arab Nufeiat and Arab Fuqara."[41]

To the south of Hadera lies the coastal plain which connects the Samaria Plain with the Sharon. The P.E.F. maps for this area show marshes and shifting sands, and hardly any settlements. This is Wadi Hawarith (the Hefer Valley), on both sides of the Alexander Creek, drawing its waters from the east and emptying into the Mediterranean. Like all the other creeks along the sea shore, the Alexander Creek was plugged up at its mouth by shifting sands which caused the level of the creek to rise and as a result a wide area was flooded and ponds and marshes were formed. The engineer who planned the draining of the area wrote: "The Alexander, which cuts across the valley, and some of the other creeks that flow into it formed marshy puddles, overgrown with wild vegetation. These wet, dark areas were the breeding ground of malaria-bearing mosquitoes and other pests, which spread over the entire valley. The banks of the Alexander were in places very high, and its bed was sometimes fully covered with wild bushes and other vegetation, so that no human foot culd find a hold there."[42]

The Sharon

The Sharon Plain stretches to the south of the Hefer Valley all the way to Tel-Aviv-Jaffa. Most of the area was poorly cultivated – the sandy soil and the marshlands left little room for agriculture. The big Swamp of Ramadan contaminated a wide area with malaria. Its waters could not find their way to the sea since the Wadi Faliq, originally opened up during the Roman days, was plugged up. To the south of it was another swamp, the Pool of Katuriya, opposite present-day Herzliya. Aside from these two big swamps there were several smaller marshes, all the way to Petah-Tikva and the shores of the Yarkon River.

The Dutch cartographer Van de Velde, who travelled throughout Palestine in the middle of the nineteenth century, got to the Sharon Plain when plowing and sowing were in progress. The soil was soft and yielding on account of the streams of water coming down from the mountains after the heavy rains. The water could be of incalculable benefit to this parched land, he thought, but it all went to waste. Only a few Bedouins, living in tents or in caves at the mountainside, made some use of it – they plowed, planted and harvested freely, since no one seemed to lay claim to the land. Then, with the harvesting over, they would move on elsewhere in search of pasture and water for their flocks.[43]

C.R. Conder described the Sharon villages in his diary (in 1874) as miserable and half in ruins, and the villagers as downtrodden and browbeaten by money-thirsty absentee landlords.[44]

In 1922, Dr. M. Sagarodski described the villages Jelil and el-Harem in the Sharon Plain: "All the way there is sandy soil, with occasional marshes in the winter... The hills are covered here and there by high grass. The sand is infertile and the pasture poor... The southern part of the Jelil land, to the west of the village, consists of nothing but bare hills and sand dunes. To the east is a fertile stretch, and it is worked by the fellaheen. In the middle of the Jelil lands is a large swamp, which once covered an area of several thousand dunam... The population on this whole terrain is very sparse – in Jelil some thirty families and in Sidna Ali (el-Harem) about fifty."[45]

Of the lands of Petah-Tikva, Moshe Smilanski had the following to say: "The spring waters spread all over the valley and turn it into a swamp. And in the swamp there are millions of malaria-bearing mosquitoes which poison the air."[46]

The first settlers of Petah-Tikva brought along a doctor from Jaffa, a Greek by the name of Mezarakis, to survey the area and advise them about its suitability. Here is the record of that visit: "The doctor stood for a long time on the roof of one of the houses, looked all around, listened carefully and finally told his companions: 'I have stood for a long time looking into the sky to see some birds, but I have seen not a one, even though seeds,

53

worms and insects of all sorts are plentiful all around. I can only conclude that the birds followed their healthy instincts and decided to stay away from here... It is a land that eateth up the inhabitants thereof,' concluded the doctor's remarks."[47]

Disregarding the warning of the doctor, the Jews bought the land and then came to plan out the settlement of the area, that had been settled by Jews before and abandoned. Here is a report of their second visit: "Judah Raab, who came back to the *moshava* after several months, did not find a soul there, not in the *moshava* and not in the village of Ummlebis, whose inhabitants all perished, except for the village guard, who was watching over the *moshava*. The good land was plowed up by the villagers from Yehudiya, who decided that the Jews had abandoned the land and would not return."[48]

The Mountainous Region

A Jew, whose name is unknown but whose testimony was accepted as valid by the British Royal Commission which investigated the conditions in Palestine in 1936, described what he found on his travels in 1913: "The area north of Jaffa, as far as Hedera and Zichron Jacob [Hadera and Zikhron Ya'akov], known as the Sharon, consisted of two distinctive parts divided by a line from south to north. The eastern part in the direction of the hills resembled in culture that of the Gaza-Jaffa area. There one could find many well populated villages with the little town of Tulkarem as their centre. The western part towards the sea was almost a desert: Sandy soil with numerous swampy stretches such as the Auja, Sidna Ali, Ramadan, Kabani and Hedera swamps and many other smaller swamps. The villages in the area were few and thinly populated. Many ruins of many villages were scattered over the area as owing to the prevalence of malaria many villages were deserted by their inhabitants who migrated to the hills."[49]

The mountain provided refuge from malaria and offered the fellaheen protection from Bedouin raiders, who came from the east and the south and took over by force the small areas suited for summer cultivation. Among the villagers there were many internal feuds (as mentioned in Chapter I) which caused villages to be

54

destroyed, but the mountain abodes were not abandoned. The lack of security prevented the fellaheen from investing much effort in ameliorating the soil and raising its yield, but wherever they found conditions that were suitable or even only tolerable, they worked the land and sometimes even cleared it of stones and sought to improve it. Various travellers – pilgrims and others – generally describe the mountain areas in more cheerful tones than the valleys and the plains along the coast.

Midway through the Nineteenth century, Robinson and Smith found that the situation of the mountain dwellers was much better than of the people in the valleys. There were field crops there and fruit plantations, and yields were generally good. The people in the valley, on the other hand, were poor and subsisted with difficulty on wheat and barley. Paradoxically the mountains which looked barren and dry had an active, relatively prosperous and free population, whereas the more fertile valleys were either deserted or very thinly populated by some indigent villagers, the lands only partially worked by people who obviously had no heart for the work, and looked more like slaves than free settlers.[50]

T. Drake found the environs of Jerusalem covered with olive and fig plantations and vineyards. The hillsides were well terraced. The fellaheen also grew wheat, barley and beans.[51]

Tristram wrote in his diary in February, 1864: "Terraces, where the ground is not too rocky, support the soil. Ancient vineyards cling to the lower slopes; olive, mulberry, almond, fig and pomegranate trees fill every available cranny to the very crest; while the bottom of the valley is carefully tilled for corn, carrots and cauliflower, which will soon give place to melons and cucumbers. Streamlets of fresh water trickled on each side of our path. The production and fertility, as evidenced even in winter, is extraordinary; and the culture is equal to that of Malta."[52]

He also visited the Nablus area:

"Having crossed the hill, we entered the rich vale of Shechem, or Nablus, clad with olives, full of gardens and orange groves with palm-trees, and watered by plenteous rills. It was the brightest and most civilised scene we had met with."[53] Conder, too, described mulberry bushes, fig trees, orange groves and well-cultivated fields which he saw in the environs of Nablus.[54]

Kitchener was impressed, as were Robinson and Smith, by the sharp contrast between the valleys and the mountain areas. After describing the desolation of the valley of Genosar, he was surprised to see that the mountains north of Meron contained many villages, Christian, Druse, Moslem and Metawi'leh.[55]

The Judean Plain

Quite different from the desolate valleys and plains was the northern part of the Judean Plain, the triangle formed by Jaffa, Yehudiya and Lydda-Ramle. Far enough removed from the Yarkon marshes to the north and from the Nebi Rubin swamps to the south, the Arab rural population developed here much better than in other areas. In addition to better sanitary conditions the area also enjoyed better protection from Bedouin raids: Jaffa protected it from the west, and two fairly large towns, Lydda and Ramle – from the southeast. The P.E.F. map shows gardens and orange groves around Jaffa, Lydda, Ramle and many populated villages. Jaffa, a growing town, provided a good market for the agricultural produce. Orange groves began to be planted in the area towards the end of the nineteenth century, and before the First World War Arab-owned orange groves covered an area of about 20,000 dunam.

But to the west of this fertile triangle were shifting sands, extending from Jaffa southward, to Gaza and beyond. Between Jaffa and Nebi Rubin the sand dunes reached seven kilometers inland, and in this space wandered the Bedouin tribe Arab es-Suteriya, which lived off its flocks and camels, and on plunder. Moshe Smilanski describes the Rishon-le-Zion lands, adjacent to 'Ayun Kara: "'Ayun Kara ceased being a spring, its waters amounted to but a trickle, and in the summer they were warm and malodorous, full of sand and swarming with leeches – in short, unfit for human consumption... And then one day came some Jewish men on horseback to look over a stretch of land some two kilometers east of 'Ayun Kara. They looked over the flora – nothing but briers, thorns and thistles – and the fauna – snakes, scorpions, foxes and jackals – and got as far as 'Ayun Kara, but

The Judean Plain. P.E.F. 1878, Sheet XIII.

found no water there, only an abundance of mosquitoes and leeches. They looked suspiciously at the sands moving eastwards,,"[56] and indeed "the shifting sands rob a fresh strip of fertile land every year, and turn it into desert. They cover trees and bushes and bury them underneath.[57]

The group of prospective settlers who purchased the 'Ayun Kara land passed Wadi Hanein (Nes-Ziona of today) and chanced upon a farmhold of a German who had purchased some land from Arabs. Instead of the owner they found a man who had leased the farm from him, and he told them that the German "had planted a fine fruit garden, had dug three wells to irrigate the garden and the vegetable patch, and had built the house. Unfortunately, the house was built close to the ponds and the marshes, and in the summertime, as the vapors rose from the marsh, he and his entire family took sick with malaria, and two of his sons succumbed to it. He then left the farm, went to Russia and settled near Odessa. This farm he leased to me... The garden is all dried up and it will bear no fruit."[58]

To the south of Wadi Hanein were the lands of Tel Deiran (Rehovot of today), and this is what they looked like in 1890: "Between the town of Ramle and the village of Zarnuqa lies a wide-open stretch of some 10,000 dunam. It is called Tel Deiran. It is waste land – not a tree, not a house, no water. The land has been this way from olden times – no one knows who owns it, it has not been worked and no *Verko* tax has been paid on it."[59]

A member of a P.E.F. expedition paints a somewhat different picture. At Zarnuqa and at 'Aqir he found olive groves, between Zar'ah and Timna there were grain fields and olive trees, but the hills were all waste, and reminded him of the saying of King Solomon, the wisest of men: "I went by the field of the slothful, and by the vineyard of the man void of understanding; and lo, it was all grown over with thorns, and nettles had covered the face thereof, and the stone wall thereof was broken down." (Proverbs 24, 30–31).[60]

To the south of Tel Deiran were the swamps around the mouth of Shoreq Creek – the swamps of Nebi Rubin. These were the property of the Turkish Government which did nothing about them. The Mandatory Government did some drainage in 1929, but the project was short-lived – the drainage canals were neglected, and the swamps returned.

Kibbutz Palmahim settled on the Nebi Rubin lands in 1949, and their first concern was to drain the swamp.[61]

Southern Judea and the Negev

Southern Judea and the Negev were not plagued by malaria as were the other parts of the country, since they had neither rich water resources nor abundant rains. As you go further south, the rainfall gets less and less, with great variations from year to year. The recurring cycles of dry and rainy years had a decisive influence on the area, and the descriptions of the southern landscape by one who happened upon it in a dry year is totally different from the description on a rainy year. The size and mode of life of the nomadic population were likewise very much affected by the rainfall.

Kitchener wrote in his diary in 1878 that when he got to Dahariya he found it completely deserted. On account of the drought the inhabitants were unable to pay their taxes, and they all left. The water shortage was very severe.[62]

On the other hand, heavy rains are known to have brought malaria even to the southern region. Conder tells of his visit in 1875 that Beit-Jibrin had suffered severely from malaria the previous Fall – he was told that 500 persons had died of it. It was caused by the "accursed" puddles that had formed in the low spots and had not dried during the summer. When Conder asked why they did nothing about draining the puddles, he was answered: "It all comes from Allah."[63]

Most of the southern areas were free of the threat of malaria, but they had another mortal enemy – the shifting sands. Conder relates that the sands were advancing at the rate of about one yard a year. They got across the northern wall of the city of Ashkelon and destroyed some flourishing gardens along their way. They covered up a fertile strip about three miles wide.[64]

In Ashdod the Conder delegation saw some fine gardens and date plantations, but there too the shifting sands were continually encroaching on the fertile area.

The village of Yavne was a depressing sight in the eyes of Flinders Petrie, though he found some cultivated fields there. But the clay huts, with roofs of stalks and grass, were wallowing in filth, even though the grain fields were among the greenest anywhere.[65]

In the year 1886 an extensive survey of Gaza and its environs was carried out by G. Schumacher. Gaza was a town of 20,000 inhabitants at the time, with wide, clean streets, despite the shortage of water. The population was poor, and it lived mostly from trade with the Egyptians. Khan Yunes was a small town of 700 souls, living in some 150 hovels. Deir el-Balah was smaller still – about 500 inhabitants in all. These were all the permanent inhabitants of Gaza and its surroundings. In the narrow strip between the coastal sands and the desert Schumacher found some fellaheen who were growing peaches, figs, mulberries, watermelons and vegetables. The Bedouins planted wheat and barley in the winter and watermelons in the summer.[66]

The Negev, which under British administration was part of the Beer-Sheba district, covers an area of 12.5 million dunam. All the flatlands of the Negev are below the drought line – their annual rainfall averages less than 200 mm. From before World War I until the establishment of the first Jewish settlements there was not a single permanent settlement in the Negev, except for the small town of Beer-Sheba. In Mandatory times the Negev was considered unsuitable for cultivation, and it was excluded from the calculations of available agricultural land.

Many different elements contributed to the decline of the Arab village. Some of them were mentioned above: the destruction of the country by invading armies, repeated raids by the desert Bedouins upon the settlers, internal disputes between rivalling villages, natural disasters such as earthquakes, locust, drought and malaria. There were additional causes: absentee landlords who owned most of the land, heavy taxes and high interest rates, which impoverished the inhabitants. We will deal with these matters in the next chapter. The Jews who arrived in the last quarter of the nineteenth century found few villages, with clay huts built on the hillsides, devoid of greenery or trees, with the inhabitants poor and listless. The waste land was in bold contrast to the historic memory of a land flowing with milk and honey and supporting millions of Jews in the period of Jewish independence.

The dismal reality confirmed the new arrivals in their belief that they were destined to revive the land, to cure its diseases, to uncover its hidden treasures and to make it fruitful once more. They believed that just as the Jewish people looked forward to its return to the Land of Israel, so the Land looked forward to the return of its sons. The first settlers were not deterred from buying marshland and infertile areas covered by stones or sand. To improve the soil and make it bear fruit again – this was the principal challenge to the pioneering settlers. The failures of earlier attempts by Americans, Swedes, Germans – who did not succeed everywhere – Circassians, Bosnians and others did not frighten them. On the contrary, they provided an added incentive to succeed where others had failed. The Jewish settler looked upon himself as coming to conquer the desert and to redeem the land from its desolate state.

Van de Velde, who fell in love with the beauty of Palestine's forests (remnants of which were still extant in the middle of the nineteenth century), compared them with the miserable stretches of cultivated land: "No human hand cultivates these forests, but none despoils them either, and so nature can flourish here without hindrance. The same riches are to be found in the other parts of the country but these are settled by people who have caused its destruction and despoliation. The unoccupied land is a blessing for the country."[67]

This was the view of the Jewish settler as well: He was going to turn the curse of the unoccupied land into a blessing.

CHAPTER THREE

THE RISE OF A CLASS OF ARAB LANDOWNERS

During the first half of the nineteenth century most of the land of Palestine lay uncultivated. Much land was abandoned by owners and workers in the wake of wars, enemy forays, epidemics and natural disasters. Problems of land ownership and maintenance arose especially in the valleys and on the coastal plain.

Robinson and Smith reported that throughout the southern coastal plain the soil was fertile and covered by high stands of grain. The land did not belong to those who worked it, but was Government-owned. However, anyone was free to plow and cultivate an unoccupied plot. Most of the land in the plains of Syria and Palestine belonged to the Government, whereas most of the territory in mountainous areas was private property.[1]

The situation was no different toward the end of the century: In 1891, Reverend George A. Post reported that large tracts of fertile land, especially in the center of the country, belonged to the Government. Some of them were settled by tenant farmers who had no right of sale, while others were uncultivated and available for rental from the Government.[2]

In 1858 the Ottoman Government published a land law which was meant to define the types of land and the ownership rights to them. Of the five categories of land defined in the law, only one – *mulk* – provided for completely private ownership. Among the four remaining categories – lands of the religious trust (*Waqf*) belonged to the religious and charitable organizations for which they had been set aside, and the other three categories were under Government control: *miri* – tillable land; *matruka* – public lands, including roads, open pasture, etc.; and *mawat* – ownerless land.

The Ottoman Government promulgated the land laws in order to register the lands in the names of their actual holders, to define these holders' rights *vis-a-vis* those of the Government, to regulate the levy of taxes and to simplify inheritance laws. The law expedited transfer and sale of land, transactions which afforded the

Treasury its chief source of income. The Government in effect removed many restrictions, but continued to reserve for itself the formal rights to the land. It was forbidden to alter the status of the land or to transfer ownership without Government permission, and no tract could be used for building or for planting orchards without Government approval. Heirless landowners were forbidden by the laws of inheritance to leave the land to others; upon their death the property reverted to the Government. A permit was required for any sale of land.

At the same time, the law stipulated that any parcel of land that lay uncultivated for three consecutive years would be taken over by the Government. Actually the law was seldom invoked against farmers who worked their land but left part of it lying fallow for several years. This, however, was not the case with the Bedouins, especially those who carried out periodic raids against their neighbors and were considered a menace to public safety. The Bedouin tribes were treated with the greatest severity, and if they neglected to work their land, it was confiscated. Other land seized was that which had been laid waste as a result of the many inter-tribal wars and had been abandoned by the warring parties.

In 1912 most of the restrictions on the sale of land that had been imposed in 1858, were lifted.

By the outbreak of World War I, thirteen offices had been set up for the registration of land, but it is not clear how effective they were. Often even land that was registered was not listed in conformity with its actual dimensions. The tax on the registration of land was on a per dunam basis. Sincethe tax was high, property owners registered fewer dunams than they actually owned, but in the property registry they described the boundaries of their tract so that the markings delineated the actual size. This procedure was the cause of much litigation when property changed hands, and was the cause of many property disputes between Jews and Arabs, as we shall see further on.

The Ottoman law of 1858 was enacted essentially for the purpose of granting to those holding and working *miri* land rights similar to those of private property owners. Thus the Treasury which suffered from a permanent deficit could increase its income. By registering land in the name of its owner the authorities gained direct access to the tax source. The stipulation that land left fallow for over three years be confiscated by the Government was meant to motivate the fellaheen to till their land without interruption, which would increase agricultural production and so provide additional tax revenue. The law as it was applied did not have the anticipated results: a) Tax collection was made more stringent, but the lion's share of the taxes collected flowed into the pockets of the collectors; b) Owners of small and medium holdings could not bear the burden of the taxes and consequently lost their property to the Government or to the very rich. As a result, independent landowners became tenant farmers on land that had once been theirs. They had no incentive to improve the land and agricultural production did not increase; c) The law accelerated the process of concentrating land in the hands of the few – a process which was already under way.

Property passed from the hands of the small holders into the hands of the owners of large estates, until they owned about half of all the arable land in Palestine. There were four principal components in the process that led to this concentration: a) The seizure of the land of the once independent fellaheen by moneylenders; b) the takeover of the land by violent or ostensibly peaceful means; c) the concentration of land in the hands of the authorities and the Government; d) the sale and granting of state lands to friends and supporters of the Government.

Seizure of Land by Money-Lenders

The landowner was taxed at the rate of ten per cent of his yield (and not of his net earnings) – the "tithe." However the tax was not collected directly by Government officials but by tax collectors who leased the concession to gather revenues in a given district. They employed assistants who determined the levy on the farmer's yield and collected it. A heavy burden of taxation fell upon the peasant, who was forced from his meager produce to allay the avarice of the tax collectors, to pay the salaries of their assistants and to make up for the petty thievery in the process of collection. And, as if this were not enough, the tax assessors would bring with them police and military personnel (the Government had undertaken to help the tax collectors in this way) in order to expedite the negotiations over the tax levy and to resolve them in a manner satisfactory to the collectors. Since the dispute over the size of the crop generally lasted a considerable time, the police and soldiers remained in the village, eating and drinking and feeding their horses at the expense of the peasants until agreement was reached. In the end the peasant was forced to pay not 10% of his crop but often as much as 30% or 40%.

After payment of his tax the poor peasant was left without means to satisty his daily needs and to purchase seeds for the coming season, and he was obliged to borrow money. The lender – generally a professional usurer, or a merchant from town – lent the money at a high rate of interest – up to 40% – until "the next threshing season." When the farmer gathered in the fruits of his labor the following year, he was once again left without enough to fill the pockets of the plunderers, let alone pay back his debts to the money lender. The solution suggested by the usurer was that the farmer get an additional high-interest loan, and the process was repeated from year to year. Eventually, when the peasant was deep in debt with no prospect of repaying it, the money lender seized his field. The new landowner did not expel the peasant from his land. The farmer continued to work it as in the past, but he was now reduced to tenancy on the land that had once been his. He paid a tenant's fee to his creditor, who henceforth had to pay taxes to the Govenment.

Laurence Oliphant, in describing the plight of the peasants, wrote that they were rapidly losing all titles to their lands, unable either to meet their tax obligations or to satisfy the exorbitant demands of the usurers. While the smallholders were being led to ruin, the number of the newly rich landowners kept growing.[3]

We have further testimony from G.A. Post, who reported that in the vicinity of the town large tracts of lands were falling into the hands of big landowners.[4] Oliphant reports that the village sheikhs were in many cases in league with the tax collectors and the usurers.[5] In many villages most of the land was the property of an absentee landlord and was worked for him by tenant farmers, while a fourth or a fifth of the land remained the property of the sheikh or a local leading family. Thus a class of landowners was established whose income was derived from the labor of tenant farmers. According to the report of the Palestine Royal Commission of 1937, citing a survey by Lewis French, the Director of Development of the Mandatory Government, in one mountainous area the effendis took over 30% of the fellaheen's land.[6] At the same time there was a movement on the part of the Jewish settlement agencies to reach into the mountainous regions, and alert effendis, aware of this trend, put aside large tracts of land to be sold at the proper time to the Jewish organizations.

The Seizure of Land by Violent and "Peaceful" Means

As a result of the internal warfare, mentioned in the previous chapter, the victors seized the lands of the vanquished, with most of the spoils falling to the sheikhs and to the heads of the ruling families of the village, or to groups of villages that had gone out to war together. In the Galilee the emirs and the beys, residents of Beirut and Damascus, seized wide tracts of land in the northern Hula and in the Hills of Naftali. In the Negev land was captured outright by Bedouins who refused to have it registered, since land registration would be tacit recognition of the Turkish regime. We are told by 'Aref el-'Aref, the governor of Beer-Sheba during the Mandatory period: "Once a Bedouin became interested in acquiring land, he would seize the tract for himself, neither seeking permission from the Government nor buying it from its rightful owner. Anyone strong or violent enough could grab lands for himself regardless of whether he was a sheikh or a pauper. And how was this effected? The Bedouin would go out to a desirable piece of land, and take possession simply by proclaiming to all present: 'This is my land!' He was not concerned about having the property registered in his name. He had contempt for anyone who might suggest that the 'slip of paper' granted by some anonymous Government official could be more effective or stronger than his own sword."[7]

Ottoman law decreed that anyone who cultivated land that had been classified as *mawat* even without Government consent was

66

entitled to receive a deed of ownership upon payment of a sum equal to the value of the property. Wealthy village notables and sheikhs made haste to work *mawat* land at least in token fashion in order to establish their ownership. During the British Mandate, even minimal cultivation of *mawat* land was discontinued, since new regulations now governed ownership of unclaimed land. Under Ottoman law unclaimed land was the property of the state and could be acquired only upon proof of right to it and payment of "*Bedel Mitel*". Under the Mandate, anyone who held land, whether acquired legitimately or not, was regarded as its owner. In any dispute between the state and the individual over the rights to a tract the burden of proof fell on the Government. Right through the Mandatory period the Government engaged in litigations claiming ownership over various areas of land. Because of a scarcity of Government officials and as a result of lengthy judicial procedures many persons were able to take over *mawat* land and claim it as their own, despite Government efforts to wrest it from them.[8]

The inhabitants of many villages on the slopes of eastern Sharon, who had for many years exploited the sandy soil of the plain for pasture, seized these large areas and claimed them as their own. When the British replaced the Turks, Government officials failed to check the way in which land had been acquired, and registered it unquestioningly as the property of the land holder.

Another way of acquiring land through "peaceful" means was through the "protection" offered by rich and powerful landowners to the fellaheen, who were afraid to register the property in their own names after the promulgation of the land law of 1858. In general the fellaheen were wary of any contact with the Turkish authorities. They knew that no good would come of having their names filed officially: The result might be either a higher rate of taxation, conscription of their sons, or both. Consequently, in many cases they denied owning property and appealed to an effendi or to some other influential person, asking him to declare that the particular plot of land was his and that the people who worked the land were his tenants. The notable who acceded to the "request" and went to the local land registry office to have his name recorded was rewarded for his pains by substantial remuneration.

Formal ownership of land was a great temptation – it afforded the opportunity to reap profit from it. In most cases, the patron lent the fellaheen money at such an exorbitant rate of interest that they could not possibly pay their debts, and thus their lands eventually became his. If, however, he was impatient and more ruthless, he commandeered the land that was now registered in his name, made tenants of the peasants and used the plots as he saw fit.

Lands of the State and of the Sultan

After the promulgation of the land law of 1858 there was an increase in the amount of land owned by the Government. It confiscated large areas belonging to the Bedouins, who cultivated only small parts of the territory over which they roamed. The Bedouins paid no taxes since their income was derived from three main sources: grazing their flocks, theft, and plunder. Moreover payment of taxes to the hated Turkish regime would be an infringement of the Bedouin's liberty.

In 1870, the Bedouin tribes of the Jordan Valley stopped paying taxes. The Government sent a commission to investigate and as a result of the investigation it decided to sell the land at public auction. The Sultan Abd el-Hamid bought most of the land.[9] In the Negev, too, the Government confiscated land that had been abandoned by warring Bedouin tribes. Such was the case in Tel-Arad.[10]

Land appropriated from the Bedouins in the Jordan Valley increased the holdings of the Sultan to about 850,000 dunam,[11] but the huge land holdings were of no great value to him unless they were auctioned off. Most of the Jordan Valley remained barren and desolate. Naguib Azouri wrote in 1905: "The Jordan Valley is very fertile, its climate is warmer than that of the Nile Delta and the river that waters it is as rich in silt as the Nile... The valley can yield as many as three crops a year... Although I have traversed this wonderful valley from north to south, I have not found a single village, nor as many as five dunam of cultivated land, nor a single meter of irrigation ditch."[12]

68

The geographic and demographic data presented by Azouri are not notable for their accuracy. There is, however, a kernel of truth in his book: The Sultan's expropriation policy led to the abandonment of arable land. After the "Young Turk" revolution, the Sultan's land holdings became the property of the state.

Land Grants and Sales for Token Payment

The faltering Ottoman rule was constantly plagued by rebellious Bedouin tribes who would neither pay taxes nor serve in the army. Moreover the Bedouin forays into settled areas spread panic and turmoil throughout the country and undermined the security of the villagers, many of whom fled, leaving behind them land and their property. The Ottoman Government was interested in maintaining a propertied class whose members would command large areas of land, pay taxes, rule over their tenants and encourage them to fight off the Bedouin raids. On top of that the Sultan and Government circles in Istanbul were in particular need of influential local people who would remain loyal to the Government. To build up a class of this kind the Ottoman Government and the Sultan sold large tracts of land to the rich and the powerful – the most influential were granted land free of charge or for a token payment.

The Sursuk family, bankers from Beirut, acquired hundreds of thousands of dunams of land in Syria and Palestine. In 1878 this family, which had branched out over the years to Alexandria and Paris, paid 18,550 pounds sterling for 230,000 dunam in the Jezreel and Zebulun Valleys. They bought land in the Yavne'el valley and in other places as well. Laurence Oliphant wrote that these bankers were the rulers over some 5,000 people living in thirty villages. He soon discovered that there was no better way to ensure the obedience of the local population than by mentioning Sursuk's name or by dropping the hint that he had the honor of being one of his good acquaintances. Oliphant added that it would be difficult to find a greater despot than this millionaire who exercised complete control over the lives of his subjects. Sursuk continued to expand his holdings from year to year until all of Galilee was in danger of falling into his hands.[13]

In 1911 the concession for the Hula Valley, which had been state property, was granted to Mohammed Omar Behum and Michel Sursuk. Together they founded the Syrian-Ottoman Agricultural Corporation, headed by Selim as-Slam, a member of one of the wealthiest and most influential families in Lebanon.

The governor of the Tulkarem District, Mustafa Aga Kabani, scion of a respected Beirut family, managed in 1841 to gain control of 10,000 dunam in the Sharon: for many years afterwards, the area was known as Wadi Kabani.[14] The 'Omri family of Syria purchased half the villages of el-Haram and Sidna Ali from the Turkish Government; the land was sold years later to the founders of Herzliya.[15]

Thus we have seen that foreclosure of land by money lenders, the seizure of land by violent and "peaceful" means and the purchase of land directly from the Turkish Government resulted in the concentration of tens and hundreds of thousands of dunams in the hands of the lawless and the powerful – marauders, wealthy city dwellers, sheikhs of Negev villages and people of influence. The Husseini family controlled about 50,000 dunam. The property of the Abd el-Hadi family, with branches in both Nablus and Jenin, was estimated at about 60,000 dunam. The el-Taj el-Farouki family of Ramle held about 50,000 dunam. The Abu Kishek family of Bedouin sheikhs ruled over tens of thousands of dunams of land between Jaffa and Herzliya. In Gaza the Shawa family controlled about 100,000 dunam. The Abu Hadra family, which stemmed from Egypt, accumulated 30,000 dunam in the vicinity of Jaffa. The Tayan family of Jaffa held some 40,000 dunam, as did the Rock and Qassar families. People of wealth in Haifa, Nazareth, Tiberias and Akko owned property that ran into hundreds of thousands of dunams.[16]

In the 1920's, after several of the large landowners such as Sursuk and others had sold land to Jews, there were still some 3,130,000 dunam in the hands of 144 large landowners. Of these, 28 landowners in the Gaza and Beer-Sheba Districts held about 2,000,000 dunam.[17]

According to the estimate of Moshe Smilanski, who was closely involved with the Arabs and knew the landowners personally, 240 families monopolized 4,143,000 dunam – about the same amount as that held by all other independent Arab farmers in the country, owners of both medium and small tracts of land.[18] Many of the large landowners were foreigners who lived in Lebanon, Syria, Egypt and other countries and who received yearly rental fees from their tenants.

Property of the Waqf and the Christian Churches

In addition to the concentration of land in the hands of the owners of large estates, much real estate was owned by the Moslem *Waqf* and the Christian churches. The *Waqf* had accumulated over a period of hundreds of years much property, especially land. During the Thirties of the present century, the *Waqf* either owned or controlled about 750,000–1,000,000 dunam of land.[19]

The activities of the Christian churches increased after the Egyptian conquest of Palestine (1831). The Egyptian conquerors, in contradistinction to the hostility shown by the Turkish rulers to members of other faiths, granted freedom of action to the churches. The routing of the Egyptian Army and the return of the Turks to power were accomplished with the assistance of the European powers. It was for this reason that Istanbul was obliged to grant greater rights to foreigners, among these a freer hand to the churches. From the middle of the nineteenth century onward churches and monasteries were built, a great network of Christian schools and charitable institutions established, and much real estate purchased. The Greek Orthodox Patriarchate, under Russian guidance, acquired both farmland and municipal tracts through grants and purchase, especially in Jerusalem and its environs. The Greek-Catholic Church also acquired agricultural land in the north of the country and in Lower Galilee. The Carmelites acquired land on Mount Carmel and in the vicinity of Haifa.

Land Sales

During the period under discussion – the end of the nineteenth century and the beinning of the twentieth – the concentrations of large holdings in the hands of the few reached its peak. The land began to lose its value as a source of income and instead became mere merchandise for sale, or the means for speculation and profit.

71

An accepted way of transferring property ownership was through a widely announced public auction. Tracts of land became available for public auction in many ways: A farm whose mortgage had been foreclosed would be sold in public auction by a bank or agent; land repossessed by Government officials for non-payment of taxes was brought to auction; land was sold to the highest bidder when the Government's coffers were empty. For many years it was a common sight to see an auctioneer walking through the streets of the cities announcing to the citizens that land was to be sold at auction that day.

Jews bought land at public auction at every opportunity. The *moshava* Rehovot was bought at such an auction.[20] In 1875, 4,000 dunam of the Arab village Majdad, near Hebron, were sold at public auction. Jews bought the land but registered it in the name of an Arab effendi, who later had regrets and bought the land for himself.[21]

A series of articles on the sale of land in the country was published in the newspaper "Hatzefira" near the end of 1884. The following villages were declared for sale: Qedesh in Upper Galilee, covering 40,000 dunam; half the village Jish (Giscala) – 19,000 dunam; half the village 'Ein Zeitun near Safed; half the village Sasa; Biram, and others.[22] Oliphant wrote that it was possible to purchase complete villages and mentions Umm el-Fahem, a village of 2,000 souls whose land was up for sale.[23]

In 1905 the Governor of Jerusalem put up for auction a section of Jericho (which was the property of the Sultan).[24] That same year, the "Majlis Idara" (Administrative Council) in Jerusalem decided to sell 30,000 dunam of land in the Hebron area.[25]

Much land was available for purchase, but the Jews had not enough money to buy. Years later Zionist leaders acknowledged that many excellent opportunities had been lost. Had they succeeded in mobilizing the necessary funds the Zionist settlement effort might have been advanced by many years.

Menahem Ussishkin, Chairman of the Directorate of the Jewish National Fund, relates in his memoirs that in 1903 10,000 dunam of land were offered for sale on the outskirts of Petah-Tikva. The Jews did not have enough money to buy the tract, but the Germans bought it and established the Wilhelma Colony. The same year one-half million dunam were offered in the vicinity of Beer-Sheba, but no purchase was made for lack of funds.[26]

A stream of offers to sell land reached Zionist institutions throughout the period of the Mandate up to the years of the disturbances in 1936–1938 and even up to the eve of the United Nations decision on Palestine in 1947.

Not only Palestinian Arabs flooded the Zionist institutions with offers to sell land; Arabs of the neighboring countries did too. On March 18, 1934 Joshua Hankin signed a contract with Syrian and Lebanese landowners for the purchase of 350,000 dunam of the Betteiha land northeast of Lake Kinneret.[27] The sale was not consummated for political reasons. The Betteiha land was within the territory of the French Mandate, and the authorities on both sides – in Jerusalem and in Damascus – opposed the deal; nor did the Jewish Agency grant its approval.

Rich Arabs from Beirut tried to do business with land held by Palestinian Arab owners of large estates who were afraid to sell directly to Jews. Eliyahu Epstein (Eilat), erstwhile emissary of the Political Department of the Jewish Agency to Beirut, reported in 1933 that a group of rich Arab merchants of that city were offering to buy land from Arabs in Palestine in order to sell it to the Jews: "Since there are many Arabs who would not want to sell their land to Jews, with the help of the aforementioned group it should be possible to arrange the matter easily..."[28]

The Jewish institutions turned down the proffered "help," whose aims were quite transparent.

CHAPTER FOUR

JEWISH SETTLEMENTS UNDER TURKISH RULE

The First Moshavot – Local Clashes and Co-Existence

The first Jewish agricultural settlements in Palestine are the result of the efforts of the "Lovers of Zion" ("Hovevei Zion") movement, which foreshadowed the Jewish national rebirth, beginning with the second half of the nineteenth century. The ideological, organizational and political transformation which this rebirth brought about took on concrete form with the establishment of the Zionist Organization in 1897. However, more than a decade passed before the Zionist Organization undertook a planned program of settlement from 1908 on.

The first settlers bought the land upon which they planned to settle with their own funds, without any assistance in planning and financing from any settlement agency. Some of them were immigrants from Russia, Rumania, Galicia and other countries, who left their homes because of anti-Semitic outbreaks, pogroms and economic hardships, but rather than follow the mainstream of migration to America they turned toward Palestine, motivated by an ideology and a national feeling embodied in the Lovers of Zion movement. Even before the so-called First *Aliya*, others turned away from the mode of life of the old *yishuv*, based on charity (the so-called "*Haluka*," or fund distribution). They organized themselves into groups for settlement and turned to agricultural pursuits. A few of the first settlers were members of the BILU society, which aimed to organize a youth movement that would realize the dream of the Lovers of Zion. Historians of the Jewish settlement point to the members of BILU as the pathfinders of the entire movement, but in fact they were very few in number, and the movement soon ceased to exist.

The organizational form which these first settlement groups assumed was from the beginning very frail. There was no technical assistance from any central agency, and each settler had to fend for himself. The arrangements for mutual aid within the group soon broke down. The Lovers of Zion movement had no organizational or financial instruments to match the magnitude of the task it took upon itself. The fund that was established in 1890 for the support of the settlements had very meager means at its disposal. Two settlements were established with this fund – Gedera, which was settled by the *Biluim*, and Kastina (later Beer-Tuviya,) which was meant to be a model colony, but was unable to continue without the aid of the Parisian Baron Edmond de Rothschild. The Lovers of Zion fund (whose headquarters were in Odessa, not in Palestine) also helped out those settlers of Petah-Tikva, who refused to accept the tutelage of Baron Rothschild's functionaries, and assisted settlers in various places with the purchase of farm equipment and draught animals.

When the means of the first settlers gave out, after the inevitable failures due to lack of experience in agricultural management under totally new conditions, the heads of the Lovers of Zion turned to Baron Rothschild, in 1883, and suggested that he take the settlements under his tutelage and assist in their development. The Baron undertook to help, contributed considerable sums of money, by the standards of those days,[1] and set up an apparatus for management, planning and agricultural training. This was the first central institution responsible for the agricultural settlement program. To be sure, it was sponsored and financed by one man and the style was philanthropic, but there were elements of country-wide planning in it, even though they were not expressed in any political program.

In 1899 Baron Rothschild suggested to the Jewish Colonization Association (I.C.A.), which had been founded by Baron Hirsch, had undertaken an extensive agricultural settlement program outside of Palestine and gave its support to a number of settlements in Palestine as well, to assume responsibility for the existing settlements and undertake to establish new ones. The I.C.A. accepted the proposal, and Baron Rothschild made a one-time grant of 600,000 pounds sterling. From 1900 on the I.C.A. was the sole agency for Jewish settlement (it remained the chief settlement factor until 1921). Its funds and policies were subject to public scrutiny, which did not prevent its officials from exhibiting a harsh attitude towards the settlers.

From 1878 until the First World War, land was purchased by three factors:

a) Societies founded by the Lovers of Zion and individual Jews of means;

b) Baron Rothschild, and, after 1900, the I.C.A.;

c) the Palestine Land Development Company and the Jewish National Fund.

In 1918 the Jewish land holdings totalled 418,000 dunam.[2]

The Jews who purchased the land were, for the main part, not Ottoman subjects, and so, according to Turkish law, could not register the land in their name. In 1867 the Great Powers obtained the right of land purchase for their subjects throughout the Turkish Empire, but Istanbul interpreted this to apply to everyone except the Jews.

In 1892 the Governor of Jerusalem, Rauf Pasha, issued an edict forbidding the sale of land to Jews, even if they were Ottoman subjects. Rauf Pasha was opposed to Jewish immigration and settlement and he saw to it that the edict was enforced strictly. This brought about vigorous protests by the Great Powers. The Turkish Government finally gave in to the pressure and in 1883 issued new regulations permitting Jews, even non-Ottoman subjects, to resume the purchase of land.[3] But even this change in official policy did not amount to much. The transfer of ownership of all *Miri* lands required a Government permit, and while in the transfer of land from Arab to Arab the permit was granted automatically, the transfer of land from an Arab to a Jew was subject to the arbitrary judgment of the local Government officials, who would raise all sorts of technicalities, unless they were softened with bribes. All in all, land purchase by Jews involved great difficulty. Often even bribes did no good, and the intervention of the Great Powers' consuls in Istanbul was called for, together with more bribes in high places.

More serious and more troublesome in the daily lives of the new settlers were the feuds with the Arab neighbors, which were very common in the early stages of settlement and would wax and wane periodically. In the course of years these feuds grew into national resistance of the native Arabs to Jewish settlement and to Zionism as a whole. In the early years there were many pretexts for such conflicts. The Jewish settlers had concepts of ownership and property rights different from the ones prevailing among the fellaheen and the Bedouins: The Jews were not familiar with the laws and customs of land purchase, the rights of tenant farmers, pasture rights, etc.

Sometimes the Jews would buy a stretch of land whose area as recorded in the sales contract did not agree with the area recorded in the books of the Government Land Registry Office. Owners of land who wanted their holdings recorded had to pay a registration tax. The tax was high, and was based on the area of the property. To evade paying all of it, owners would often record a smaller area, but would describe the boundaries of their holdings by reference to various landmarks (trees, wadis, etc.) so that in case the land was sold the buyer would know what belongs to him and would correct the record in the registry office accordingly. But sometimes the seller would obliterate the landmarks and then claim that the sale referred only to the land as recorded in the registry office. An argument would ensue and would often lead to conflict and prolonged litigation. In some cases a compromise would be reached, but sometimes the seller would lose the case in court and a long-standing feud would be born.

There were quarrels between the new settlers and their neighbors over grazing rights. It was accepted practice that once the land owner was done with his harvesting, anyone could bring his flock to graze on the stubble-field. The new settlers saw in this practice an infringement of the owners' property rights. They would expel the shepherds by force and confiscate their mules or part of their flock "to teach them a lesson." The Arab neighbors considered this to be a denial of legitimate rights.

There were feuds over the use of water sources. The Arabs looked upon all sources of water as gifts of nature, freely available to all. But the new settlers, who had developed and extended some water sources for purposes of irrigation, would refuse to have them considered public property. The Arabs, on the other hand, would insist on their natural right to use all water sources freely.

The Arabs were familiar with the old-type Jewish community, but a Jewish settler who worked the land with his own two hands was something totally new to them. The new settler was not only a stranger himself – his ways were strange as well: A man who is a property-owner (every Jew was considered to be a property-owner) insists on working himself and refuses to give work to the one who is meant to do it – this they could not fathom. But with the passage of years the *moshavot* began to employ considerable numbers of Arab workers, and the tension between the Jewish settlers and their neighbors subsided.

At first the Jewish settlers guarded their property themselves. Previous to their arrival the accepted practice was that strangers would be dependent on the local sheikhs and strong-arm men for the safety of their lives and property, and handsome fees would be paid for this "protection." The refusal of the new settlers to avail themselves of this "service" aroused the ire of the local strong-arm men, who would proceed to rob and attack the settlers, in order to prove to them that their "protection" was not to be dispensed with, that the settlers' lives and property would not be safe without it. In most cases the settlers gave in, and called in Arabs to take over the guard duties. However, after some years when theft and armed robbery did not halt, despite the heavy sums paid out to the watchmen (who would often themselves be involved in these burglaries), the settlers turned the guard duties over to the "Hashomer" (The Watchman) society, newly founded in order to provide Jewish watchmen for the new settlements. Quarrels broke out anew, and there were many cases of provocations and trespassings. The "Hashomer" people responded sharply, and this sometimes led to bloodshed. At the same time the "Hashomer" showed understanding for the accepted custom of grazing the flocks on fallow land and on stubble-fields, and so some of the tension between them and the neighbors was relaxed. But when the Arab shepherds, who considered this concession a sign of weakness, began to graze their flocks upon planted fields, the "Hashomer" people again responded firmly. In all, the arrival of Jewish watchmen on the scene brought about an overall improvement in the relations with the Arab neighbors.

The factors mentioned above, and many others besides, lay behind the frequent clashes and conflicts in the early years of Jewish settlement, but side by side with the tensions other types of relationships developed as well: Arab workers were employed in the *moshavot*; trade relations developed between the settlers and their neighbors, both the fellaheen and the town dwellers; some forms of mutual aid took shape; the Jews refrained from forbidding the flocks from grazing on stubble-fields, and even got to understand that, as they develop water resources, provision should be made for their use by the Arab neighbors as well. Mutual relations became more complex, with both positive and negative elements present, but so far these were basically relations between neighbors – as yet the national factor played no part.

Petah-Tikva appears in the annals of modern Jewish settlement as the first *moshava*, but it should be noted that its establishment was preceded by the purchase of the Motza tract (1860) and the founding of the agricultural school at Mikve-Israel. Rachel Danin relates of the purchase of the Motza land: "There was a drought that year and many of the Arab land-owners had forsaken their lands and had left them in the hands of relatives. They themselves had gone off to the Hauran in search of sustenance. Arabs came with offers of land sales at a low price. My grandfather and my uncle bought up some small disconnected land parcels, without much thought and without any system. Later on, when they were forced to buy up some of the missing parcels that fell in between the pieces they had bought, they had to pay exorbitant prices."[4] In the riots of 1929, the Arab neighbors of Motza attacked the *moshava*, laid it waste and murdered some of its inhabitants.

In 1866, Carl Netter, the head of the French *Alliance Israelite Universelle*, obtained 2,000 dunam of land from the Turkish govenment for the founding of the agricultural school Mikve-Israel, south of Jaffa. The land, leased for 99 years, had previously been worked by Arabs of the village of Yazur, who looked upon the leasing as an act of injustice. This led to clashes between the students and staff of the school and the villagers. Netter appealed for help to the Turkish police, which dealt harshly with the villagers, adding to their embitterment. They tried to interfere with the farming program of the school, but finally a compromise was reached: The villagers were compensated with 1,600 dunam of Government land at Beit-Dajan, and the conflict was settled.

Netter acted firmly toward the Yazur fellaheen, basing himself on his French citizenship and the support of the French consul. Not so Y.M. Pinnes, one of the leaders of the Russian Lovers of Zion and their representative in Palestine, who aimed to advance the cause of Jewish settlement by establishing friendly relations with the Arab neighbors, and therefore shied away from any appeal for help to the Turkish police. He was very cross with Netter for having expended large sums on bribing Turkish officials, instead of paying the Yazur Arabs in full for the land they had worked, even though the land was actually Government property.[5]

The incident did not look so grave to the British scholar, T. Drake, who was in Palestine at the time in behalf of the British Palestine Exploration Fund. In 1872 he wrote of the Arabs' objections to turning over the land they worked to the school, even though the land belonged to the Government. They were particularly wrought-up, because they had intended to plant a grove there and then sell it to residents of Jaffa, as they had done with similar stretches before, in this way profiting from land which they did not own. When they were given 1,600 dunam of Beit-Dajan land as compensation, they were not satisfied and claimed that they were ruined economically, while in fact they were able to save 65,000 piasters (520 pounds sterling) for the purchase of a tract of 4,000 dunam which the Government had put up for sale.[6]

The first stretch of land acquired by the Petah-Tikva settlers, in 1878, was purchased from the village of Ummlebis. There were 32 fellaheen in that village, who were leasing land from the effendis Antoin Tayan and Selim Qassar.[7] The village lands extended in the past over 100,000 dunam. In the course of the years the land passed from had to hand, the original inhabitants became impoverished and dwindled in number, until there remained only one, Hamed el-Masri, who owned 14,000 dunam of land. Hamed, too, got into difficulties and fell into the clutches of the loan-shark Tayan, to whom he was forced to mortgage a good part of his property.[8] He could not meet the payments on the mortgage, and the land was turned over to Tayan. Trying to get the land back, Hamed took Tayan to court, and in order to cover the litigation costs he sold 3,500 dunam of his holdings to Qassar. As was often the case, the effendi Tayan bribed the Government officials and the judges and won the case, and Hamed was left without the land he had mortgaged to Tayan and also without what he sold Qassar. As a result his son Ahmed, his family and his slaves remained on the land as tenant farmers of the two efffendis.

At first the Petah-Tikva settlers intended to buy the big holding of Tayan, but when they came to the village and saw the sick and miserable tenant farmers – because "the land was either clay or a black, thick swamp,"[9] – they changed their minds and bought Qassar's smaller holding instead, since it lay south of the swamps and was further away from the malaria nest.[10]

When more settlers came to Petah-Tikva, they purchased Tayan's land after all – 8,500 dunam of it. This brought them into conflict with the villagers of neighboring Yehudiya, and the tension lasted for a number of years. The Yehudiya fellaheen claimed that Qassar and Tayan had sold to the Jewish settlers mortgaged land belonging to the fellaheen.[11] In the meantime, the fellaheen failed to pay their taxes, and the Government put the land up for sale. The Jews bought up the disputed plots, paying for them a second time, and the fellaheen agreed to give them a *qushan* (Certificate of Ownership). However Rauf Pasha, the Governor of Jerusalem, who was opposed to land sales to Jews, refused to ratify the *qushans.*[12]

Again a dispute flared up because of ignorance of the accepted practice. It was customary that if a fellah worked a piece of land in the summer, he was entitled to plant on it winter crops as well. The Petah-Tikva settlers, unaware of the custom, demanded that the fellaheen vacate at once the land which they sold. Since the governor refused to ratify the *qushans,* the fellaheen were fortified in their refusal to turn over the lands, even though they had been properly sold and paid for in a public sale. An area of 5,000 dunam was involved.

The dispute continued, and the Yehudiya fellaheen were supported in their claim by Ibrahim Abu-Rabah, a member of the notable family of Halidi, who was looked upon as a holy man by the Arabs of the region, and who was opposed to land sale to Jews on religious grounds. He had an interest in sharpening the conflict, since the sheikh had received a flour mill as a gift from Rauf Pasha, bordering on the Petah-Tikva, and while he was at it he usurped 200 dunam of Petah-Tikva's land.[13] The dispute reached the courts, and the enmity between the new settlers and the Arab village was intensified.

In the spring of 1886 shepherds form Yehudiya put out their flock to pasture on land of the *moshava*, and they were chased off by the Petah-Tikva watchmen, who took away a few of their donkeys. The next day the fellaheen came to ransom their donkeys, as was the custom, but the sides could not agree on a price and the Arabs left in a rage.

It so happened that a day after the failed negotiation over the donkeys, most of the Petah-Tikva men had gone to Jaffa. The Yehudiya villagers took advantage of the fact and attacked the *moshava*. They struck and wounded some old men and some women, plundered and demolished property and made off with the flock of the *moshava*. When the men came home at the end of the day, they found the *moshava* in a state reminiscent of a *shtetl* after a pogrom. The settlers and the representatives of the Lovers of Zion appealed to the Russian consul, who turned to the Turkish authorities. The villagers were forced to return the flock, and thirty of their men were arrested.

After a number of quarrels and fist-fights Abu-Rabah decided to intervene, and got the sides to agree to a compromise: The Yehudiya villagers agreed to recognize the ownership rights of the *moshava* over 4,000 dunam of the disputed land, while the remaining 1,000 dunam would remain in the hands of the village. Abu-Rabah got his reward as well: From then on he received an annual stipend from Baron Rothschild's treasury, and he continued to play the role of mediator, prevailing on the Arabs to settle all disputes by peaceful means.[14]

The disputes with the neighbors came to an end, and the new settlers stayed on, even though malaria was rampant. The Government gave the *moshava* a 50-year concession over the

Ummlebis swamp, covering an area of 1,558 dunam, on the condition that it be drained within five years.[15] In 1921 the Mandatory Government ratified the lease and extended it to 99 years.

In September 1902, after the I.C.A. took over the responsibility for 28 settlers' families (the others preferred to carry on by themselves, with some assistance from the Lovers of Zion), the chief administrator of the I.C.A. in the Judea district, Isaac Levi, bought an additional 1,200 dunam from Salim Qassar, situated in the village of Mir, some five kilometers east of Ummlebis. The deed states: "...including 300 dunam of swamp-land."[16]

Rishon-le-Zion was established in 1882 on a stretch of 3,340 dunam purchased from Musa and Mustafa Dajani, members of a rich and influential family of big land-owners, whose children and grandchildren later continued to sell land to Jews. Three years after the *moshava* was founded, the Dajanis sold to the settlers some of the swamp-land of 'Ayun Kara, whose inhabitants deserted it on account of malaria.[17] Five thousand dunam of Beit-Dajan land, 4,000 of which had been purchased by the fellaheen from the Government less than twenty years earlier (as attested to by Drake - see above), came into the possession of one Alexander Rock, who sold it to the *moshava*.[18]

The neighbors of Rishon-le-Zion had no land claims against the *moshava*, but a dispute broke out between the *moshava* and the villagers of Sarafand el-Harab, when the latter put their flocks out to graze on Rishon-le-Zion's land. The settlers seized the flock and refused to return it until the fellaheen signed an undertaking to maintain good-neighborly relations. The undertaking was signed and was honored for many years.[19]

Fifty years later, as the Jewish Agency tried to prove to investigators of the Mandatory that no Arabs had been dispossessed by Jewish settlement, Jewish Agency officials instituted a search as to how and from whom land was purchased and who occupied it previously (see Chapter Five). In looking into the acquisition of the Rishon-le-Zion land they found that the land sold by the effendis Dajani had been waste and uncultivated, and that the Arab notables had received the land as a gift from the

Turkish Government.[20] It was customary for the Turkish Government to give away stretches of waste land to its influential Arab supporters.

The Jubilee book of Rishon-le-Zion refers to a land purchase of 600 dunam "from the *Mufti*" – however without stating which *mufti*.[21]

In addition to the land which the Rishon-le-Zion settlers purchased, they received from the Government a concession over 21,000 dunam of sandy soil lying between the *moshava* and the sea. The Ottoman Administrative Council in Jerusalem ratified the concession on June 4, 1915, and so did Sir Herbert Samuel, the High Commissioner after the British conquest.

Neighboring Arabs presented various claims to parts of this area, and arguments over these claims continued for a long time. In the meantime the British Army requested that part of the area be set aside as a rifle range. Claims and appeals continued until 1942. Finally, on December 22, 1942 an agreement was signed between the Mandatory and Rishon-le-Zion, dividing an area of close to 17,000 dunam half-in-half – 8,473 to the Government, for the rifle range, and 8,473 dunam to the *moshava*.[22] Some Jaffa Arabs laid claim to 600 dunam, and the Government recognized their right to part of it. After some time the Arabs sold their plots to new inhabitants of Holon and Bat Yam.

In Chapter Two reference was made to Wadi Hanein, which had been abandoned by its German owner after two of his sons died of malaria. The German, whose name was Reissler, migrated to Russia, and in Odessa he met the *Hovev Zion* (Lover of Zion) Reuben Lerer, who owned some fields and vineyards in the vicinity of the city. When Lerer heard Reissler's story and that he owned 2,000 dunam of land in Palestine, he suggested that they make a trade: He will trade Reissler his farm near Odessa in return for the land in Wadi Hanein. The German agreed readily, and a deal was concluded. When Lerer got to Palestine and laid claim to the 2,000 dunam he acquired, the fellaheen of Sarafand el-Harab demanded a part of the land, claiming that Reissler had robbed them of it. Lerer turned to the Russian consul for support, the dispute reached the courts, and Lerer was finally awarded only 1,421 dunam, losing

572 dunam.[23] A group of settlers joined Lerer, and they founded the *moshava* of Nes-Ziona.

The investigation initiated by the Jewish Agency in 1930 (mentioned above) found that the Arabs of Sarafand el-Harab had sold the settlers of Nes-Ziona an additional 4,500 dunam near the swamp: The local inhabitants, like Reissler, intended to leave the malaria-infested region and move to Qastina. The new settlers dried the swamps, the Qastina move did not materialize, the Sarafand el-Harab fellaheen remained where they were.[24]

In the course of years Nes-Ziona became the only *moshava* with a mixed Jewish-Arab population. Effendis purchased land from fellaheen who were neighbors of the Jewish settlers, and built their houses right inside the *moshava*. Among these effendis was Abdul Rahman el-Taji el-Farouqi, a member of the Supreme Moslem Council, who built "a magnificent palace on one of the hilltops."[25]

In 1883 the Jewish settlement took a further step southward: The Baron's officials decided to build a model community and established the *moshava* Ekron on an area of over 2,000 dunam. The annals of the *moshava* contain descriptions of unsuccessful agricultural experiments, mutinies against the Baron's administrators, etc., but not of any conflicts with the neighbors.

In the years 1882–1884 three settlements were established in the vicinity of Lake Hula: Rosh-Pinna, Yessud-Hama'ala and Mishmar-Hayarden.

On the slope of Mount Canaan and further to the north-east was an Arab village called Ja'una. A few years before Rosh-Pinna was founded, a group of Safed Jews, led by Elazar Rokah, tried to settle on some Ja'una land, right inside the village. The fellaheen, who lived in extreme poverty because their rocky soil gave very poor yields, heard of the fertile stretches availabe in the Hauran and decided to send half their inhabitants to acquire some of the land there. They sold half of the village lands, about 2,500 dunam, to the Jews from Safed, and used the money to equip the villagers who were leaving for the Hauran. The effendis in the neighborhood, for whom some of the Ja'una inhabitants worked as farm hands, foiled the plan of the remaining villagers to follow their brethren to the Hauran, by informing on them to the authorities that they were leaving in order to evade military service.[26] As a result, the second half of Ja'una's population remained in the village, and the settlers from Safed lived right with them. In fact they preferred living in a mixed Arab-Jewish village rather than on their own, because they were afraid that they would be unable to cope with the Bedouin raids, which were a frequent occurrence. After a year of plentiful yields came a year of drought. The fellaheen mortgaged their lands to money lenders, but the Jews refused to do it and left the village.

In 1882 a group organized by the Lovers of Zion of Rumania arrived in Palestine. They bought some lands from inhabitants of Safed in the same area and established the *moshava* of Rosh-Pinna. Like all the other communities that were established in the first wave of Jewish settlements, Rosh-Pinna soon found itself in grave financial straits, because of inadequate capital and lack of farming experience. The settlers turned for help to the Baron Rothschild, who acceded to the request of the Lovers of Zion to take the *moshavot* under his tutelage. In order to put the *moshava* on a sound basis and to be able to plan for future expansion, the Baron's official Joshua Ossovetski bought 3,300 dunam of land from two Safed effendis, Abdul Hadra and Hajj Teleb Badour, an additional 3,700 dunam from Ja'una, as well as some other land in the vicinity.[27] Ahad Ha'am noted in the year 1900 that Rosh-Pinna's holdings came to 34,000 dunam, out of which 9,000 were later set aside for the founding of Mahanayim.[28]

Relations between Rosh-Pinna and Ja'una were very good, and the village never had any claims against Rosh-Pinna. On the contrary: Margalit-Kalvarisky established the first modern Arab school in all of Palestine in the village of Ja'una, and this contributed greatly to the maintenance of friendly relations between the village and the *moshava*.[29]

But some serious clashes did occur between Rosh-Pinna and the Bedouin tribe Arab el-Zangariya over the sources of water. There were three springs in the Rosh-Pinna area. The settlers concentrated the spring waters in an open canal which was used for irrigation, and also dug a pond for watering their flocks. In normal years the neighboring fellaheen watered their flocks there as well, and there was no room for argument. But the situation was different in a dry year, when fellaheen and Bedouins from a wide area around would come with their flocks to the pond. "To the east of Rosh-Pinna," one of the early settlers wrote, "there is a Bedouin tribe, Arab el-Zangariya. The tribe owns a lot of livestock, its land is very good for grazing, but they have no sources of water. Every summer the tribesmen pitch their tents near the Jordan and make use of its waters for their livestock. Now that the Almighty has provided them with a ready-made ditch dug by the Jews, they no longer need bother to go to the Jordan for water."[30] The "waters of strife" caused many brawls which, fortunately for the settlers, did not lead to bloodshed. Once the Bedouins realized that the Jews were out to defend their land and their water and were not giving in to violence, they had no choice but to come to terms with the *moshava*. An agreement was reached whereby the settlers were permitted to take their flocks out to pasture on the rich land of the Bedouins, and the Bedouins in turn were permitted to water *their* flocks at the water sources of the *moshava*.

In 1883 the *moshava* Yessud-Hama'ala was founded on the western bank of Lake Hula. The population of the lake's bank, as of the Hula Valley as a whole, was very sparse. No permanent settlement could hold out there for any length of time because of the debilitating effects of the prevailing malaria, and only the most down-trodden of Bedouin tribes or nomads that came from distant lands in search of a livelihood managed somehow to hold on for a while. On the western bank of the lake there were ez-Zubeid Bedouins who had arrived in Palestine from Egypt in the wake of the armies of Ibrahim Pasha. In 1858 the Turkish Government proclaimed the Land Law, which called for the registration of all lands, but the Bedouins feared that this would require them to pay taxes and to serve in the army. Like Bedouin tribes elsewhere, they tried to find a man of influence who would have the land registered in his name and would extend his protection over them, so that they would be considered his tenant farmers.

The Bedouins were apparently loath to turn to the Safed effendis for fear that they would dispossess them of their land altogether, and so they decided to turn to a Safed Jew named Samuel Abu, a recent arrival from Morocco, who served as French consul in Safed and was respected by the Turkish authorities. He registered the land in his name and paid the required taxes. According to one version he received from the tribe a stretch of 2,500 dunam in return for his services, but according to another version he paid for the land its full price.[31] According to a third version, Abu was a friend of Abd el-Kader el-Hassani, the refugee rebel from Algeria, to whom the Sultan gave asylum and assigned some land to him and his followers. According to this version, it was el-Hassani who helped Abu purchase the tract of land on the bank of Lake Hula.[32]

The sons of Samuel Abu tried to farm the land with the help of Safed Jews and some Arab tenant farmers, but they failed and the land was put up for sale. In 1882 delegates of the settlement society established by the Lovers of Zion of Meserich and Brest-Litovsk arrived in Palestine in search of land for settlement. They bought the land belonging to the heirs of Samuel Abu and founded Yessud-Hama'ala.

Relations with the neighboring Bedouin tribe were good. The tribe which controlled large stretches of land was getting smaller and smaller on account of the malaria, and it moved its tents as far as possible away from the deadly lake and nearby swamp. But the new *moshava*, as did the other new settlements, got into conflict with some of its other neighbors – in this case not over rights to land. A quarrel broke out between the *moshava* and the nearby Mugrabi village of Teleil, because of ignorance of Arabic and of the prevailing local customs. Three Algerians, mounted on horses, rode into the tree nursery of the *moshava*, out of curiosity, and while doing so trampled on some of the saplings. The gardener got angry, bawled them out and insulted them, using words he himself did not understand. A brawl developed and blows were exchanged. One of the intruders who was badly hurt died of his wounds. The inhabitants of Teleil attacked the *moshava* to avenge the blood of one of their own. The Mugrabis were numerous, they had lethal weapons, and the life of the settlers was in danger. At the last moment one of the Teleil notables intervened and prevented further bloodshed. He proposed that the dispute be settled by having two of the Teleil men appointed as watchmen in the colony.

The Yessud-Hama'ala people agreed, and a *sulha* was arranged between the neighbors.[33]

In 1901 the *moshava* decided to drain the Hula swamp, in order to rid the area of malaria and the black-water fever. They worked out a plan to widen the Jordan River, and with the help of the I.C.A. they obtained a concession from the Turkish Government for the execution of the project. The settlers dug drainage ditches with their own hands, and part of the swamp was dried. After they prepared the soil for cultivation, the Teleil fellaheen occupied it by force and began to farm it, but they neglected the drainage ditches, and before long the dried land turned into a swamp once again.[34]

The beginnings of Mishmar-Hayarden date from 1884, when a new arrival from the United States, Mordekhai Lubavski, bought a stretch of land on the banks of the Jordan with the intention of setting up a hostel for travelers between Palestine and Syria, which he decided to call "The Lily of the Jordan." But his plan came to grief, and he was forced to leave. His holdings, as well as some additional tracts, were bought up by prospective settlers who called their *moshava* Mishmar-Hayarden ("Watch over the Jordan.") The Lovers of Zion took the settlement under their wing and supported it. The *moshava* suffered great hardships because of economic deprivation, isolation and frequent raids by marauders from both sides of the Jordan, however there is no record of any conflicts over land throughout its history.

The year 1882 saw also the founding of Zikhron-Ya'akov, to the south of Mount Carmel and on the edge of Samaria. A society of Rumanian Lovers of Zion bought 5,000 dunam of land from the French consul Germain, who had worked only one-fifth of the area with tenant farmers.[35] Baron Rothschild took the *moshava* under his tutelage, following which his officials purchased some additional land on the coastal plain, near the Arab village of Tantura. This was strewn with ponds and marshes, and having them drained by the new settlers brought great relief to the entire region, including the Arab villages of el-Fureidis and Sindiyana.

This *moshava* was the Baron's special favorite, and his officials poured large sums of money into all sorts of fanciful plans for its development. Most of the work was done by Arabs, fellaheen from the neighborhood and some of the former tenant farmers of the consul, who were glad to exchange their former miserable lot for regular wages assured by the Baron.

Gedera was founded with Lovers of Zion funds on 3,000 dunam of land purchased by Pinnes from the French consul in Jaffa, Polivierre. Polivierre had purchased 3,800 dunam in partnership with an Arab named Husni, and when they divided the land between them, Polivierre got 3,000 dunam of poor soil and Husni – 800 dunam of fertile soil. When Husni learned that Polivierre's poor soil had been sold, he claimed that the 3,800 dunam had actually never been divided between himself and his partner and demanded that it now be divided half-in-half, so that his share in it would be 1,900 dunam. A series of trials began, and it ended only after the Lovers of Zion fund agreed to buy Husni's 800 dunam as well, as a cost of 18,000 francs.[36]

After the purchase was completed it came to light that the land actually belonged to the village of Qattra. According to Granovsky, who cites Philip Baldensperger as his authority, the Qattra villagers became involved in a murder charge, and in order to avoid punishment they disclaimed ownership of the land on which the murder had occurred. The Government authorities stepped in and assigned the land to the neighboring village of Mughar.[37]

It would seem that the Mughar villagers sold the land, which was not really theirs, to Polivierre. As long as the Qattra villagers continued to work the land, even though only as tenant farmers, they had no complaint about having been dispossessed, but when the Jewish settlers were about to take over, the villagers refused to leave. Abraham Moyal, who represented the Lovers of Zion in the area, wrote to Dr. Leon Pinsker:

"...The Qattra people lost the land to their creditors and without it they could not subsist even for one year. As long as it was owned by M. Polivierre they did not feel the gravity of their loss, because he allowed them to continue working it as tenants, but now that they realize that we intend to work it ourselves... they are up in arms – for how else will they sustain themselves?[38] We have found no evidence that the Qattra villagers were compensated in any manner and that the injustice toward them was rectified.

90

After the founding of the first settlements there came a halt to the establishment of new ones. The brief settlement experience showed that with the settlers' own meager capital, with no knowledge of the local conditions and with no agricultural expertise it was impossible to found a village whose inhabitants would be able to earn their own livelihood. On the other hand, the takeover by the Baron, who administered the settlements through a ramified and wasteful officialdom that showed no understanding for the settlers, caused the settlers to stop working with their own hands and to lose their pioneering spirit.

At the same time the Lovers of Zion movement in the Dispersion grew in numbers, and there were people eager to come to Palestine and to settle on the land. The center of the movement was in Russia, and for many years the Russian Government refused to recognize it and to grant it the authority to raise funds for settlement in Palestine. Finally in 1890 recognition was granted, and the same year "The Society for the Support of Israelites, Tillers of the Soil and Craftsmen, in Syria and Palestine" was founded. The Society, or as it came to be known the "Odessa Committee for Palestine" (Odessa was where its headquarters were located), decided to initiate a program of practical activity by establishing a settlement fund. Its first aim was to centralize all future land purchases, so as the eliminate all land profiteering. In 1891 the Palestine Office of the Lovers of Zion was established in Jaffa, headed by Ze'ev Tiomkin, who invited Joshua Hankin to work with him.

The office flourished for but a brief period, in which it founded two *moshavot* – Rehovot and Hadera – both with funds of the settlers themselves.

In 1891 the Deiran lands, south of Nes-Ziona, were purchased. The land had been on public sale in 1873 and was then bought by Tayan, the Jaffa Christian Arab, who had sold some of the Ummlebis land to the founders of Petah-Tikvah. Tayan sold the land to Butrus Rock. In 1889 German missionaries from Jerusalem, who had established the Schneller orphanage there, sought to buy this land for an agricultural school they planned to build. Eisenberg, one of the Nes-Ziona settlers, persuaded Hankin to acquire the tract from Rock,[39] and it eventually became the property of the Warsaw society, "Menuha ve-Nahala," which established the *moshava* Rehovot.

Some of the parcels in the tract, which covered an area of 10,500 dunam, were worked by 42 families of the Bedouin tribe Arab el-Suteriya. According to the map of the British Palestine Exploration Fund, the Bedouin tents extended over all the sand dunes south of Jaffa up to the Rubin Creek.[40]

In March 1892, a year after Rehovot was founded, a conflict ensued between it and the neighboring village of Zarnuqa, part of whose inhabitants had come into Palestine from Egypt with the army of Ibrahim Pasha. The conflict was not over land, but over pasture rights. It all began with a "normal" event for those days: The Arabs put their flocks out to pasture on the land of the *moshava*; its watchmen seized the flock and locked it up. The sheikh of the village came the next day to pay the fine and ransom the flock. While the negotiations over the ransom were going on, one of the young men of the *moshava* insulted the sheikh, who returned to his village in a rage. While the men of the *moshava* were out in the fields, the sheikh collected the villagers who broke into the moshava, released the flock, broke windows and caused other damage to property. The men hurried back from the fields, called for help from the neighboring *moshavot* and attacked the villagers. The two camps fought on, until the Zarnuqa villagers were forced to withdraw. The battle led to a prolonged court trial which cost thousands of francs.[41] The *moshava* decided to boycott the village, and for two years there was great tension, until the neighbors finally made up.

A more serious dispute arose with the tribe of Suteriya. Part of the land which the *moshava* purchased was being worked by Suteriya tenant farmers, who refused to vacate it. "They received compensation," writes Moshe Smilanski, one of the early settlers of Rehovot, "but they were not satisfied and wanted part of the land. They lodged their complaint not against the sellers, who made a handsome profit on the sale, but against the buyers, the *moshava*. They realized that the law was not on their side, so they decided to gain their ends by force."[42] In 1893 the villagers launched a fierce

92

attack against the *moshava*, with the women following the men in order to be in on the plunder. A clash ensued, and the attackers were made to flee. In the wake of this outbreak came the intervention of Abu-Rabah, whom the Arabs regarded as a saint, and a compromise was worked out: Beside the compensation money which the Bedouins had received, they were paid an additional sum which enabled them to dig a well on their land, and good-neighborly relations were established.[43]

The year 1891 saw the acquisition of the largest tract of land since the Jewish settlement in Palestine began: Joshua Hankin bought 30,000 dunam of land from the Christian effendi Selim Khuri, and the *moshava* Hadera was founded. Khuri owned large tracts of land in Syria and in Palestine. He owned a palace in the village of Burj, situated on a hill at the foot of the mountains of Samaria, near present-day Binyamina, where he would come from time to time to collect the rents from his land holdings.[44]

This purchase, the largest so far, had however a serious drawback: Most of the land was an uncultivable swamp. It had hardly any permanent inhabitants, except for a few families belonging to various small tribes. They were mainly shepherds, and they also raised water buffaloes and sold reeds growing in the swamp.[45] Most of these were newcomers in the area. The Bedouin tribe Arab el-Damair had come from Egypt with Ibrahim Pasha's army, and the tribe of Nufeiat had come some twenty years earlier from the area south of Emek Hefer, from the oak forests that had covered the Sharon Valley at the time – as indicated on the map of the Palestine Exploration Fund. After the forests were destroyed by the coalers who cut down the trees to turn them into coal, the sandy soil was exposed and was no longer suited for pasture. The Bedouin tribe was forced to move northward, and it landed in Huzera, on the edge of the swamp, where there was good pasture after the swamp waters receded. The Fuqara, another small tribe, were there as well. The only permanent village was es-Sarcas, settled by Circassians, whom the Sultan had given asylum in 1878, but they suffered severly from malaria, and only a few remained.[46]

In its first few years Hadera, in common with the other Jewish settlements, had its share of feuds over grazing rights, burglaries, etc. The swamp was considered to be ownerless, and the Bedouins felt free to avail themselves of the wild vegetation growing on it in abundance. When the Hadera settlers began cultivating the area, the Bedouins continued to graze their cattle on the fields, and even to cut some of the yield, as if the land continued to bear nothing but wild vegetation freely available to all. This caused many feuds and frays between the Bedouins and the settlers, who, in 1910, turned over the guarding of the field to the "Hashomer" organization.

For many years after its founding Hadera knew no conflicts over land. The first claims began to appear only fifteen years after the moshava was established. In 1906 Bedouins of the Arab ed-Damair tribe forcefully seized 360 dunam of Hadera's land. The settlers lodged a complaint in court. The Bedouins hired lawyers and bribed the Turkish officials – a common practice in those days. The litigation took a long time – the Jews did their share of bribing as well. Many scuffles took place while the litigation was in progress. The police and the army would come to investigate, in the meantime feeding themselves and their horses at the expense of both the Hadera settlers and the Bedouins. The trial was very costly to both sides, and finally the moshava won the case.[47]

In 1911 a land dispute broke out between Hadera and the fellaheen of Kafer-es-Sarcas. After the swamp next to their village was dried by the I.C.A., the villagers began plowing up the area. At the same time ten plowmen of the moshava, protected by three members of "Hashomer," went out to plow up the land and so establish ownership rights to it. The villagers attacked them and tried by force to prevent them from plowing. A scuffle developed, in which the Hadera plowmen and the watchmen had the upper hand, and the fellaheen were chased off. Some time later an agreement was signed, determining clearly the boundary line between the moshava and the village.[48]

For many years Hadera enjoyed a respite from land disputes. This lasted until the 1930's, when claims to land and complaints about dispossession became the stock-in-trade of the Arab political leadership in its struggle against the Zionist endeavor (See Chapter Five).

The opening of the Palestine Office in Jaffa, headed by Ze'ev Tiomkin, and the founding of Rehovot and Hadera on an area of 40,000 dunam presaged a renewal of activity with increased momentum by the Lovers of Zion, who received official approval from the Russian government to establish a fund for settlement in Palestine. But the high hopes which these events raised soon came to nought. Rumors of impending large-scale land purchases brought on a wave of profiteering and sharp competition between land brokers, who caused the demand for land to increase by artificial means. Prospective Jewish buyers lost large sums of money because of all sorts of shady deals. As a result of these dubious activities land purchases came to a halt, and many prospective settlers left the country.

The great spurt of activity on the part of the Jewsih community brought about a reaction among the Arabs, which for the first time assumed the nature of organized opposition to Zionism, to *aliya* and to Jewish land acquisition. In 1911, 500 Arab notables from Jaffa and Jerusalem signed a petition against Jewish immigration and land sale to Jews and sent it to the central Turkish Government in Istanbul.[49] Following this petition the Governor of Jerusalem received instructions to forbid land sale even to Jews who were Turkish subjects.

In the slump period which followed the failure of the Jaffa Palestine Office (Tiomkin left the country after a brief stay) and lasted until the *moshavot* were handed over by the Baron to the I.C.A., very few new settlements were established, and even these became involved in conflicts with their Arab neighbors – sometimes "ordinary" disputes and sometimes disputes over land.

In 1892 Noah Karlinski, the son-in-law of Y.M. Pinnes, bought 7,500 dunam of land of Kafer-Saba, with the intention of founding a Lovers of Zion settlement. The settlers tried to plant vineyards and to grow spices, but they failed and the land was sold to the I.C.A. In 1903 it was turned over to the settlers of Petah-Tikvah with the idea of establishing a new settlement for their sons. The previously mentioned memorandum of 1930 relates that some fellaheen laid claim to parts of this tract, but it transpired upon investigation that all the claimants who had sold some of the land had left a part of it for themselves and stayed on in their village. Since all the village land was *musha'a*, i.e. undivided land, it was now divided afresh among all the village's inhabitants.[50]

A violent clash occurred in 1910 between the watchmen of the temporary encampment (before the settlement was established) and the Arabs of Qalqilya. The guard was mixed – two Jewish watchmen and several Arabs. In one of the encounters with some Arab herdsmen, who put their flock out to graze on the fields of the new settlers, one of the Arab watchmen was assaulted by the herdsmen. The watchman fired at the attackers, and one of them was killed. That night – we read in the "Book of Kefar-Saba" – a band of Arabs from Qalqilya, armed with rifles, pistols and clubs, launched an attack on the settlement, where only one family was living at the time, in addition to the two Jewish watchmen. They kidnapped the watchmen and took them to Qalqilya. It was one of the Bedouins who called up the Petah-Tikva watchmen for help, and only thanks to the connections between Abraham Shapira of Petah-Tikva and one of Qalqilya's notables were the prisoners released.[51]

The *moshava* Metulla, in Upper Galilee, was founded in 1896. A long-drawn-out feud ensued between the new settlers and the Druse tenant farmers who had worked the land previously. The tenant farmers refused to give up their right to continued cultivation and accused the Jews of dispossessiong them. Bloody frays occurrred as the Druse repeatedly attacked the new settlers in the fields and in their homes. Reports of the conflict spread throughout the country, and it was the subject of heated discussion in the Zionist movement. A solution was finally arrived at, but the Metulla incident exerted a great influence on future land purchase practices and on the relations with the tenant farmers.

The em-Mutallah land belonged to a Christian named Jabur Bey, and for many years it was worked by Christian tenant farmers. During the massacre of the Christians in Lebanon (1860) the farmers feared for their lives and fled. When the first French expeditionary force arrived in Lebanon to re-establish order, many of the Druse who took part in the massacre ran away from their native villages. Among these were the inhabitants of the village

Meri, who went to em-Mutallah. They asked Jabur Bey to receive them as tenant farmers, and this is how they established themselves in the new domicile.

When the Druse Rebellion broke out in 1895, the men of em-Mutallah joined the rebels. The land lay waste, as the women were unable to cope with the work. Jabur Bey then proposed to Joshua Ossovetski, one of the officials of Baron Rothschild, that he buy the land, and so the land of em-Mutallah became the property of the Baron. Ossovetski put 60 families there, and Metulla was established (1896).

After the Druse Rebellion was put down, the Druse villagers returned and demanded back their rights as tenant farmers. When Ossovetski got wind of this, he called in the Turkish authorities, who came to arrest the Druse as deserters and rebels. Ossovetski took advantage of the fact that the Druse were in danger of being arrested and he offered them compensation for leaving the place, which they readily accepted.[52]

Isaac Epstein, a well-known educator who lived in Upper Galilee at the time, voiced sharp criticism of Ossovetski's actions and of the land purchase practices in general. He demanded a more humane attitude toward the previous occupants, urging that they be given not only money as indemnity, but alternate tracts of land so that they could continue to derive their livelihood from them. Epstein published his critical article in the monthly "Hashiloah," edited by Ahad Ha'am, and it made a deep impression on the agencies involved in land acquisition.[53]

Ahad Ha'am, who visited Palestine in 1901, was also very critical of the Baron's officials, "who refuse to compensate the tenant farmers properly, even though this forces them to pay out 4,000 francs (about 200 pounds sterling) to Arab strong-arm men, who provide protection against the attacks of the Druse villagers."[54]

According to the testimony of a Metulla settler,[55] the Druse used their compensation money to buy land in the Hula Valley, near the sources of the river Dan. The Druse, who were mountain dwellers, could not adjust to the climate in the valley, and in addition they were badly hit by malaria. Several of them died, and the others left and returned to Metulla to claim their erstwhile rights. But the

Baron's officials would not have them back, and they also refused the Druse demand for additional compensation with which they could buy some land in a hilly region. After eight years of feuds and clashes a compromise was finally reached in 1904 through the good offices of Isaac Levi, one of the top I.C.A. officials. The tenant farmers received an additional 60,000 francs for the purchase of land on the slopes of Mount Hermon.[56] This did not put a stop to attacks on Metulla, but with the passage of time good relations were established between the neighbors.

Many years later Margalit-Kalvarisky wrote of the Metulla events: "I am certain that from the very first steps in Metulla not everything we did was right, and these unjust deeds were the cause of the troubles. Ossovetski took advantage of the Druse Rebellion to buy the village lands from the effendi and to expel the Druse tenant farmers, and this was the cause of the many raids on the *moshava*. Only some years later did the Baron's officials come to grasp the facts of the situation, and they compensated the previous inhabitants. This brought about improved relations between the Druse and the Jewish settlers of Metulla, so much so that when we were in the midst of a litigation with the Catholic bishop of the valley, who was out to rob us of a thousand dunam of land, the Druse came to our assistance by offering to expel the bishop and his people and by testifying in court in our favor."[57]

In 1896 two additional *moshavot* were established in the southern part of the country: Hartuv and Kastina (Beer-Tuvya). In Kastina a land feud broke out between the *moshava* and one of its neighbors, the sheikh Abd el-Hadi from the village of Hammama, the sheikh claiming that the *moshava* occupied some of the *Waqf* land. Even though the agronomist who was in charge of establishing the new settlement on behalf of the Jaffa office of the Lovers of Zion had clear evidence that the sheikh's claim was unfounded, he agreed to pay the sheikh 320 francs as indemnity. The sheikh agreed to accept the money, but demanded in addition a stretch of land as well. Since no agreement could be reached, the *mufti* of Gaza was called in to act as arbitrator. The *mufti's* judgment was that the sheikh's claim was without foundation, since the Jews were settling on land which they rightfully bought. A day after the judgment was

98

issued the sheikh and fifty armed Arabs attacked the *moshava*. In the course of the skirmish which ensued some shots were fired, and one of the Arabs was injured and died of his wounds. The feud was escalated – the Arabs were out to avenge the blood of their comrade. A series of court trials ensued, some bribe money changed hands, until the Sheikh Abu-Rabah intervened as mediator, and it was agreed that 2,500 francs would be paid to the family of the deceased. The agronomist was forced to leave the country, and tempers quieted down.[58]

The I.C.A. – First Attempts to Compensate Tenant Farmers

Toward the end of the nineteenth century, as has already been mentioned, Baron Rothschild decided to merge his settlement activities with those of the I.C.A. and to hand over the settlements in his care to the I.C.A. Most of the Baron's officials joined the staff of the I.C.A. and a joint administration was established.

After the handover of Baron Rothschild's land holdings, the I.C.A. became the largest landowner in Palestine, with some 151,000 dunam of land in its possession.[59] After the merger, on January 1, 1900, further land purchases were made at an increased pace.

Baron Rothschild, who refused Dr. Herzl's offer to join the Zionist Organization and to become identified with its political aims, favored a policy of slow, quiet, well-planned settlement, which he believed would further the Zionist aim more than political activity. The transfer of the colonies to the tutelage of the I.C.A. in no way decreased his interest in their further development. He continued to influence the policy of large purchases in concentrated blocks, which would eventually serve as bases of economic and demographic power and would be able to offer protection against any possible obstruction by the Arab neighbors. He probably foresaw the eventual merging of such settlement centers into a Jewish administrative entity. This future prospect underlay the decision to purchase a large tract of 80,000 dunam in the Golan (1891) and the efforts to begin concentrating land holdings in the Lower Galilee, undertaken by the Baron's chief official in that area, Ossovetski. With the same idea in mind the I.C.A. continued

99

to buy up land in the lowlands of Samaria, near Zikhron Ya'akov, from Atlit to Hadera.

The man who further developed these ideas of concentrated land acquisitions was the agronomist Chaim Margalit-Kalvarisky. When the *moshavot* were transferred from the Baron's tutelage to the I.C.A., its managing director, H. Frank, put him in charge of the Lower Galilee settlements and gave him a free hand in planning their development and in making additional land purchases. He planned to buy up most of the lands in the Akko district and establish some settlements there on a sound economic foundation, so that in time Jews would constitute the majority of the population in the district and would have a good claim to the appointment of a Jewish district governor. (Some ten years later Dr. Arthur Ruppin drew up a similar plan for the creation of Jewish-owned land concentrations, which would lead to the formation of Jewish autonomous districts).

Kalvarisky was critical of the patronizing way the Baron's officials were handling the *moshavot*, as well as of the policy of developing commercial crops and of employing Arab hired labor, with the settlers turning into supervisors and employers. He was hoping that under the new regime of the I.C.A. the settler's farmhold would be based mainly on field crops and livestock, from which the settler would be able to earn his livelihood without the interference of advisers, bureaucrats and merchants, and without requiring outside support. He aimed at developing a new type of settlement, where the settler would be able to live completely off his farm and the labor of his own hands.

About half of the Lower Galilee lands which the I.C.A. acquired were purchased by Joshua Ossovetski before the merger with the I.C.A. In April, 1900 Kalvarisky wrote to the I.C.A. head office in Paris: "Frank, Ossovetski and Co. bought in our behalf the lands of Sejera, Umm Jubeil, Zebeih and Mes'ha – 35,000 dunam in all."[60] Ossovetski's land purchases brought in their wake some severe conflicts with the tenant farmers and with the Turkish officials, and Kalvarisky had his work cut out for him trying to settle the disputes, while saving the lands the I.C.A. was in danger of losing, and to establish friendly relations with the neighbors. These efforts sometimes succeeded and sometimes did not, as will be related below. By 1904 the I.C.A. holdings in Lower Galilee came to 70,000 dunam.

The Lower Galilee lands were acquired from various owners. Only a few of the villages had been settled for a long period of time. A short time previously – a mere forty years earlier – refugees from Algeria, Abd el-Kader el-Hassani's men, had settled in the four villages Kafer-Sabet, Ma'ader, Shara and Ulam. About half the land of these villages was the property of the emir 'Ali el-Gezari ("The Algerian"), Abd el-Kader's son. Two villages – Kafer-Kamma and Sharona – were settled by Circassians some twenty-five years earlier.[61] On the elevated plain was Kafer-Miser and on the banks of the Jordan was Ubeidiya – two Egyptian villages founded some 60–70 years earlier. In the center of the plain was the Zebeih tribe which occupied *Jiftlik* land.

At the eastern end of the plain and along the slopes down to Lake Kinneret were the Bedouin tribes Delaike and Delaike-Sahu. Uncultivated stretches were used for grazing and occasional cultivation. On the banks of the Jordan was the property of a Persian effendi – Umm Juni.

Most of the land in the region did not belong to those living on it, but to rich landowners who were collecting a rental from the tenant farmers. The Sursuk family (already mentioned in these pages,) which bought 10,000 dunam from the Sultan, the mufti of Tiberias, the Sa'id family of Tiberias (one of its members was the mayor of Tiberias), the Fahum family of Nazareth, the Beidoun family of Akko, an effendi named Barbur, 'Ali, the son of Abd el-Kader – these were the owners of the cultivated lands, while the lands of the Bedouin tribes were recorded in the name of the sheikh, or belonged to one of these families.

The landowners were eager to sell their property and were not averse to circumventing laws and regulations of the Turkish regime to achieve their end. However, the large-scale sales caused a ferment among the fellaheen, the tenant farmers and the Bedouins living off these lands.

Of the 70,000 dunam that were bought, 18,000 were at the disposal of the two Delaike tribes of Bedouins, who in 1886 consisted of 695 souls.* Another 8,900 dunam were worked by the Arab village el-Sejera, but the land belonged to the French consul in Beirut who acquired it the way money lenders were accustomed to acquire land. After this tract was sold, the villagers had a total of 2,200 dunam left. The fellaheen of Lubiya worked 7,000 dunam, the fellaheen of Mes'ha another 7,000, and the Bedouins of the Zebeih tribe – 6,000. The land was undivided *Jiftlik*.[62] Another 6,000 dunam bought from Barbur was worked by 40 tenant farmers of Kafer-Yeima.[63]

When the I.C.A. surveyors arrived to measure out some of the tracts, they were attacked by the fellaheen of Lubiya and Ubeidiya and the Bedouins of the Delaike and Zebeih tribes. The surveyors sustained injuries and were chased off.[64] They asked the police for help, but the *kaimakam* of Tiberias, the emir Amin Arselan, sided with the Arabs and in fact was actively involved in inciting them. Arselan, even though a Druse and a Turkish Government official, opposed the sale of land to Jews on Arab nationalistic grounds, because Jewish settlement – so he claimed – would change the character of the area and would "bring about denationalization," as he was later quoted by Kalvarisky.[65]

The mufti of Tiberias owned 3,000 dunam of land at Umm Jebeil between Mes'ha and Sejera, which he sold to the I.C.A. When the Circassians of Kafer-Kamma learned of the impending sale, they made priority claims on the land and obtained a judgment from the court in Tiberias, giving them a first option on the land to be sold. Their claim was supported by Arselan.[66]

The events of Lower Galilee evoked a sympathetic response on the part of the Arab community. In 1901 a group of Arab government officials sent a petition to the central Turkish authorities in Palestine protesting the sale of land to foreign nationals, even if they came into the country legally, because the sale provided a loop-hole for illegal entrants to remain in the country.[67]

In an attempt to reach a peaceable solution to the problem of the

---

* According to Z. Vilnai (in the *Encyclopedia of the Land of Israel*), who is basing himself on the *P.E.F. Quartellyy*, 1887, p. 187.

tenant farmers, the I.C.A. appointed Margalit-Kalvarisky to take charge of the Lower Galilee settlements. Kalvarisky was at the time the I.C.A. representative in Rosh-Pinna, where he succeeded in establishing friendly relations with the fellaheen of Ja'uni and even opened a school for the children of the village, as was related earlier.

Some time later Kalvarisky wrote: "At first, when Jews came to establish a new settlement, there were feuds and clashes. Not always were we in the right. I recall what happened with the establishment of the Lower Galilee settlements of Sejera, Yavne'el, Mes'ha, Beit-Gan, Menahamiya and others. Most of the land which the Jews bought from effendis and Beirut merchants was worked by tenant farmers. Neither Ossovetski, of Baron Rothschild's staff, nor the sellers had any interest in what would happen to these tenants. Ossovetski only wanted them off the land for which he paid the full price. A feud developed between Ossovetski's men and the villagers. The district governor sided with Ossovetski, but Arselan, the *kaimakan* of Tiberias, supported the villagers. Ossovetski was fired on and he called in the police, who put many of the villagers in jail. Things were approaching an open rebellion, at which time I cabled Paris and asked for authority to intervene and to settle the dispute. In less than three weeks an agreement was reached, and within two months four new settlements were founded – Sejera, Yavne'el, Mes'ha (Kefar-Tavor) and Menahamiya. All this was accomplished by a fair approach to the tenant farmers and by modest compensation which they were paid in response to their claims."[68]

Kalvarisky's efforts to settle the disputes by the payment of compensation did not always work out well. The border feud between the *moshava* Sejera and the Arab villages el-Sejera, Tur'an, Kafer-Kanna and Kafer-Sabet continued for many years.[69] When the settlers of Sejera began to plow up land that was bought from the village of Lubiya, the fellaheen attacked the *moshava* and killed one of the settlers. Following this incident the Sejera settlers invited the "Hashomer" to take responsibility for guarding the *moshava*. The settlers tried to take the dispute to court, but court expenses were too high and the settlers gave up their right to the disputed tract.[70]

Wherever the landowners calculated that for the money from the sale they could buy larger land holdings elsewhere – in Syria or in Trans-Jordan – it was possible to come to an agreement.

The emir 'Ali, who – as has been mentioned – owned about half the land of the four Algerian villages, sold his Kafer-Sabet and Shara lands to the I.C.A. But the land was "musha'a," i.e. owned jointly with the fellaheen, and it was necessary to compensate them so that they would agree to separating their holdings from the land bought by the Jews.

As has been mentioned, the fellaheen of Kafer-Sabet were among those who attacked Sejera. They did not acquiesce in the sale, however after years of clashes the I.C.A. finally reached an agreement with them and paid them compensation (see below). The Shara villagers, too, at first refused to agree to the separation, but a few years later they agreed to hand over their land in return for double the area in Syria, near the Algerian settlements there. This was the first time that Algerian fellaheen were moved across the border and settled near their brethren.[71]

The land upon which Yavne'el was founded was occupied by forty families of the Delaike–'Issa tribe, and they now moved to Trans-Jordan.[72] Sheikh 'Issa of the Delaike tribe sold his land because he apparently wanted to get out of the sight of the Turkish authorities. "...At the time of Umm Juni (1909)," writes the "Shomer" Zvi Nadav, "the sheikh and some of his men went into hiding east of the Kinneret – the Turkish authorities were out to arrest him on a charge of murder and other crimes."[73]

Sheikh Hussein of the Delaike-Sahu tribe, who sold land on which the *moshava* Kinneret was founded, moved to Trans-Jordan. Of his son, the "Shomer" S.D. Yaffe wrote in his memoirs: "Hussein sold his land and moved with all his men to Trans-Jordan. However his son Canj apparently did not want to give up his fiefdom in the Yavne'el and Kinneret area. He organized a gang of marauders, who robbed travellers and stole flocks of sheep and cattle."[74]

In 1909, the *moshava* Mes'ha reached an agreement with the Zebeih tribe concerning a disputed tract of a thousand dunam.Joshua Hankin carried on protracted negotiations with the sheikh of the tribe over handing over the area which the I.C.A. bought from the Govenment, and which was not separated from the land owned by the tribe. Every time they seemed to be nearing an agreement the sheikh would change his mind and demand a higher indemnity. After the "Hashomer" took over the guarding of the *moshava*, the Mes'ha settlers decided to go out in force into the field and plow up the land which they had rightfully bought. The settlers and the watchmen of "Hashomer" were prepared to defend themselves against a possible attack, but at the very same time Hankin was in the sheikh's tent, and an agreement on compensation was reached.[75]

The I.C.A. bought 10,000 dunam near the Jordan River from the Sursuk family for the founding of Menahamiya. One of the members of the family had bought the land from the Sultan, and the deed which Sursuk handed to the buyers stated that there were 10,000 dunam. But upon surveying the fields it was found that there were only 6,000. It turned out that Sursuk had really bought 10,000 dunam, but on part of the land near the river crossing the Government decided to establish a new village, Jisr el-Mejami, which was intended for the military guard that would control the Trans-Jordan Bedouins who were raiding the area. The officer in charge was authorized to requisition stretches of land from the nearby villages, among them some of the land which Sursuk had sold to the I.C.A. A prolonged litigation between the I.C.A. and the Government ensued and lasted until the outbreak of the World War, when the issue lost all relevance.[76]

In 1905 the I.C.A., purchased 3,000 dunam from the Persian effendi of Umm Juni. (Three years later the I.C.A. sold this tract and an additional 3,000 dunam of Delaike land to the Jewish National Fund. The kibbutzim Degania and Kinneret – which, like Sejera, were to play a major role in the history of Jewish settlement – were established on these lands). The Persian effendi, 'Ali Rida Irani, was a trustee of the Bahai sect, the son of a refugee who had left Persia because of religious persecution.

One of the founders of Degania wrote about Umm Juni: "The Umm Juni lands made up about half of the village lands. The other half was worked by Arab tenant farmers by most primitive methods. They were paid for their labor with part of the crop and a meager sum of money. The tenants who had worked the land which the Jewish National Fund purchased received compensation and left. With the remaining ones we maintained good-neighborly relations."77

In 1910 the I.C.A. bought the land of Sharona, a village founded by Circassians, who had moved on elsewhere. Their place was taken by Arab fellaheen, who had received or bought the land – this point was never cleared up – from the Circassians. In the files of the P.I.C.A. we find a declaration by the village head and the villagers, dated 1329 by the Moslem count – 1910 A.D. – that they have no claims regarding the Sharona land; a declaration by the villagers of Kafer-Kanna and Hadita verifiying the borders described in the deed and stating that they had no claims; and an accounting of the indemnity paid to the fellaheen by the I.C.A. for damages caused while establishing the demarcation lines.[78]

Several years after the I.C.A. purchases, a Russian Zionist society bought 6,000 dunam of land along the shore of Lake Kinneret, north of Tiberias. The seller was a German. As will be recalled, Germans bought up tracts of land, following the establishment of the Templar settlements, outside these settlements as well. In most cases the German owners were unable to hold on to their property and they sold it to Jews. This is what happened in this instance, and the land was used for the founding of the moshava Migdal in 1910.[79]

The various resolutions of the land feuds and the employment of Arab workmen and guards in the moshava did not make for a lasting peace between the new settlers and their neighbors. Any small incident was sufficient to cause the enmity of the Arabs to flare up anew.

In 1909 the Jewish Watchmen's association "Hashomer" was founded, and all the moshavot of Lower Galilee went over to the employment of Jewish watchmen. The Mugrabi and Circassian villages, which until that time had a monopoly on guarding these moshavot, did not easily give up their positions of strength and their incomes. Instances of theft, armed robbery and murder

106

became more and more frequent, and the members of "Hashomer" reacted firmly, though they were careful not to engage in indiscriminate acts of revenge. In the course of time the neighbors adjusted to the new situation, and learned to appreciate the Jews' ability to defend their lives and their property. Some form of *modus vivendi* was worked out, with alternating quiet periods and times of tension.

The idea behind the purchase of large tracts of land in the Lower Galilee during the years 1899–1904 also guided the I.C.A. land purchases in the foothills of the mountains of Samaria and the efforts to obtain concessions from the Government for draining the swamps from Atlit to Hadera. Zikhron-Ya'akov, Bat-Shelomo and Shefeya in the north and Hadera in the south were to serve as cornerstones of continuous land holdings, extending from Atlit at the sea shore in the north, reaching into the Samaria foothills in the east and continuing on the Hadera in the south. The acquisition maps of the Baron and of the I.C.A. (later also of the P.I.C.A.) show clearly that the main land-buying effort was concentrated in two zones: the Galilee (especially Lower Galilee) and the Samaria coastal plain. The I.C.A. continued to assist the settlements founded by the Baron in the South, but the main initiative for new settlement was in these two areas. The difference between them was that the Galilee lands were suitable for immediate settlement, while the coastal lands required very extensive preparation which took many years.

In 1902 the chief executive officer of the I.C.A., H. Frank, contracted with Hafez Beidoun, in his own name and that of his brother Zaqi of Akko (it will be recalled that the Beidoun family also owned lands in Lower Galilee, which it sold to the I.C.A.), for the sale of 2,911 dunam of land, on which the *moshava* Binyamina was later established.[80]

Sidki Pasha, the brother of Jamal Pasha, sold to the I.C.A. 4,000 dunam of the lands of Burj, which was added on to Binyamina's holdings. Jamal Pasha, who was one of the three rulers of Turkey after the "Young Turk" revolution, was giving out land with a free hand. His brother Sidki was one of the beneficiaries, and he sold his land to the I.C.A.[81]

In 1903 the I.C.A. bought 7,858 dunam of land in the village Marah from Fuad Sa'ad, and the *moshava* Giv'at-Ada was established on it. The tract had been abandoned in 1873, and Sa'ad had bought it at a public auction. Eight hundred dunam was swamp, and the rest very meager land, worked by tenant farmers who left it after the sale to the I.C.A.[82]

The same year the I.C.A. also bought the lands of Atlit and obtained a Government concession over 3,403 dunam, of which 1,510 were swamp-land. A hundred families were living there, suffering heavily from malaria.[83]

To the south of Atlit the I.C.A. bought the Tantura tract which suffered badly from flooding and lack of drainage and was not considered fit for cultivation. In 1896 the notables of Tantura signed over their rights to the Smali Swamp to Baron Rothschild.[84] In 1921, when the I.C.A. decided to drain the swamp, it presented a plan for the drainage project to the District Commissioner. Among the expenses listed were: 700 Egyptian pounds as compensation and 1,200 Egyptian pounds as loans to the tenant farmers.[85]

In 1914 the I.C.A. obtained a concession from the Turkish Government over 25,510 dunam of Caesaria sand-dunes and Kabara swamps (the swamps covered 6,000 dunam). The concession was ratified by the Mandatory Government in November 1921 and in the agreement between the Mandatory and the I.C.A. a stretch of 2,500 dunam was allotted to the fellaheen who had occupied the swamp-land.[86]

In the hope of rehabilitating the entire area the I.C.A. obtained a concession over an additional 362 dunam of swamp-land, where years later (1929) Pardes-Hana was founded.[87] More land was later bought there by private individuals, and the area of the *moshava* came to 16,702 dunam. Forty percent of this land had been abandoned, and on the remaining 60% there were 140 families. Of these, 70 left before the purchase, five remained (two of them planted orange groves), and the lot of the other 65 is not known.[88]

The extent to which the whole area was neglected and forsaken can be learned from the memoirs of the "Shomer" Yigael. In 1912 Hankin bought 11,368 dunam of the lands of Karkur and Beidous from Mustafa Pasha and from Qasem Abd el-Hadi.[89] The purchase was made in behalf of the Palestine Land Development Company. The place was desolate, and Yigael undertook to guard it – he had agreed to go to so forsaken a spot because he was fleeing from the threat of revenge resulting from a blood-feud.

Here is what he writes in his memoirs: "Karkur was a ruin of a village, belonging to three landowners. The nearest neighbors were three Turkmenian families, who had come here from the Jezreel Valley, where they had quarrelled with their neighbors and were afraid of revenge. It then happened that one of them killed one of the others, and the murderer came to my room in search of shelter."[90]

Up to the end of the First World War the I.C.A. bought up a total of 350,000 dunam of land. Together with the concessions its holdings came to 400,000 dunam.[91]

Even during the war years the I.C.A. maintained contact, through Joshua Hankin and his assistants, with potential sellers. Negotiations were conducted mainly with Algerian land-owners, heirs to the property of Abd el-Kader, who were living in Syria and were out of touch with their holdings in Palestine, now that a border came between them and the Mugrabi villages. Some of the fellaheen were also interested in moving to Syria and joining their families there. In October 1920 the British authorities re-opened the land registration books, and land sales were renewed. In May and June 1921 nine land owners in Kafer-Sabet sold land to the I.C.A. (among the sellers listed in the P.I.C.A. archives is one named Zina bint Abd el-Kader...)[92] The emir Said Abd el-Kader, who lived in Syria, conducted an active correspondence with Hankin and sold land to the I.C.A. On July 7, 1921 Hankin reminded Abd el-Kader that he promised to come to Tiberias and take care of the formalities around the sale of his lands in the Tiberias and Safed districts. Kalvarisky wrote to him on May 28, 1922, pointing out that he was demanding 1,301 Egyptian pounds more than was due him, nevertheless he would send him an additional 500 Egyptian pounds.[93]

In the Mugrabi village Ulam the heirs of the emir 'Ali owned 10,175 dunam of land, and the fellaheen – 8,225 dunam. On June

20, 1924, a contract was signed between 'Ali's heirs, with the approval of the emir Said, and the representatives of the I.C.A., Isaac Levi and Rosenheck, concerning the sale of the emir's lands.[94] A year later, 14 fellaheen sold 2,209 dunam to the I.C.A., and the remaining fellaheen were left with 6,000 dunam.[95]

With the advent of British rule the activities of the I.C.A. were slowed down, and a change occurred with the founding of the P.I.C.A. (Palestine Jewish Colonization Association) in 1924. The practices of the I.C.A. – P.I.C.A. regarding the Arab neighbors of the *moshavot* and the tenant farmers were the subject of criticism by the Mandatory Government and the inquiry commissions which visited Palestine in the 1930's. More about that later.

Beginnings of Political Arab Opposition to Jewish Land Purchases

Arab opposition to land sale to Jews on national political grounds became more and more pronounced as Jewish settlement, directed by the Zionist Organization, came to be more and more an expression of Jewish national aspirations. The Jewish-Arab confrontation, which became more pronounced in later years, was foreseen in the early stages of Jewish settlement by two men – a Jew and an Arab.

As far back as 1891 Ahad Ha'am wrote: "We are accustomed to think of the Arabs as uncultured desert dwellers, a people similar to an ass, who see nothing and perceive nothing of what is going on around them. This is a grave error. The Arab, like all the Semites, is a clever and cunning man... The Arabs, particularly the town dwellers, see and understand very well what we are doing and what we are aiming at, but they are quiet and pretend to know nothing, because they do not consider themselves threatened by our actions so far... But if there should come a day when the developing Jewish community begins to press upon the Arabs, they will not give up their positions easily...''[96]

On the Arab side the man who foresaw the coming confrontation was Naguib Azuri, a Government official in the Jerusalem District, who was forced to emigrate to Paris because of his opposition to the Turkish regime. Azuri published a book on the revival of the Arab nation, which appeared in Paris in 1905. In the preface he

110

wrote: "Two mighty processes, similar in content but opposite in aim, are now taking place in Asian Turkey – the revival of the Arab nation, and the re-awakening of a long-dormant desire of the Jews to re-establish the ancient kingdom of Israel on a large scale. These two movements are bound to come into conflict, until one of them overcomes the other..."[97]

Ahad Ha'am's prophetic words of warning succeeded to some extent in implanting an understanding for the Arab neighbor in the minds of the Zionist leaders, and to raise their awareness of the moral aspects of their activities. However the continuation of Jewish settlement added fuel to the confrontation, which could only have been avoided by the abandonment of the idea of the Jewish Return.

Azuri's book was the expression of the beginnings of the Arab national ferment, which developed a growing opposition to the Zionist endeavor as Jewish settlement became more and more rooted in the country. The "Young Turk" revolution accelerated the growth of Arab national consciousness. In Palestine this heightened consciousness took the form of opposition to Zionism, to *aliya* and to Jewish settlement. The acquisition of the Fuleh (later Merhavya) lands was a signal for the first mobilization of the educated Arabs – professionals, journalists, political leaders – in a campaign against the realization of the Jewish national aspirations. At the same time the Arabs used the Zionist issue to test the nature of the new regime in Istanbul, to see to what extent it was ready to take account of the desires of the Arab population.

The year 1908 marks the beginning of land buying and settlement activity by the organized Zionist movement. The Palestine Office was established for this purpose, with two executive arms: the Jewish National Fund, which was founded back in 1901 for the purpose of buying lands for national ownership and establishing settlements on it (the separation between land-purchasing and the allocation of budgets for settlememt did not take place until 1921, when the Palestine Foundation Fund – "Keren Hayesod" – was created for the latter function), but remained inactive until 1908; and the Palestine Land Development Company, which was created as a stock company and was meant to buy land and to prepare it for

111

settlement, both for the Jewish National Fund and for private individuals, with the idea of centralizing all land purchases in public hands so as to avoid possible land speculation.

In 1910 Joshua Hankin, in the name of the I.C.A., bought from Elias Sursuk of Beirut 9,000 dunam of land in the village of Fuleh. But the I.C.A. did not ratify the purchase, and Hankin turned to Ruppin suggesting that the Palestine Land Development Company buy the land. Ruppin had difficulty financing the purchase, but after prolonged efforts he succeeded in working out a deal for a joint purchase: part of the tract was bought by the P.L.D.C. and another part – 3,240 dunam – by the Jewish National Fund. The land was to be used for the building of a cooperative settlement according to the plan worked out by Franz Oppenheimer.[98]

The Ottoman law did not recognize the Company as a legal body authorized to buy land, so the sale was recorded in the name of Eliyahu Krause, the director of the Sejera farm. But the *kaimakam* of Nazareth, Shukri el-'Asli, who was an Arab nationalist and an extreme opponent of the Zionist effort, refused to register the land in Krause's name. Elias Sursuk used his influence on the *wali*, urging him to persuade Shukri to cooperate; Hankin tried to use his connections for the same purpose, but el-'Asli was adamant in his refusal, claiming that he was acting on instructions from Istanbul.[99]

In the meantime Hankin saw to it – according to the testimony of Sa'adia Paz, who took part in the first occupation of the Fuleh land – that the tenant farmers who worked the land were paid compensation.[100]

When the Jewish workers, accompanied by members of "Hashomer," came to take possession of the land, the *kaimakam* of Nazareth dispatched six policemen with orders to drive the Jews off. Hankin lodged a complaint with the *mutissarif* of Akko,[101] while Sursuk kept pressing the *wali* in Beirut to approve the transfer of the land to the Jews. While all this was gong on, el-'Asli resigned from his post to run for the Turkish parliament, and the settlers took possession of the land.

While the negotiations were in progress el-'Asli told a Jewish official of the Anlo-Palestine Bank in Haifa that he would fight to his last drop of blood to prevent the Jews from taking over the

112

Fuleh lands.[102] After he resigned his Nazareth post, he continued his active campaign against the sale and published sharp attacks on Zionism in various Istanbul newspapers.[103] He continued to be an active leader in the Palestinian Arab national movement.

After the Jews took possession of the Fuleh lands there were frequent clashes between the "Hashomer" watchmen and the Arab neighbors, mostly because the latter continued to graze their flocks on the cultivated fields. A sharp conflict broke out between the watchmen and the villagers of neighboring Solam, not over land but because a gang of robbers was operating out of Solam and the "Hashomer" watchment interfered with their activities. One night three Arabs attacked the watchman Yigael who was guarding the settlement. In the ensuing fray Yigael fired a shot and killed one of the attackers. The threat of blood vengeance increased the tension between the settlers and the neighboring village. Yigael was arrested and tried. The family of the deceased was paid an indemnity and Yigael spent eleven months in jail, after which he moved to the village Marah, to get away from the threat of revenge (see above).[104]

Even after the purchase of Fuleh became an accomplished fact, it served as the focus of an extensive campaign on the part of the Arabs against the sale of land to Jews. Cables were sent by Arab notables from Nazareth and Haifa to Istanbul, protesting the sales. A delegation of Arabs from Aleppo and Beirut appeared before the Minister of the Interior and demanded that he ban the sale of land to Jews because "they are a threat to the Empire."[105]

In 1910 a society was established in Haifa with the aim of "taking firm step that will lead to the Government prohibiting land sales to Jews."[106]

The Arab newspapers which began to appear in Palestine at this time published sharp articles against Zionism and the sale of land. An active role in this campaign was played by the Christian Arabs. The writings of the editor of "El-Carmel," Naguib Nasser, who until recently had been an agent of the I.C.A., were especially sharp.[107] It is not known why Naguib Nasser went through such a total change. It may be that in the course of his work for the I.C.A. he came to realize the threat to the Arab position contained in the

Jewish purposes; it may be that he left the I.C.A. for other reasons, and his change of heart was due to some personal grievance against his former employers.

On March 31, 1911, some 150 Arab notables from Jerusalem, headed by Ragheb Nashashibi, sent a cable to the Turkish parliament protesting the land sales to Jews.[108] Even moderate Arab leaders, such as the mayor of Jerusalem, Hussein el-Husseini, who thought that the Arabs had much to learn from the Jews, expressed their apprehension over the land sales: "All this nothwithstanding, we must keep a watchful eye on the Zionists, for, if things continue as they are now going, all our land will before long pass into their hands. Our fellah is poor and down-trodden, and a poor man is ready even to part with his land to keep body and soul together. For this reason the Government must pass a law against land sales to Jews, taking into account the conditions in the country."[109]

In July 1913 the Arab leaders tried to call together in Nablus a convention of representatives of all the towns of Palestine to organize the struggle against Zionism and against the sale of land to Jews.[110] The attempt failed and the convention never took place, but from that time on the transfer of land to Jews became one of the main issues in the mobilization of the Arab national movement against Zionism and Jewish settlement.

CHAPTER FIVE

THE MANDATE DURING THE YEARS 1920–1935

The Acquisition of the Jezreel and Zebulun Valleys – Displacement of Tenant Farmers as the Focus of Arab Resistance

At the end of World War I, with the tranfer of Palestine to British trusteeship under the League of Nations Mandate, Jewish settlement was freed from the limitations that Ottoman laws and edicts had imposed.

The hopes raised by the signing of the Feisal-Weizmann Agreement that the Zionist undertaking would win Arab acceptance proved to be unfounded. The strong opposition of the Palestinian Arabs was decisive.[1] The Palestinian-Arab national movement began to emerge as an independent Palestinian political party that sought self-rule in the country – in a word Arab majority rule.

The Palestinian-Arab nationalist struggle for self-rule was aimed first and foremost at Zionism in all its aspects. It fought against the political obligations that Britain had undertaken in conformity with the Balfour Declaration and the League of Nations Mandate, and it opposed Jewish immigration, land acquisition and settlement.

The opposition to Jewish land purchases by the Arab political leaders was premised, *inter alia*, on a contradiction (as they saw it) implicit in Article VI of the Mandate. This required the Mandatory to encourage "close settlement by Jews on the land, including State lands and waste lands not required for public purposes," as long as "the rights and position of other sections of the population are not prejudiced." Their argument was that the purchase of land by Jews *per se* prejudiced the position of the existent Arab population.

The efforts of the Zionists to have the Mandate implemented, in letter and in spirit, and of the Arabs to have it annulled, were directed at the British Government in London and, to some extent, at the Mandates Commission of the League of Nations. However the execution and interpretation of the laws that the Mandate established were left to the British officialdom in Palestine. In addressing itself to the apparent contradiction in Article VI of the Mandate, the Mandatory enacted laws concerning the transfer of real property, so as to protect the rights of tenant farmers and small landholders (fellaheen).

The Jews feared that these edicts might be expanded or interpreted in a fashion that would block land purchases. They were not opposed to measures that would protect the fellaheen and the tenant farmers against discrimination and eviction. They were prepared to compensate the displaced farmers adequately and such offers were made repeatedly. The Arab leadership, however,

115

remained adamant in demanding a total ban on the sale of land.

Until the publication of the White Paper of 1939, which forbade the sale of land to Jews on 95% of the country's area, the Arabs were unsuccessful in their attempts to force the Mandatory to forbid land sale to Jews. Nevertheless Arab efforts to make displaced tenant farmers the focus of their struggle to forbid the sale of land added a human dimension to their maximalist political demand. The point stressed was that the sale of a particular plot of land dispossessed so many and so many tillers of the soil, and so, under British rule, Arabs were being uprooted from their land.

Along with the political struggle, the Arab Executive urged the fellaheen and the tenant farmers not to sell land to Jews; to refuse to accept cash indemnities; and to forcibly oppose the evacuation of their land. The British authorities, whose prime responsibility was to ensure law and order in the country, became an active factor in the disputes over land. The enforcement of the laws and regulations pertaining to the transfer of land were the responsibility of the Land Department; the courts were called upon to intervene and to render judgment in the litigations which arose; and the police were summoned when one of the parties to the conflict failed to obey a court order and sought to take the law into its own hands. The quarrels often became violent and resulted in bloodshed. Long-standing feuds over land challenged the authorities and the prestige of the British. Therefore it was not surprising that the Mandatory maintained strict supervision over land transfers from Arabs to Jews from the very beginning.

The Zionist Movement, aware that it would be unable to reach an accommodation with the Arab aspirations, imposed limitations on itself in regard to land purchases, so that in no case would the individual Arab be dealt with unfairly. The Jewish settlers were imbued with the belief that their efforts would bring about real improvement in the condition of the Arab fellah and tenant farmer. Thus the Zionist Organisation agreed to cooperate with the Palestine Government in observing the existent legal limitations on the transfer of real property, provided they were not used as an instrument to limit or block Jewish settlement.

In 1918, after the conquest of Palestine by the British Army, the

116

military authorities had found the Land Register records in a state of utter chaos. For this reason, and because the military authorities did not consider the Balfour Declaration binding policy (most of the senior officers were emphatically anti-Zionist), they closed the Land Register and forbade all sale of land. With the coming of the first High Commissioner, Sir Herbert Samuel, and with the establishment of civilian government, the Land Register was re-opened in October 1920 and the sale of land allowed. However in order to prevent speculation and to safeguard the homestead of the fellah the High Commissioner promulgated an edict forbidding the sale of more than 300 dunam of land or the sale of land worth more than 3000 Palestine Pounds (LP.), without his prior permission. Smaller tracts of land, or transactions involving less than LP. 3000, required the assent of the District Commissioner. Fellaheen were permitted to sell their land, provided they retained enough land for their livelihood. According to Turkish law it was forbidden to sell land to corporations. This ban was lifted and corporations were free to purchase land within the bounds of the new regulations.

Before the Land Law was decreed, Joshua Hankin began negotiating for the purchase of the Jezreel Valley. It was his life's dream. When only a young man of 27, he succeeded in contracting with the Sursuk family to buy 160,000 dunam in the Valley. He suggested to Ze'ev Tiomkin, the representative of the Lovers of Zion in the country, that he raise the money and consummate the purchase. But in that year, 1891, the *aliya* was spontaneous and unorganized and consequently speculation in real property was rife. As a result the Turkish authorities banned *aliya* and the sale of land. The proposed purchase fell through.[2]

On August 27, 1920 Hankin signed a contract in Alexandria with Nagib and Albert Sursuk, confirming the terms of an agreement dated December 18, 1919 for the purchase of 71,356 dunam in the Jezreel Valley.[3]

On April 19, 1921 Arthur Ruppin, who was in charge of land settlement on behalf of the Zionist Organization, wrote to the Main Office of the Jewish National Fund at the Hague: "The fact that the seller (of the lands in the Jezreel Valley) personally undertook to leave land for his fellaheen is a matter of considerable importance.

Thus the seller has retained some 6,000 to 8,000 dunam near Afula, and about 4,000 to 5,000 dunam in the Nuris sector. He will rent the land to the fellaheen who were previously his tenants for a nominal sum, or perhaps at no cost. In this way the fellaheen will be justly compensated."[4]

Sursuk lived up to his agreement only in part – he alloted only 2,000 dunam to the fellaheen. On May 12, 1921 Ruppin wrote to the Main Office of the Jewish National Fund: "We bought 23,676 dunam in Ma'alul, Sufsafa and Umm Qebi, of which 6,000 dunam will be given to the Arabs – leaving us 17,676 dunam. In the Nuris sector we purchased 29,454 dunam, of which 2,000 dunam are mountainous, and 4,000 dunam are allotted to the Arabs – leaving us 23,484 dunam. All told, there will be 41,160 dunam available for cultivation."[5]

As will be recalled, the law decreed that the sale of parcels of land larger than 300 dunam required the prior permission of the High Commissioner. The Secretariat of the Palestine Government kept an eye on such sales. On July 7, 1921 the Commissioner of the Northern District wrote to the Chief Secretary's Office: "In Ma'alul there are 87 families, numbering 450 souls. Sursuk left them 2,000 dunam and the Palestine Land Development Company, the purchaser of the land, has leased them an additional 3,000 dunam. The fellaheen are demanding that the land be given to them in perpetuity free of charge. I advised them that I would be responsible for the implementation of such an agreement. The fellaheen agreed. In Jinjar there were thirteen families who had been living there only a few years. The Company alloted 1,300 dunam for them – 100 dunam per family. In Tel el-Ferı there were fourteen families. In Jalud, nine families."[6]

The Director of the Land Department, in a letter to the Chief Secretary, expressed himself approvingly of the allocation of 3,000 dunam, with an option to buy. He then explained that the inhabitants of Jinjar, Tel el-Ferr and Jalud never owned their land and so were not entitled to as generous a settlement as the inhabitants of Ma'alul. The former had worked the land for only a few years and consequently the land was to be leased to them for a six-year period, with an option to buy.[7]

On December 28, 1921 Dr. Arthur Ruppin signed an agreement with Sa'id A'id el-Khuri, who represented the seventy families of Ma'alul. It provided for the leasing of 3,000 dunam to them for six years, with an option to purchase at the end of that period.[8] In addition the Palestine Land Development Company agreed to supply water to Ma'alul from the two wells of 'Ein Beida, in the same quantity that they had been using prior to the agreement.[9] The 70 tenant farmers had paid no rent for the preceding six years, yet 22 families out of the 70 demanded at the time of the purchase that the Jewish National Fund sell them the entire 3,000 dunam outright. Dr. Ruppin was opposed to selling the land, which was meant for 70 families, to 22 well-to-do farmers. In the end the negotiations broke down without an agreement having been reached, and the tenant farmers paid no rent until 1934.[10]

While the negotiations were going on, the herdsmen of Ma'alul kept invading the hill lands of the Jewish National Fund near Nahalal, claiming grazing rights there. Several times were the intruders haled into court and fined. On a few occasions they appealed, but the verdict was always against them.[11] These trials kept cropping up until May 22, 1932.

In order to put an end to the dispute, the Jewish National Fund offered to give 1,500 dunam of land in the plain to the fellaheen of Ma'alul, on condition that they acquire a tract of 1,000 dunam of land in Yafia (south of Nazareth) and transfer it in exchange to the Jewish National Fund. Thus the offer constituted a gift of five hundred dunam to the people of Ma'alul. The offer was made conditional on their desisting from grazing their flocks on the hill lands. It was accepted in principle, but then the fellaheen notified the Jewish National Fund that they did not have the money to buy the land in Yafia. The Director of Development agreed to give the fellaheen the money,[12] but this agreement also fell through. Finally the Jewish National Fund transferred the land to the Arabs and received in return a government franchise on land in the Beit-Shean Valley (See below).

As to the other two small groups of fellaheen in the Nuris (Harod) sector, the fourteen families of Tel el-Ferr and the nine families of Jalud, the negotiations with them took a different turn.

119

Tel el-Ferr co-opted a few additional families in order to swell their claims for reimbursement, and the total number of families came to 31. Joshua Hankin was of the opinion that it was preferable to pay off the fellaheen in cash, so that they might lease new lands in an Arab area, rather than to rent them lands adjoining the Jewish settlements. He argued that these neighbouring lands would be needed for future development.

Originally the Jewish National Fund had contracted to acquire 4,000 dunam in the Nuris sector to be rented for a six-year period to the tenant farmers, but Hankin persuaded them to accept a cash settlement instead, which included a loan to each family to build a house wherever it decided to settle.[13]

In Jinjar (Ginegar), the Jewish National Fund purchased 4,470 dunam of land, and rented it to the thirteen families, who were settled there.[14]

In 1924 Linda and Nicholas Sursuk sold 15,500 dunam of land near Afula to the P.L.D.C. Hankin reached an agreement with the sixteen tenant farmers who were affected by the sale to pay them reparations ranging from LP. 50 to 150, depending on the size of the plot cultivated. He continued to negotiate with the remaining tenant farmers on the same basis.[15]

The Jewish settlers set out to plough the vacated areas. When they came to the fields they were met by a volley of stones from the former tenant farmers and other villagers. A brawl with stones and sticks ensued when suddenly a shot was fired and an Arab was killed.

Sa'adia Paz, a member of *Hashomer*, and a man by the name of Segal were arrested and charged with murder. The testimony in court showed that the two had not even been at the site when the shooting occurred. Nevertheless the court sentenced Paz to six months imprisonment and Segal to a year. The judge, in setting forth the reasons for his verdict, explained that the defendants had shot their rifles in the air and thus had spurred others on to using their weapons in earnest. Thus they were the proximate cause of the Arab's death. The family of the deceased received a cash indemnity.[16]

Five years later the Shaw Commission thoroughly investigated the incident. Charles Passman, the Managing Director of the American Zion Commonwealth, the corporation for which the Palestine Land Development Company had bought the land, took the witness stand.

Passman testified that the land was bought in 1924. A written commitment was made to the Chief Secretary of the Government, Sir Gilbert Clayton, "that we would satisfy the tenants,... that we were to offer to the tenants either lands in any place outside Afula or monetary compensation in accordance with the [area] the tenant worked."

"... There were 54 tenants... With about 40 or 42 agreements were made immediately."

One of the members of the Commission asked Passman whether they had preferred money to land. Passman replied:

"They all preferred cash." The following exchange took place:

"'Now, what about the remaining 12?'

"'The remaining 12 refused to accept either land or cash.'

"'Why?'

"'They claimed that some people in Jerusalem told them... not to give up the land.'

"...'Who were the people?'

"'We have seen a number of people from the Arab Executive calling at Afula village at the time of the transaction...'

"'Now, with regard to those who did elect to take cash, how was the transaction carried on?'

"'They signed before a Notary a document that they have been compensated for their tenant rights and that they have no further claims. These documents were filed with the District Commissioner.'"[17]

Passman then described how the Jews had gone out to plow the land and how the tenant farmers had greeted them with a hail of stones. A conflict ensued: Twenty Jews were injured and an Arab was killed. After this event twelve intransigent farmers sought a settlement on the terms given to the others. They received compensation and the disturbances ceased.[18]

Hankin bought 16,482 dunam of land in Kefar-Yehezke'el and in Tel-Adashim. In his account of expenditures the following item appears: "transfer, commission, indemnity to the fellaheen – 11,537 Egyptian pounds."[19]

In the sector of Hartiya, Harbaj and Sheikh-Ibreiq (today Sha'ar-Ha'amakim, Kefar-Hassidim and Alonim), Hankin bought 25,560 dunam of land from the Sursuk family. On these lands there were 54 tenant farmers. They were compensated by the payment of LP. 5,450.[20] In the sector of Jedda, Tel-Shamam and Qamon (today Ramat-Yishai, Kefar-Yehoshua and Yokne'am), the Sursuk and Touwini families sold 28,000 dunam. There were 76 tenant farmers who received compensation amounting to LP. 4,441.[21]

In Jebata and Ikhnefis (now Gevat and Sarid), the Sursuk family sold 24,000 dunam to the Jewish National Fund. Fifty-seven tenant farmers received payment of LP. 2,032.[22] The amount of payment was determined by the use that the farmer put the land to – more was paid for cultivated than for grazing land.

In August 1935 the Palestine Land Development Company bought 64,588 dunam of land in the Haifa Bay area from the Sursuk family, from Mary Bustros, and from Nahle Touwini. There were only three settled communities in all the Haifa Bay area: a Bedouin encampment in the village of Jidru, comprising 117 families, and two villages, Majdal and Kufreta, on the hills adjacent to the bay area, that numbered 96 tenant farmers.[23]

Most of these lands were bought on behalf of the American Zion Commonwealth and other private companies. The A.Z.C., which had sold some of its properties to private settlers, went bankrupt, and in the end most of its holdings were acquired by the Jewish National Fund. In the inquiry of the Shaw Commission mentioned above, the members of the Commission continued to question Charles Passman, the Managing director of the A.Z.C., about the lands of Jidru, Majdal and Kufreta. The questioning brought out that there were 90 tenant farmers in Jidru and 96 in Kufreta. Those in Jidru were really nomadic Bedouins, squatters who claimed that the land belonged to them. They were offered a lease of one hundred dunam of land per family for a period of six years, or a cash indemnity. They preferred the cash.

One of the Commission members asked for proof that an offer of land had indeed been made. The Jewish attorney for the defense,

Boyd Merriman, promised to produce such evidence the next day. The proceedings of the Commission were conducted as a court of law. There was a Jewish attorney for the defense as well as an Arab one. In reply to further questions Passman informed the Commission that the farmers all received cash indemnities and were satisfied. There were no problems. Finally the tenant farmers moved to the nearby villages of Shafa-'Amr and Damun, and continued to cultivate the land. With the money they received they built houses for themselves. The witness himself had seen their houses and their cattle.

On the following day, Boyd Merriman, the attorney for the defense, produced, as promised, a document executed by Nahla Touwini (the Seller) and by Charles Passman, Mordekhai Saks, Akiva Ettinger, and Ernst Wallenstein on behalf of the American Zion Commonwealth, the Palestine Land Development Company, the Jewish National Fund and the Meshek Company (the Buyers). It provided that one hundred dunam of good land would be leased for a period of six years to each family at a rate of 6% of the purchase price. During the six-year period the lessees had the option to buy the land at the original purchase price. The document was included in the record of inquiry of the Shaw Commission.[24]

The 117 tenant farmers of Jidru received a total of 3,568 Egyptian pounds as indemnity; and the tenant farmers of Majdal and Kufreta received 6,156 Egyptian pounds.[25]

In 1928 the Palestine Land Development Company completed its purchases in the Zebulun Valley with the acquisition of the "Persian Gardens." In the account that it submitted to the Haifa Bay Development Company one finds a long list of indemnity payments to the tenant farmers who had lived there. The total payment amounted to LP. 1,750.[26]

Some time later the land was sold to the Jewish National Fund. In 1938 Kibbutz Ein-Hamifratz settled there.

Land purchases for the period under discussion amounted to 216,800 dunam of land in the Jezreel Valley and 44,588 dunam in the Zebulun Valley, making a total of 261,388 dunam.[27]

The years 1924 to 1926 were marked by an increase in the

acquisition of land by Jews and by economic prosperity. In the years 1927 and 1928, however, there was a general depression. Then came the bloody riots of 1929, when 133 Jews were killed and 339 wounded.[28] In the wake of these riots committees of inquiry followed one after the other.

In October 1929, a British Parliamentary Commission, presided over by the Chief Justice Walter Shaw, arrived to investigate the riots and the tensions between Jews and Arabs.

Pursuant to the findings of the Shaw Commission, Sir John Hope Simpson was dispatched to Palestine in May 1930 to survey the cconomic condition of the coutnry. His primary aim was to investigate the condition of the fellaheen, in order to make recommendations as to how to implement the conclusions of the Shaw Commission.

In June 1930 an International Committee was sent to investigate the rights and the claims of the two parties to the Western Wall.

During a three-month period, October to December 1929, the Shaw Commission carried out a far-reaching investigation of the causes of tension between the Arabs and the Jews. Representatives of both sides were interrogated at length.

Both sides soon became aware of the main thrust of the investigation. The far-fetched accusation that the Jews were plotting to seize the mosques of el-Aqsa and the Dome of the Rock was not taken seriously by the members of the Commission. At most they understood it as a ploy to arouse sympathy in the Moslem world. Likewise the demand of the Palestinian Arabs for self-government, when not all the neighbouring Arab States had yet achieved full independence, did not have much chance of impressing the Commission. Therefore the Arabs focused their attack on *aliya*, Jewish purchase of land and the threat of expropriation. They charged that in the first instance the fellaheen would be displaced, and in the final analysis the Arab community would be totally uprooted from its lands. These fears were expressed both in moral terms and as a question of national survival for a people dwelling in its land. The Arabs felt that this approach was most likely to be effective in the effort to gain public support in Britain and in the world. It should be remembered that

124

policy in Palestine was not formulated solely by the British Government in London. The Mandates Commission of the League of Nations served as a kind of supreme supervisory body. Many countries were represented on this Commission, including members of the British Commonwealth, and winning their favor was a prime object of the political activity by both Jews and Arabs.

The Shaw Commission began placing more and more stress on the question of land purchases and on the alleged displacement of the fellaheen. On November 10, 1929, when the investigation proceedings were at their height, Ruppin noted in his diary: "The Commission has broadened the framework of its inquiry. Arab witnesses are making all kinds of accusations against Jewish settlement on land, most of them unfounded. I must prepare material to refute them."[29]

The Political and Settlement Departments of the Jewish Agency requested the active land-purchasing agencies, the Jewish National Fund and the Palestine Land Development Company, to make a detailed survey of the number of displaced tenant farmers, of the monies paid them, and of what happened to them thereafter.

The Shaw Commission worked quickly. It finished its investigation in less than three months. The Jewish representives did not manage to prepare data based on exact and detailed surveys to refute the accusations leveled against Jewish settlement.

Ruppin did appear at a closed session of the Commission and he refuted the Arab accusations, but a well-documented memorandum, accompanied by accurate and detailed statistics, was submitted by the Jewish Agency to the Mandatory only in May 1930, in anticipation of Sir John Hope Simpson's mission. (The Report of the Shaw Commission was published on March 31, 1930).

The Shaw Commission considered the claims of both sides, but it made its recommendations mainly on the basis of data submittted by officials of the Mandatory Government, rather than by those furnished by either of the two sides.

Government officials in the Northern District furnished a list of displaced people in the Jezreel and Zebulun Valleys. Their information came from the village heads of the vicinity. They reported that 1,806 families in the two valleys were displaced by Jewish settlement. The list was attached to the Report of the Shaw Commission as an official exhibit.[30]

One may judge the extent of exaggeration by the village heads by noting the following item: The exhibit contains the statement that 280 families were evicted from Tel el-Ferr and Jalud, whereas the District officials had reported that the two villages contained 23 families, and that in order to increase their claims for compensation they had co-opted another eight families, making a total of 31 families at the most.

While the figure for displaced families in the official report was quite high, the Shaw Commission stated very clearly that the Jewish Companies had behaved correctly in making all their acquisitions: "We think that the Jewish Companies are not open to any criticism in respect of these transactions. In paying compensation, as they undoubtedly did, to many of the cultivators of lands which they purchased in the Plain of Esdraelon [Jezreel Valley] those companies were making a payment which at the time of the transactions the law of Palestine did not require. Moreover, they were acting with the knowledge of the Government."[31]

On the other hand, the Shaw Commission found that while the tenant famers had been dealt with fairly, the Arab claim that the purchase of land by Jews constituted a present danger to Arab national survival had substance. "The sale of the Sursuk lands and other Jewish land purchases in districts where the soil is most productive* were regarded as showing that the immigrants would not be content to occupy undeveloped areas and that the economic pressure upon the Arab population was likely to increase."

"In other words, those consequences of Jewish enterprise which have most closely affected the Arab people have been such that the Arab leaders could use them as the means of impressing upon their followers that a continuance of Jewish immigration and land purchases could have no other result than that the Arabs would in

* The Commission report makes no mention whatsoever that before the land became the most fertile in the country the Jewish settlers had reclaimed the swamp lands of the Jezreel Valley.

time be deprived of their livelihood and that they, and their country, might ultimately come under the political domination of the Jews."[32]

The conclusions reached by the Shaw Commission were ominous for the future of the Zionist effort in general, and for the continuation of *aliya* and settlement in particular. The Report went on: "...The position seems to be that, taking Palestine as a whole, the country cannot support a larger agricultural population than it at present carries unless methods of farming undergo a radical change."[33] The Report acknowledged that experiments were being carried out with a view to achieving greater intensification of the agricultural economy, but their success was doubtful. It therefore recommended that the Mandatory monitor land transfers from Arabs to Jews very closely. In plain language, the intent of the Report was to forbid sale of land to Jews.

The British Government adopted the report of the Shaw Commission and decided to send an expert on settlement to investigate the situation in the country, specially to determine the economic absorptive capacity of Palestine. He was to establish the amount of arable land available to the indigenous farmers, the Arabs, and the number of additional farmers that could settle on the available land. The British Government expressed its intent to shape its policy in accordance with his forthcoming recommendations.

The man chosen for this task who seemed suitable for it was Sir John Hope Simpson. After World War I, he had been sent to Greece by the British Government to help the Greek Government resettle Greek refugees who had been driven out by the Turks. Simpson arrived in Palestine in May 1930. He toured the various regions of the country and surveyed it by plane, determining areas suitable for cultivation. Considerable data were made available to him by the Mandatory Government. He also invited Arab and Jewish representatives to meet with him and state their views. Ruppin recorded in his dairy that he had had long talks with Simpson. At times, he was under the impression that Simpson understood the essence of Zionism and thus realized that the Zionistt effort did not aim to deny Arabs their rights.[34]

The Shaw Commission Report and the ideas known to be current in the Colonial Office concerning the future of the Zionist undertaking provided the Political Department of the Jewish Agency with good guidelines as to the probable course of Simpson's investigation. It was also clear that his conclusions would be drawn from the answers he would get to the following questions: How much arable land was there in the country? How many landless Arabs were there? What would be the influence of Jewish settlement on the Arab fellah?

In May 1930 the Jewish Agency expressed its point of view in a Memorandum to the Mandatory Government, setting forth its demands in the matters of *aliya*, settlement on land and the preservation of the letter and the spirit of the Mandate. Relying on the evaluations of its experts, the Jewish Agency presented estimates of the amount of arable land extant and of the portion that was available for new settlement. It also enumerated the advantages accruing to the Arab population as a result of the Zionist effort.[35] Among other matters the Memorandum contained data on the total number of tenant farmers who had resided in the Jezreel and Zebulun Valleys, on the amounts they had received as reimbursements, and on how they had fared in their new homes. These were areas that the Shaw Commission had regarded as crucial in proving that Jewish colonization endangered the future of the Arab community in the country.

The following, in brief, are the data that were submitted: 261,388 dunam were bought in the two valleys. The total number of tenant farmers on these lands was 641. They cultivated or used for grazing a total of 140,650 dunam. Thus about half the area had no settlers on it – the land was either lying fallow, or swampy, or covered with shifting sands. The tenant farmers were compensated to the extent of LP. 26,735. In addition, 30 Ma'alul families received 3,150 dunam of cultivable land, for which they paid no rent, and also received a cash indemnity of LP. 325. Thirty-nine families in Nuris were offered a lease on 3,100 dunam of land, but they preferrred to take a cash indemnity of LP. 585. The residents of Jinjar received 1,300 dunam cultivable land, free of rent. The amounts of rent which the Jewish National Fund waived and which would have been paid to the former owners came to LP. 2830.[36] Some time later Dr. A. Granovsky made a final calculation that 688 tenant farmers received LP. 27,434 as indemnity.[37]

The average payment to a tenant farmer was about forty pounds, but this average does not describe the true situation. Many payments were of the nuisance variety: Rather than get involved in protracted eviction proceedings against tresspassers, herdsmen, and others with dubious claims, the Jewish settlement agency would pay them off with a small sum. Thus, those with legitimate claims received an average of LP. 60 to 80 or even more, depending on the area they had cultivated.

Now, some fifty years later, it may seem strange, even incredible, that such sums could be regarded as fair payment to the displaced tenant farmers. The Simpson Report set forth the inventory value of the fellah's farm and his net income. It also gave figures for the tenant farmer and his homestead.

The Simpson Report estimated the value of the fellah's farm at between LP. 51 and LP. 62.[38] The annual income of the fellah who cultivated 100 dunam of land was LP. 11.80, according to the same Report. A tenant farmer who cultivated an area of similar size had an average annual income of LP. 3.60. 30% of his gross income went for rent to the effendi (the feudal landlord), taxes, and other levies, so that he and his family had very little to live on. Thus, a lump payment of LP. 40 to LP. 100 as an indemnity was the equivalent of ten to twenty years' net annual income or, alternatively, it was a sum that enabled the fellah or the tenant farmer to buy another homestead elsewhere. The Government, at that time, was ready to sell land to all comers at a price of LP. 1.25 to LP. 1.50 per dunam, payable over a period of thirty years. Thus the tenant farmer was enabled to become an independent fellah or he could easily settle elsewhere as a tenant farmer on leased land.

Somewhat later the Jewish Agency furnished Simpson with a detailed account of what happened to the 688 tenant farmers who were displaced from the Jezreel and Zebulun Valleys. Simpson included the account in his Report: 437 tenant farmers continued as such in other villages; 89 herdsmen continued to care for their flocks; 4 became craftsmen, 50 – urban laborers, 14 – mrchants, 4 –

129

vegetable hawkers, 10 – camel riders, 2 – dairymen; 37 had died, and the fate of 41 was unknown. Of the total of 688 tenant farmers 154 bought houses and tracts of land.[39] Those who remained farmers settled in Shafa 'Amr, Damun, Sasa, Usha, Wadi 'Ara, Jenin, Yafia, the Beit-Shean Valley, Iksal and other places.[40]

There was a considerable discrepancy between the figures that the Jewish Agency submitted and those that the Shaw Commission received from other sources. The testimony of the village chiefs before the Shaw Commission was that there were 1,806 tenant farmers in the Jezreel Valley at the time in question. The disparity in the figures was due to differences in the definition as to who was a tenant farmer. The general understanding in the Arab villages was that a tenant farmer was one who hired a plot of land for a number of years, cultivated it, and paid a tenant's rent. He was free to do with the land whatever he pleased: He could sublease it to someone else or he could hire laborers to farm it. Many tenant farmers hired a sharecropper, who would plow, sow, reap, and be paid with a portion of the crop. After the season was over the tenant farmer had no obligation whatsoever to employ the sharecropper further, nor was the sharecropper obliged to continue if he wished to find another place of work.

When the Government had promulgated the Protection of Cultivation Ordinance, which dealt with the rights of tenant farmers, it did not include "*harats*" (sharecroppers) among them. It is possible that had the Jewish agencies been more liberal and indemnified the sharecroppers as well, they would have allayed to some extent the bitterness of those who left empty-handed. But even though they did not satisfy everybody, Simpson summed up the situation by noting: "The Jewish authorities have nothing with which to reproach themselves in the matter of the Sursuk lands. They paid high prices for the land, and in addition they paid to certain of the occupants of those lands a considerable amount of money which they were not legally bound to pay."[41]

Simpson sought to amend the law pertaining to tenant farmers. A 1927 law provided that land could not be transferred without first securing for the tenant farmer other land elsewhere. Experience showed – Simpson noted – that whenever cash or land was proposed to tenant farmers, they preferred cash.[42] A 1929 amendment to the law provided for the formation of a judicial committee within the Land Register which was charged with handling the claims of the tenant farmers. It required the buyer to send formal notice to the tenant farmer of his intent to purchase the land. If the tenant farmer had been on the land more than five years, the buyer had to pay an increased indemnity. These requirements and others merely heightened the trend among tenant farmers to prefer money to land as reparations. In consequence Simpson recommended that the buyer be required to give the tenant farmer a year's notice of his intent to purchase. This would enable the tenant farmer to calculate accurately his overall expenses which the buyer would be required to cover, including the value of the amelioration of the land during the farmer's tenancy. This would constitute a fair indemnity.[43] He did not recommend that the sharecroppers be compensated.

As to future land purchases for Jewish settlement, Simpson found that no land whatsoever was available for new settlement of any kind. A long-drawn-out debate between the Government and the Zionist experts was carried on as to the amount of cultivable land in the country. The Government experts regarded the existing condition as unalterable, whereas the Zionist experts sought to prove on the basis of exhaustive surveys that many areas not under cultivation could be made cultivable by draining swamps, reclaiming land covered by a variety of wild grasses, clearing land of stones, and uncovering fertile areas covered by shifting sands.

To prove that there was insufficient land for the fellaheen living on it Simpson relied on a study of 104 villages, made by Government officials. On the basis of this study he generalized as to the state of agriculture in the entire country. There were 23,573 families in the villages investigated – of these, 16,633 cultivated some land, while 6,940 were landless. In other words, 29.4% were landless. "Everywhere," Simpson wrote, "there is this complaint that many of the cultivators have lost their land. Doubtless this 29.4% includes these landless men who previously were cultivators."[44]

Government statistics showed that there were 86,980 families of fellaheen in the entire country. Simpson considered these 104 villages as representative of Arab agriculture in the country as a whole and concluded that only 70.6% of the population, or 61,408 families, owned land, while the others were landless.

In estimating the amount of cultivable land in existence Simpson relied on data suplied by the *Geographical Review*, an American journal. Map No. 4 in that publication showed a total of 6,544,000 dunam of arable land in the whole country.[45] Since the Jews had bought about a million dunam, the Arabs were left with a little more than 5.5 million dunam. Simpson figured out that a fellah family needed 130 dunam, but even if one allowed only 90 dunam per family, as was done in the case of the 104 villages, the fellaheen would require more than eight million dunam of land.[46] As a result of his findings Simpson reached the conclusion that Jews should not be allowed to buy any more land and that land transfers should be approved only in rare cases.

About the same time that the Simpson Report was published the British Colonial Secretary issued the document known as the "Passfield White Paper" (October 1930), setting forth Britain's policy in Palestine regarding the Zionist project and the rights of the Arabs.

The White Paper adopted the recommendations made by the Shaw Commission and by Simpson. It reported: "It can now be definitely stated that at the present time and with the present methods of Arab cultivation there remains no margin of land available for agricultural settlement by new immigrants, with the exception of such undeveloped land as the various Jewish agencies hold in reserve."[47]

The Arabs had accused the Jews of making land purchases for political motives, i.e. to gain control of the country. Passfield agreed with this, and suggested that Jewish aspirations for new settlement be met by lands already in the hands of the Jews.

The Zionist leadership had demanded that the Government allocate land from its holdings for the purpose of Jewish colonization, as provided for by Section VI of the Mandate. The demand referred specifically to lands in the Beit-Shean Valley, and in the southern part of the Jordan Valley. With regard to this

132

demand, the White Paper stated: "It is an error to imagine that the Palestine Government is in possession of large areas of land which could be made available for Jewish settlement. The extent of unoccupied areas of Government land is negligible. The Government claims considerable areas which are in fact occupied and cultivated by Arabs. Even were the title of the Government to these areas admitted, and it is in many cases disputed, it would not be possible to make these areas available for Jewish settlement, in view of their actual occupation by Arab cultivators and of the importance of making available additional land on which to place the Arab cultivators who are now landless."[48]

The White Paper repeated Simpson's calculations that the Arabs held 5,500,000 dunam of land and that 29.4% of the Arabs were landless. Unlike the findings of the Shaw Commission and of Simpson that the Jews had compensated the Arabs generously, beyond their legal obligations, the White Paper found: "Some of the attempts which have been made to prove that Zionist colonization has not had the effect of causing the previous tenants of land acquired to join the landless class have on examination proved to be unconvincing, if not fallacious."[49] The White Paper goes on: "Consideration must also be given to the protection of tenants by some form of occupancy right, or by other means, to secure them against ejectment or the imposition of excessive rental."[50]

As to the sale of land to Jews, the White Paper ruled: "Transfers of land will be permitted only in so far as they do not interfere with the plans of that authority. Having regard to the responsibilities of the Mandatory Power, it is clear that this authority must be the Palestine Administration."[51]

In addition, the White Paper adopted Simpson's recommendation that a Director of Development be appointed, who would be responsible for resettling the landless farmers and for determining whether any land remained for the continuation of Jewish settlement.

The Zionist movement and the Jewish community in Palestine regarded the White Paper as a death blow to their aspirations for a national homeland, and immediately launched a political campaign against it. The Arabs mounted a counter-campaign to defend its policies, charging that *aliya* and Jewish land acquisitions were uprooting them from their homeland.

The members of the Arab Executive found it convenient to ignore the fact that most of the land purchases were from large landowners. George Antonius admitted as much some years later when he wrote: "The peasants have had no say in the great majority of the land transactions which have led to their eviction. The landowner who had the legal title disposes of the land at his discretion, and one of the provisions of the deed of sale is that the land is to be surrendered to the purchaser free from all occupants of rights or tenancy."[52]

The efforts of the Zionist Movement were finally crowned with success. On February 13, 1931 the British Prime Minister, Ramsay MacDonald, sent a letter to Dr. Chaim Weizmann in which he renounced in effect the political line taken by the White Paper and reaffirmed Britain's obligation to the Jews under the Mandate. In response to Simpson's conclusion that many Arabs remained landless as a result of Jewish land purchases the British Government decided to determine the exact number of such landless individuals, to take the necessary steps to solve the problem, and at the same time to facilitate further Jewish settlement.

On June 26, 1931 the Colonial Secretary appointed Lewis French as Director of Development in Palestine. French was an agricultural expert who had formerly served in India. His Letter of Appointment set forth two primary tasks:

a) To compile an accurate list of Arabs who had been displaced from their lands; to suggest where they could be resettled; and to estimate the required budget.

b) To prepare a survey of Government lands available for allocation to Jewish settlement, after the displaced Arabs were resettled.

In addition he was asked to report on hill lands and sources of water supply.

French arrived in Palestine on August 20, 1931. He was requested to file a preliminary report by December 31, 1931. The

Mandatory sought to provide French with two advisors – a Jew and an Arab. The Arabs refused to appoint an advisor, because the letter of appointment mentioned the MacDonald letter, which the Arabs regarded as a retreat from the Passfield White Paper. The Jewish Agency demanded the right to participate with the development authorities in evaluating the Arab claims. Since this demand was denied,[53] it, too, refused to name an advisor.

French began his investigation at a time when the Wadi Hawarith (Emek Hefer) affair was at its height.

The Wadi Hawarith Affair (Emek Hefer)

Like other large-scale projects, the plan to purchase the lands of Wadi Hawarith antedated World War I. In 1910, Ruppin and Hankin traversed the area between the sea and the slopes of the Samarian hills, and were impressed in equal measure by its fertility and by its desolation. They agreed that the land should be acquired for Jewish settlement.[54]

In 1914 Hankin signed a preliminary agreement to purchase a part of the valley from a few of the owners, but the outbreak of the War set it to nought. In 1921, the representatives of I.C.A., Kalvarisky and Rosenheck, wrote to their head office in Paris that they were being pressed to buy the land of Wadi Hawarith on which a man named Arieh held a mortgage of 300,000 francs.[55]

In 1927 Hankin again sought ways to purchase the land, which covered an area of 30,000 dunam and which would ensure the continuity of Jewish settlement from Zikhron-Ya'akov, Atlit-Kabara and Hadera southward.

As was the case with most of the land in the valleys and in the plains, the ownership of land in Wadi Hawarith originated in armed conquest. Oral tradition as preserved among the Arab elders told of a certain Bedouin chieftain from east of the Jordan, named el-Harati, who invaded the shore lands, drove out the inhabitants, and robbed them of their land. Tristram, who toured the area in 1864, described the destruction and the desolation after the conquest, thus confirming the tradition. (See Chapter One). In 1869 one of the descendants of the Bedouin chieftain sold the Wadi Hawarith land to a Lebanese Christian by the name of Antoin

Bashara Tayan.[56] Tayan had bought up many tracts of land in the country, including – as mentioned earlier – the land on which Petah-Tikva was later to be founded. In addition to Tayan's property there was a 10,000-dunam parcel of land owned by Mustafa Aga Kabani, a Beirut Moslem, who was a Turkish Government official. He acquired the land in the 1830's, in collusion with senior Turkish officials, as some sort of reward for his services to the State.[57] This part of the valley is called Wadi Kabani.

There was a mortgage on the 30,000 dunam of land owned by Tayan, and it could not be bought except at a public auction. It was clear that were the lands to be sold at a public auction the Jewish National Fund would be the successful bidder. Arab politicians brought pressure to bear on Tayan's heirs to refrain from a public sale, but the heirs had previously signed an agreement with Hankin that they would offer the property for sale at a public auction and that Hankin would have an option to buy.

In accordance with the provisions of the law, the sale was advertised in the Arab press, and criers made the news known in the streets of Nablus and Tulkarem. The lawyer representing the sellers was 'Auni Abd el-Hadi.[58] A public sale was held, and the Jewish National Fund bought 30,718 dunam of land in Wadi Hawarith. On May 27, 1929 the land was registered in the Tulkarem Register in the name of the Jewish National Fund, Land Certificate No. 206/29.[59]

When the tenant farmers of Wadi Hawarith learned of the impending sale, the village chiefs sent a memorandum dated October 10, 1928 to the head of the Land Department of the Palestine Government in which they wrote that 239 families, numbering nearly 1000 souls, drew their livelihood from cultivating the land of Wadi Hawarith and from growing livestock. They owned 1,500 cows, 50 camels, 32 horses, 600 goats, 150 donkeys and 300 water buffaloes. They contradicted Tayan's claim that he owned 30,000 dunam of land: He owned only 5,000 dunam – the rest was owned by the inhabitants by virtue of the work they invested in reclaiming, developing and cultivating the land.[60]

Indeed the records of the Turkish Registry Office showed that

136

only 5,000 dunam were registered in Tayan's name, however the markings on the official map indicated an area of 30,000 dunam. As will be remembered, it was customary under Turkish rule for the owner to register only a part of his actual holdings. Along with the registration a map would be attached which would indicate the true size of the parcel. It was common practice at the time of sale to give a deed to the property in accordance with the size as shown on the map.

The tenant farmers knew that only 5,000 dunam were registered in Tayan's name, and they argued that all the rest was property without owner. They based their claim on an old Turkish law that anyone could seize *mawat* land ("dead land"), reclaim it, and gain title to it by paying a certain sum into the Government treasury. The tenant farmers of Wadi Hawarith either paid no rent at all or did so at very irregular intervals, because the owners were spread over many countries. Their point was, therefore, that the land was really without owner, and the fact that they had cultivated it gave them title to it.

Word of the affair reached the neighboring villages. Among the villagers on the slopes of the Hills of Samaria were some who occasionally came down into the valley to cultivate tracts of vacant land. Two of these villagers, Hussein el-Mahmud and Mohammed Mah'adur, notified the District Commissioner of Tulkarem on December 11, 1928 that a portion of the land that had been allegedly sold belonged to them. They charged that Hankin had bribed the village chiefs of the village 'Atil to bear false witness as to the true boundaries of the land belonging to Tayan's heirs, that the surveyors had included in the deed of sale land belonging to the two of them.[61]

On January 13, 1929 the District Court of Nablus sent the District Officer of Tulkarem to investigate the complaint. The District Officer, accompanied by Michel Tayan representing the Tayan heirs and Fuad Abd el-Hadi, checked the boundaries to see if they accorded with the data on the map that was attached to the deed of record. He confirmed that the area was 30,826 dunam; that there had not been any false witness; and that the complaint was unfounded.[62]

On October 24, 1929 Abdallah Samara from Tulkarem filed a claim in his own name for 5,000 dunam, and additional claims in the names of five other fellaheen to various other tracts of land. At the trial four claims were denied outright, and a fifth was held over for further hearing. The court ruled that Samara's claim would be heard separately because it involved a boundary dispute.[63]

On November 16, 1929 the judge of the Nablus District issued a judgment of execution ordering that the tract in question be evacuated by all inhabitants and that possession be transferred to the Jewish National Fund. Ten days thereafter the village chiefs of Wadi Hawarith and other fellaheen from the vicinity filed a claim of ownership of the property and requested that the evacuation order be vacated.[64]

One year prior to the time that the land had been offered for sale and prior to the registry of the transfer of the land, Hankin located 140 of the tenant farmers of Wadi Hawarith. He sent them notice of the intended transfer of the property from the Tayan family to the Jewish National Fund. The law relating to tenant farmers, first promulgated in 1921, was amended several times. At first it had required that the tenant farmers be assured of an equivalent plot of land elsewhere. Since in practice in almost all cases the tenant farmers preferred cash reparations to alternate land, a settlement would be reached between the parties before the Government agencies even knew that a land sale was about to take place. In order to remedy this situation and to assure governmental supervision, the Government issued an amendment to the law, requiring prior notice of an intended sale of land be given at least one year before the actual transfer of title. The amedment was to enable the tenant farmer to prepare his accounts, to estimate his costs for the amelioration of the land, and to determine the amount of reparation that he would request. The amendment became law only in 1929, but its terms were known, and so Hankin sent out notices of proposed transfers of title even before the amendment became law. Eighty-four tenant farmers actually received notice, but for some reason 56 did not, and so were not required to vacate the premises. But Hankin paid them compensation and they promised to remove their tents from the fields. On the other hand, the tenant farmers who had received notices refused to accept a cash payment. Hankin intended to continue negotiating with a view to reaching a mutually agreed settlement, as was his custom.[65] In the meantime new claims began to come in from all sides. Many of the claims were instigated by the Arab leadership, which was interested in making the problem of the tenant farmers a prime political issue.

With the approach of winter, while the Jewish National Fund was making preparations to plow the land, the tenant farmers began plowing every piece of land in sight. Hankin declared before a court that, while the law did not require the payment of indemnities to herdsmen and sharecroppers, the Jewish National Fund was ready to make payments to them as well. He also brought suit against the tresspassers.

The case was heard by the presiding Chief Justice of the Nablus District, A.H. Webb, on November 30, 1929. After hearing the testimony of the witnesses and the arguments of both sides, he ruled as follows: The land had been acquired legally. There were two groups of tenant farmers on the land in dispute. One group had received proper notice of the intended sale, as required by law, and the second group had accepted indemnity payments of their own free will. Therefore, all the land was to be vacated and turned over to the Jewish National Fund.[66] Attached to the decision of the Court was a list of the names of the 84 tenant farmers who had received due notice, and a list of the names of 56 tenant farmers who had received cash indeminities, a total of 140 tenant farmers, all residents of Wadi Hawarith.[67] On the same day that the judgment was handed down, the Court furnished the District Commissioner with a copy of its decision, explaining the reasons for it. It added that about one hundred tenant farmers would have to be evacuated and that an effort should be made to secure alternate land for them.[68]

After the ruling of November 30, 1929 was handed down, the Commissioner of the Haifa District asked for insturctions from the Chief Secretary of the Mandatory as to how he was to proceed. A similar request was made by the Director of the Land Department. The Chief Secretary replied in a secret letter, dated December 14,

1929, that he recommended that the 7,000 dunam of land, known as the "Lands of Qaqun," be transferred to the tenant farmers.[69]

The Chief Justice's decree stirred up activity in the Colonial Office in London as well. On December 18, 1929 Lord Passfield sent a letter to the High Commissioner, Sir John R. Chancellor, asking for information about the events in Wadi Hawarith and what he intended to do in the matter. The High Commissioner replied with a thirteen-page typewritten letter dated March 1, 1930, describing the history of the area's ownership, the claims of the tenant farmers, and the Mandatory Government plans for a suitable solution to the problem.

These were his conclusions:

1) The Jewish National Fund is entitled to the land.

2) The Arabs are claiming 6,000 dunam of land, but their attorneys are dubious as to the chances of winning their case in court.

3) Should they win, there is doubt whether there would be money to buy the land.

4) No general order of evacuation had been issued.

5) The Jewish National Fund is amenable to an interim agreement.

The High Commissioner concluded by stating that the Government Council was of the opinion that the evacuation could no longer be delayed. Consequently, he had instructed that the tenant farmers settle on the 6,000 dunam which they were claiming and on the additional 5,000 dunam that the Jewish National Fund had offered.[70]

On February 12, 1930, Colonel Frederick P. Kisch, the head of the Political Department of the Jewish Agency, met with the High Commissioner and offered on behalf of the Jewish National Fund to lease to the tenant farmers a tract of 5,000 dunam of land for a period of two years, until a permanent arrangement could be reached. Kisch protested that the 56 tenant farmers, who had already received reparations, would have long ago evacuated their land had it not been for the incitement by Arab leaders. He added that certain British officials also encouraged them not to comply with the court order. The High Commissioner requested that the

Jewish National Fund give the land to the tenants in perpetuity, but was met with a refusal.[71]

On March 1, 1930 the Officer of the District Court of Nablus advised the Acting Chief of Police that in accordance with the decree of the court of November 30, 1929 he had ordered the tenant farmers to concentrate their holdings on an area of 6,000 dunam that were under litigation, and a further area of 5,000 dunam that the Jewish National Fund had offered to place at their disposal.[72]

Thus the 6,000 dunam were ruled to be land in dispute, and whoever was in possession of it would remain on it until final adjudication. This could take years, because appeal could be carried to the King's Council in London. The Jewish national institutions protested against the one-sidedness of such a situation and on June 15, 1930 the Jewish National Fund offered a plan to solve the problem along one of two possible alternatives: It offered to lease to the tenant farmers 5,000 dunam of arable land and 2,000 dunam of grazing land in place of the 6,000 dunam that were in litigation; or, alternatively, to lease them 4,000 dunam in the Beit-Shean Valley.[73]

The Arabs refused both offers. The Jewish National Fund demanded that the authorities evacuate the tenants from the land that it had purchased, except for the tract that it had offered to lease to them.

On July 26, 1930 the District Commissioner of Haifa advised the Chief Secretary of the Palestine Government that the Arabs had concentrated their holdings in the area that the Jewish National Fund had agreed to lease to them. He convened the representatives of both sides, Hankin and Attorney A. Ben-Shemesh, representing the Jewish National Fund, and the village chiefs representing the tenant farmers. The village chiefs signed a document in which they agreed to remain within the confines of the leased area for the duration of the lease. They further undertook to vacate the land upon the expiration of the lease.[74]

The tenant farmers, however, did not abide by the terms of the agreement and did not evacuate the 6,000 dunam under litigation. On August 14, 1930 Justice A. Plunkett of the Nablus District

141

issued an Order of Evacuation to *all* the tenant farmers in the area.[75]

The tenant farmers vacated the land as ordered. Eight of them filed a claim to 5,000 dunam of land. The claim was denied, and they appealed to the District Court of Nablus. The appeal was denied on December 12, 1932.[76]

The Arab political leaders were not ready to concede a Jewish "victory." They urged the tenant farmers to return to the vacated land and promised to enlist the aid of the neighboring villagers.

In September 1930, when the plowmen of the Jewish National Fund entered the area, they found the empty tents of the tenant farmers. They loaded them on trucks and took them outside the boundaries of the Jewish National Fund lands. The tenant farmers were gathered there as if to receive their property – the tents. The Jews were not in any way apprehensive, especially as they were accompanied by two British soldiers. Suddenly a group of Arab women advanced toward the plowmen and the soldiers, and attacked them with a hail of stones. The plowmen retreated, but the soldiers, in trying to disperse the women, wounded a few of them and arrested three.

Another group of plowmen, who were scheduled to start plowing in another part of the tract, were met by a mob of 300 Arabs who attacked them with cudgels. In a report submitted right after the attack, Hankin wrote: "The two soldiers couldn't hold out by themselves and had to retreat to seek help from the Army. One of the plowmen went on horseback to seek reinforcements. He was attacked by the Arabs and barely escaped. Shots were fired at our house and the rider. After lunch we began to plow once again. We were attacked by a larger number of Arabs."[77]

The plowmen worked under the protection of the British Army. The Jews did not use firearms. As a rule both Jews and Arabs were careful not to use fireamrs for fear of fatalities that would lead to blood feuds. But in the Wadi Hawarith incident shots were fired by Arabs. Since most of the participants in the fray were not local Arabs, the consequences of a blood feud would not fall upon them. Luckily no one was killed.

On October 12, 1930 Hankin reported to the Jewish National

Fund: "The sheikhs and some of the Arab tenant farmers paid me a visit. After a long discussion I understood that they had no intention of ever evacuating the land and that the Government had tacitly given them permission to remain on it until the matter would be adjudicated. I told them that if such was their attitude, they would not get one more dunam from us, but if they wished to live in peace with us, not only would we agree to their holding the 6,000 dunam till the end of the litigation, but, in addition, we would lease to them another 5,000 dunam for a 23-month period; we would waive the LP. 3,600 they owed us; we would give them an interest-free loan of LP. 1,000 for 23 months; and we would sign an individual lease with each one of them. The offer was made conditional on their withdrawing the cases then in court, except for the trial concerning the 6,000 dunam, and on their undertaking not to bring any new actions against us. They rejected the offer."[78]

The tenant farmers persisted in turning down all reasonable offers. The Arab leadership was heartened by the conclusions of the Shaw Commission, by those of Simpson, and by the publication of the Passfield White Paper. The conclusions were critical of Zionist land purchases and accepted the Arab argument of displacement and uprooting. The Shaw Report, in dealing specifically with the Wadi Hawarith dispute, opposed giving the tenant farmers alternate land lest they be dispersed and lose their tribal identity.[79]

The problem of the tenant farmer, which the Shaw Commission considered, related essentially to the past, since it pertained to the purchases of the Jezreel and Zebulun Valleys during 1921–1924, but it became a live issue with the land purchases in Wadi Hawarith, which served to demonstrate the effect that Jewish land purchases had on the fellaheen and the tenant farmers. At the same time, after the 1929 riots the Jewish organizations showed an increasing reluctance to give tenant farmers alternate lands near Jewish settlements. The creation of a continuous stretch of settlement along the coast became a prime security aim. The Wadi Hawarith land dispute inevitably turned into a political one. The more that the Arab leaders, encouraged by pro-Arab British investigators, statesmen and officials, turned the quarrel into a strategic political weapon, the more determined did the Jewish leadership become to prevent the incident from becoming a brake on continued Jewish settlement and the development of the Jewish National Home.

The Arab press dealt at length with the various aspects of the incident. It wrote about the evacuation order that the tenant farmers received; it set forth in detail the counter claims that were filed; it repeated the allegations of the tenant farmers that they were the rightful owners of the land, since they had lived on it for generations. Arab public figures presented memoranda to the Government, which warned that the Jews were gaining dominance over poor fellaheen through land purchase. They denounced Hankin as "that horrible land broker," who bribed Arabs to submit false affidavits about lands that were not theirs. Protest meetings were held throughout the country in support of the tenant farmers of Wadi Hawarith. Not only did the neighboring villagers urge them not to abandon their plots, but they themselves also laid claims to additional tracts of land in Wadi Hawarith. Thus the number of claimants grew from month to month.

In addition to initiating litigation against the Jewish organizations and settlers, the Arabs did damage to property. During the night they would steal into the orchards and groves and uproot the trees. In the course of the Wadi Hawarith dispute 24,000 eucalyptus saplings that had been planted to combat malaria were uprooted.[80]

Some of the Arab leaders, such as the spokesmen for the Arab Executive and their supporters, had a material interest in prolonging the dispute. Among them was Abdallah Samara from Tulkarem, who had filed a claim to part of the land. In addition he actively incited the villagers to join the tenant farmers of Wadi Hawarith in their struggle whenever the Government attempted to carry out court rulings. Arlosoroff noted in his diary: "About a year ago Abdallah Samara, one of the Mufti's neighbors and cronies, agreed to hand over to the Goverment a tract of his own land. His intent was that the Government would permit Arab villagers to set up their tents on it. There is no doubt that this man is partly responsible for the present dispute, just as he was for earlier ones. He eggs the Arabs on to demand lands, so that at the

144

appropriate moment he will be able to buy their legal rights from them. Then he will turn around and sell these rights to the Jews."[81]

'Auni Abd el-Hadi was a founder of *Istiqlal* and some years later a member of the Arab Higher Committee. Something about his character may be learned from the proceedings of an appeal, brought by Ismail Mohammed el-'Ufi and heard in the District Court of Nablus on February 12, 1932. El-'Uti claimed from the Jewish National Fund 5,600 dunam of land for himself and for 174 other Arab claimants. His suit was denied in the lower court. On appeal, the Jewish National Fund was represented by Dr. A. Ben-Shemesh and by Mr. Eliasberg. 'Auni Abd el-Hadi was the attorney for the plaintiffs. When Dr. Ben-Shemesh called an Arab witness to the stand, el-Hadi called out to him: "How much money did the Jews pay you for your false testimony?" The witness rplied: "How much money did they pay you for helping Hankin concentrate his acquisitions in one area?" A disturbance broke out in the courtroom, and the proceedings were suspended. The clash prompted some comments in the Arab press, but the united front against the Jews helped el-Hadi suppress the matter. Dr. Ben-Shemesh later confirmed that Hankin had employed el-Hadi to help him concentrate land holdings in one area, and had paid him a fee.[82]

The High Commissioner Sir Arthur Wauchope wrote to the Colonial Secretary that el-Hadi was prominent in anti-Government protest activities. He noted that the press had mentioned him as having been employed by the Jews and as having carried out the public sale of the Wadi Hawarith lands. Wauchope agreed that the publicity given the matter would not solve the problem of Wadi Hawarith, but felt it should make protesters from Egypt and Iraq lower their tones.[83]

A moderate Arab, such as As'ad el-Shuqairi, the *Mufti* of Akko (who had sold some of his holdings in Haifa to the Palestine Land Development Company – See ch. 7),even though he was of the opinion that the tenant farmers of Wadi Hawarith had been treated fairly, made common cause with those who argued that land purchases by Jews necessasrily resulted in displacement of Arab farmers. In an interview conducted by Tuvya Ashkenazi, el-

145

Shuqairi said: "There is displacement... True, not in Wadi Hawarith, but I refer to those displaced in the Jezreel Valley. The solution is not in the fifty pounds that is given to every tenant farmer, but in alternate land. Here is the sticking point: The Jews have done much to develop the country, but they must enable the Arabs to participate in their efforts so that the benefits will accrue to all inhabitants, irrespective of religion or race..."[84]

The Government could not afford to countenance the violation of law and the disregard of decisions rendered by its courts. It sought a solution that would satisfy the tenant farmers, and yet would leave its prestige, as the agency responsible for public order, unimpaired.

On February 18, 1932 an agreement was signed by the Jewish National Fund and a representative of the Mandatory, in the name of the High Commissioner, whereby the Jewish National Fund undertook to lease 2,965 dunam of land to the tenant farmers from December 31, 1931 to September 30, 1933. It was hoped that this would allow sufficient time to arrive at a permanent solution.[85]

On August 18, 1932 the Commissioner of the Northern District called in the representatives of the tenant farmers of Wadi Hawarith and made them the following offer:

* Every tenant farmer who vacated his land would receive twenty to sixty dunam in the Beit-Shean region.

* The Government would drain swamp areas near the area of settlement, and would install irrigation pipes.

* The Government would deep-plow the lands.

* The Government would furnish seeds, and supply the settlers with expert guidance.

*The Government would pay the settlers travel fares to and from Tulkarem, whenever they had official business there.

* The Government would pay the settlers LP. 2,300 for their unharvested summer and winter crops.[86]

In addition Moshe Shertok advised the Directior of Development that the Jewish National Fund would pay the tenant farmers an indemnity of LP. 3,000.[87] The tenant farmers rejected the proposal.

On May 2, 1932 the Director of Development, L. Andrews (who replaced French in October 1932), reported to the Colonial Office

146

in London, that he was preparing a detailed plan to resettle 109 families from Wadi Hawarith. He proposed to buy 7,165 dunam of land in the Beit-Shean Valley. A budget of LP. 30,000 would be required. He requested Treasury approval for his plan.[88]

At the end of 1933 the High Commissioner reported to the Colonial Office, that the Bedouins of southern Hawarith were evacuated peacefully on June 16. The Jewish National Fund paid them LP. 4,300 and the Government, for its part, added LP. 2,000.[89] The District Commissioner of Nablus informed Andrews that the Bedouins set up 139 tents on the new tract, and that the population numbered 113 families, or 563 souls.[90]

Despite the fact that the Government had provided an alternate settlement area, the evacuation of the Bedouins evoked a wave of protests. An English official in Iraq reported to the Colonial Office that the evacuation prompted hostility to the Jews in Iraq. Violently anti-Zionist diatribes were being preached in the main mosque in Baghdad, causing Jews to fear for their safety. He added that there were voices calling for a boycott against the Jews.[91]

In the end 199 Bedouins of Wadi Hawarith, who had been recognized as being entitled to resettlement, refused to accept 10,000 dunam of land in the Beit-Shean area, despite the favorable terms – fifty dunam of irrigated land per family. Ninety families from the northern part of Wadi Hawarith chose to receive from the Jewish National Fund 240 dunam, plus a lease of 2,695 dunam. The Jewish National Fund paid the Bedouins a sum of LP. 1,800 to cover the cost of moving, and an additional LP. 1,800 for their unharvested crops.[92]

Dr. Tawfik Canaan, an Arab publicist, who had himself sold Beit-Shean land to the Jewish National Fund (see Chapter 9), harshly criticised the Government's arrangements with the Jewish settlement organizations. He charged that it was using Government funds to settle the evacuees on Government land, and in this way was imposing a heavy burden on the taxpayer.[93] He also chided the Government and the Jewish settlement organizations for the niggardly allocation of 240 dunam to the 109 Bedouin families of Wadi Hawarith. Canaan did not mention the Government's offer to settle them in the Beit-Shean Valley; nor that the Jewish National

Fund had leased them land in Wadi Kabani, and thus they would continue as tenant farmers without suffering any worsening of status.

The Dimensions of the Tenant Farmer Problem

Lewis French was appointed by Lord Passfield, the author of the White Paper. Armed with the findings of the Shaw Commission and of Simpson, French arrived in Palestine on August 20, 1931. He devoted most of his efforts to locating the tenant farmers, ascertaining their numbers, and establishing their rights. The District Officers and officials of the Land Register were required to gather information about tenant farmers and displaced persons from the village chiefs. They made it publicly known that they would hear any claim and would forward it to the Development Department. As will be remembered, the Mandatory had wanted to appoint a Jewish and an Arab adviser to the Development Commissioner, but both the Arabs and Jews refused to nominate candidates. Notwithstanding, the Jewish Agency demanded that in the event of a charge of displacement against a Jewish settlement organization, such charge should first be submitted to a committee, which would examine the validity of the claim. The demand of the Jewish Agency was met in effect when Justice H.B. Webb, known for his impartiality, was appointed the President Justice of the Land Court, attached to the Development Department. Justice Webb used to forward the claims to the Political Department of the Jewish Agency. He would note the comments made, would examine the arguments of the claimant and would then deliver his verdict.

On September 15, 1931, Dr. Chaim Arlosoroff, the head of the Political Department of the Jewish Agency, convened a group of lawyers and land experts to examine the documents hidden away in the archives of the P.L.D.C., P.I.C.A. and the Jewish National Fund that touch on claims of allegedly displaced Arabs, to complete the files, whenever necessary, and to put them in order.[94]

Zvi Wolff, the liaison contact man of the Jewish National Fund with the Arab villagers in the Jezreel Valley, a man of considerable experience, made an over-all survey of the number of fellaheen and tenant farmers who might make claim and of the area of land involved. On December 7, 1931, he submitted the following table to Hankin:[95]

District or Region	Tenant Farmers	Land Owners	Totals
Haifa	495	70	565
Safed	48	122	170
Nazareth	332	6	338
Tiberias	29	62	91
Beit-Shean	90	8	98
Jenin	57	–	57
Tulkarem	560	19	579
Grand Totals	1,611	287	1,898

The 1,611 were tenant farmers in the Jezreel and Zebulun Valleys who had received indemnities. Some of them had bought land and built houses, as had been reported to Simpson. (See above) Half of the tenant farmers in the Tulkarem District came from Wadi Hawarith. (Negotiations in the matter of Wadi Hawarith were still going on) It should be noted that the number of fellaheen-landowners was relatively small – 287. The Jewish organizations judged that some of them would present claims, which they were prepared to consider.

The Jewish Agency study led to the conclusion that there were at most 1,898 possible claimants, of whom some had already been indemnified, and some were in the process of negotiating a settlement. And yet Lewis French stated in his first report to the Colonial Office, dated December 31, 1931, that 3,172 claims had been filed.[96] The Jewish Agency was taken by surprise, because it had maintained close contact with Justice Webb, who, prior to adjudication, submitted all claims to the Jewish Agency for its comments. The Court's files contained only 2,722 cases in various stages of investigation. The Jewish Agency protested the exaggerated figure and charged that French had included a thousand claims that had been made by the village chiefs without a shred of evidence to support them, and in the meantime Arab propagandists were making effective use of French's figures. A few months later it became clear that the Jewish Agency's statement

149

had been well-founded.

On July 14, 1932 the High Commissioner reported to the Colonial Office the number of claims that had been filed with the Development Department by April 1932 and the court's decisions in each case. There were a total of 2,722 claims filed; 249 were found to be justified; 1,021 were denied; and 1,452 were still under review.[97]

In April 1932 French submitted his second report. It included his recommendations for resettling the Arab families and his conclusions as to how much land was available for new settlement; what the sources of water were; the amount of land owned by the Government; what the possibilities for development were; and how large a budget would be needed for resettlement.

His recommendations for the continuance of Jewish colonization were similar to those of the Shaw Commission and of Simpson: He concluded that no Government land was available for settlement. He recommended strict supervision of land sales, especially in the coastal region, where Jewish ownership of citrus groves had reached 30%-40% of the total, and 50% was a foreseeable figure for the near future.

On the other hand, French noted a process of concentration of real property in the hands of a few effendis, and the consequent displacement of the fellah from his land. He reported that in one of the hill regions 30% of the land of the fellaheen had come into the possession of the effendis over a thirty-year period. "References are made from time to time in the Arabic press to the part played by some members of the Supreme Moslem Council or the Arab Executive in sales by Arabs to Jews; from which it is not unfair to infer that in some leading Arab quarters such disposals of surplus lands are viewed with no disfavour. *But the chief risk – an ever-present one – is that the progress of comparatively large growers, backed by plentiful financial resources, which weigh the scale so heavily against the independent small Arab proprietor, will mean the entire and permanent displacement of the latter from the soil.*"[98]

He further recommended that all sales of land be supervised, including those concluded between Arabs. But as early as 1930 the

Arab Executive voiced its disapproval of this suggestion.[99]

The true interest of the Arab leadership, most of whom were large landowners themselves, can be readily understood. Arlosoroff commented to the High Commissioner Arthur Wauchope on French's report: "The Arab leadership for years has been attempting to create a complex of fear in the hearts of the Arabs and of all who examine the situation from the outside. The French report has given this fear official written support. Throughout his report the Jews are described as baleful financial ogres endowed with great power, whose main aim is to uproot the defenseless Arab landowner from his small holding..."[100]

French's recommendations for the resettlement of Arabs throw some light on the indemnities that Jewish organizations were paying toward resettlement. In estimating a resettlement budget for the tenant farmer, French recommended that in addition to the land, the tenant farmer be paid LP. 20 for a house, LP. 30 for work animals and equipment, LP. 20 for the support of the family for a period of eight months, – altogether LP. 120. But, as noted above, the Jewish organizations had often made such resettlement allocations before French had even begun his investigation. It may be of interest to note for purposes of comparison that in Greece the resettlement of refugees from Turkey after 1923 was budgeted at less than the equivalent of LP. 104 per family.[101]

In October 1932 Lewis French resigned and was succeeded by Lewis Andrews. Justice Webb continued to hold hearings on land claims. The Chief Secretary of the Government reported to the Colonial Office in October 1932 that 3,175 claims had been filed; 368 were approved; 1,781 were denied; and 1,026 were still under review.[102]

In 1933 the Jewish Agency submitted a memorandum to the Government in which it took issue with the far-fetched conclusions that French had reached in his reports. It sought to set the problem of the tenant farmers in proper perspective. By that time almost all of the adjudications of claims had been made. As of March 6, 1933 a total of 3,188 claims had been filed; of these, 570 were approved, 2,519 were denied and 99 were under review.[103]

The memorandum went on to dispute Simpson's claim that

29.4% of all the Arab fellaheen were landless. Simpson had reached this conclusion on the basis of a sampling taken in 104 villages, from which he generalized to the whole country, that Jewish land purchases left the Arabs landless. But in fact of all the claims only 570 were found to be valid. Even if one were to double this figure, the 29.4% would melt down to 1.9%.[104] The memorandum went on to say that even those litigants whose claims were found to have merit fell into two categories: those who had been harmed in the past, and those who were being presently harmed. Among the claims disallowed by the Director of Development were individuals who owned land elsewhere. Some were prosperous and owned hundreds of dunams of citrus groves, others owned land in Trans-Jordan.[105]

For the information on prosperous claimants the Jewish Agency relied on Yosef Nahmani, an employee of the Jewish National Fund in Galilee, who knew many of the claimants personally. As early as October 1931, he wrote to the Legal Committee of the Jewish Agency: "It is rumored that the Government has decided to take back lands from the Jews and return them to their original owners. What an absurdity: Arabs who have left the country for good, have settled in Trans-Jordan, and are landowners there, have submitted land claims to the District Commissioner in Tiberias. They claim that they have been displaced from their lands, but in fact they demand that lands which their fathers had sold be returned to them. Here is an example: The father of Mohammed el-Khatib, the sheikh of the 'Arab ed-Dalaike tribe, together with others, sold the land on which Yavne'el has been located for the last 35 years. Now his son has filed a claim as a displaced person. The members of the tribe have done the same. But Mohammed el-Khatib has lived in Sehor el-Ghor in Trans-Jordan for the past fifteen years, where he owns about 1,000 dunam of land. He is convinced that the Jews are about to leave the country..."[106]

The Arabs were very critical of the Government's definition of a "landless person," used by the Government in determining the legitimacy of a claim for resettlement or any other form of indemnity. The definition – Dr. Tawfik Canaan wrote – considered as landless anyone removed from the land when it passed into

Jewish hands, without having been given other means for his support, or without having obtained suitable employment. Thus the following categories were excluded from the definition:

A. Arabs who have become landless because they cannot pay their debts to the Government's Agricultural Bank.

B. Arabs who, because they have become landless, have been forced to leave Palestine and to migrate to Trans-Jordan or to other countries in search of a livelihood.

C. Tenant farmers who have become laborers.

No wonder that only 565 Arab claims were recognized and all the others denied.[107]

In addition to the many claims filed, numerous attempts were made by Arabs to seize plots of land, over which the squatter would claim ownership and thus be recognized as a displaced person entitled to indemnity. Also, the Supreme Moslem Council helped prepare legal claims against individual Jewish landowners in the hope that they would win land awards. The process began in 1929, as unrest within the Arab community grew prior to the outbreak of the riots. Its intensity was steadily increasing until 1936, the year of the Arab revolt against Zionism and British rule in Palestine.

For many years, the *moshava* Hadera, whose lands had been bought in 1891, was not troubled by land disputes and by claims of displaced people. In 1929 the neighboring Arabs began filing claims on lands that the *moshava* had allegedly stolen from them. The Arabs from Fuqara filed a claim for 5,000 dunam; those from Arab ed-Demair claimed 150 dunam; and the Nufeiat Arabs seized a tract of 1,200 dunam. The latter claimed that the land belonged to them, and they were adamant in their refusal to leave.

The claims of the Fuqara and el-Damair Arabs were disallowed in court.[108] The trial on the claim of the Nufeiat Bedouins was held on July 24–31, 1930. The Court found against them. They appealed, and a Court of Appeals with A. Plunkett, 'Ali Hasne Effendi and A. De Frites as judges heard the case. Judgment was rendered in Nablus on December 5, 1930 denying the appeal. A copy of the decision was forwarded to the Colonial Office, which received ongoing information on the situation in the country in general, and especially on the cases before the Land Court.[109]

The Nufeiat Bedouins, according to the P.E.F. Map of 1878, were totally new to the area north of Hadera – they had been encamped south of Wadi Hawarith. Nevertheless they persisted in claiming that the land sold in 1891 belonged to them. The Bedouins might have abandoned their claim, had it not been for the support of the *Waqf* and the Supreme Moslem Council.

The archives of the Political Department of the Jewish Agency contain a copy of an interesting letter that the Managing Director of the *Waqf* sent to the Supreme Moslem Council, dated February 12, 1935. He wrote that the costs of the trial were being financed by Hajj Tahar Qaraman from Haifa, and that there was an agreement between Qaraman and the plaintiffs that, in the event that they succeeded in their law-suit, he would take title to half the land and the Bedouins – to the other half, and Qaraman would permit the Bedouins to cultivate his half as tenant farmers, if they so wished.

In 1930, Qaraman sought to withdraw from the entire matter. He proposed to the *Waqf* that it reimburse him for his costs in the trial and assume his rights under the terms of his agreement with the Bedouins. The Managing Director of the *Waqf* wrote to the Supreme Moslem Council: "A victory for the Jews in this case will be a very severe blow to the Arab cause. The Jews, by offering a little money and a portion of the tract of land, are trying to seduce the Arabs into accepting the arrangement. If the Supreme Moslem Council intervenes in the matter it will succeed in thwarting any such arrangement which is definitely not in the Arab interest."

The *Waqf* proposed: "...to come to an agreement [with the Bedouins] as to the whole tract of land on the condition that the *Waqf* take title to half the tract as reimbursement for the trial costs that Hajj Tahar Qaraman had incurred, and that will be incurred during the balance of the trial. Title to the other half of the tract will be taken by the [Supreme Moslem] Council at a reasonable price which it will pay after the court awards the land to the Bedouins. In addition, the Council will undertake to keep them on as tenant farmers on the second half of the tract at the current rental rate."[110]

Two things stand out in this letter: a) *Waqf* warning the Council

The Plain of Sharon. P.E.F. 1878, Sheet X. The Nufeiat Tribe is located to the south of the Alexander Creek.

that there is a "danger" that the Jews will not only pay indemnities, but will leave the Bedouins a portion of their lands; b) in place of Hajj Tahar Qaraman's offer to finance the trial in return for half the tract of land, the Council, in addition to taking title to half of the land, proposed to buy the other half "for a reasonable price," with the Nufeiat Bedouins being reduced to a state of serfdom.

The archives of P.I.C.A. contain many files of litigations with the individuals who had sold lands in the past and who suddenly "recalled" that their signature on the document of sale had been forged; that they had never sold the land; that they had been swindled out of their property.

In 1935, the 'Arab ez-Zebeih Bedouins near Kefar-Tavor, who had received a cash indemnity some thirty years previously, seized lands belonging to the neighboring *moshava*. They heard that the Jews were anxious at almost any price to stay out of land disputes, and that they were willing to pay indemnities even on baseless claims to achieve that end, and so they confronted the residents of Kefar-Tavor with a *fait accompli*.

On January 19, 1936 the P.I.C.A. representative wrote to the Political Department of the Jewish Agency: "The 'Arab ez-Zebeih Bedouins occupied the lands of the Mes'ha (Kefar-Tavor) farmers and plowed them. They hoped that a violent clash would occur with killed and wounded, and that the incident would evoke a strong echo throughout the country. We suspect that they acted on the advice of the Supreme Moslem Council. Az ed-Dim el-Q'ssam* visited them twice."[111]

A land controversy that perturbed the country for many years beginning in 1931 involved the region of Hartiya, Qusqus and Tabaun. The trials of Wadi Hawarith, the Nufeiat Bedouins, and others, moved tenant farmers to file land claims based on alleged rights acquired by occupancy or grazing of the lands in question. The tract that belonged to Hartiya, Sheikh-Ibreiq, Qusqus, Tabaun and Harbaj (to-day Sha'ar-Ha'amakim, Giv'ot-Zeid, Alonim,

* The leader of an extremist Moslem Arab band who carried out terrorist acts against Jewish settlements in the Fall of 1935, and was a precursor of the 1936 riots.

156

Tiv'on and Kefar-Hassidim) were partly covered with bushes and forests. At the time of the purchase, Hankin paid indemnities to the tenant farmers and the herdsmen and obtained signed releases from them. On December 20, 1931 Hankin wrote to the Palestine Land Development Company: "The 28 names listed below are those of individuals who each received reparations at the time. Now they have come up with new claims."[112]

When the Jewish National Fund sought, at the beginning of 1935, to take possession of the lands of Hartiya, the Zubeidat Bedouins attacked the plowmen, who were forced to call for police assistance. Sixty mounted policemen appeared and a battle ensued, in which a policeman shot and killed an Arab. In August of the same year Bedouins again clashed with Jewish watchmen in Qusqus and Tabaun, and again an Arab was shot and killed. The man who fired the shot was sentenced to ten years imprisonment.[113]

The quarrels would die down for a while and then flare up anew from time to time, until 1939. A report to the Political Department of the Jewish Agency states: "Until January 1939 disputes arose from time to time. The members of the Zubeidat tribe would round up some fellaheen and have them file land claims, when at the most they had in the past only grazed the land sporadically. The Jewish National Fund allotted them grazing land bordering on the lands belonging to the Germans (in Bethlehem-in-Galilee). Rafiq Beidun, a commissioned police officer, urged the Bedouins not to abandon their claims. Attorney Salomon lodged a complaint with the Commissioner over the intervention of a commissioned police officer in the matter."[114]

The incidents mentioned above were selected from a large number of land cases tried in court during a period which witnessed a radical change in the attitude of the British Government to the Zionist effort in Palestine, a change which finally crystallized in the White Paper of 1939.

The entire subject of displaced tenant farmers, which was raised with such a fanfare of publicity by the Arabs, by a part of British officialdom in the Mandatory Government and by the Colonial Office in London, died down to a whisper in 1935.

The Director of Development, Lewis Andrews, reported in April

12, 1934 that, in accordance with Insturction No. 487, dated June 25, 1931 (the date of French's appointment as Director of Development), the Land Court had investigated the claims of displaced persons. It summed up the situation as follows: The number of tenant farmers recognized as having been displaced (including 199 tenant farmers from Wadi Hawarith) – 584; the number of Arabs presently cultivating Jewish land, who should be taken into account as potential displaced individuals – 237; the Ez-Zubeid Bedouins of the Safed District – 68; all told – 889 families. The Director of Development reported that 18,200 dunam of land were acquired in the Beit-Shean Valley. Part of the above-mentioned displaced families would be settled there.[115]

This was the plan of action that the Director of Development proposed after he had examined all the claims. But in fact, of the 889 candidates for resettlement only 348 accepted the land and the accompanying budget as offered by the Development Department. The rest refused.[116]

In 1936 the Mandatory Government submitted a memorandum to the Peel Royal Commission, dealing with the problem of the displaced farmers. The memorandum declared that until January 1, 1936 3,261 claims had been filed. 2,607 were found to be groundless, and only 654 were considered valid. Among those recognized as displaced families were the 199 families from Wadi Hawarith. They had been offered 10,000 dunam of land in the Beit-Shean Valley, but they turned the offer down. Ninety of these families, from the northern section of Wadi Hawarith, were settled by the Development Department on a tract of land in the Tulkarem region known as "Sheikh Mohammed's Swamp." The swamp was drained and 1,571 dunam of land were made fit for cultivation. The remaining 109 families, from the southern section of Wadi Hawarith, received from the Jewish National Fund 240 dunam of land and a lease on cultivated land in Wadi Kabani. The memorandum went on to relate that 68 families of the ez-Zubeid tribe received land from the P.I.C.A., after the Government had given the P.I.C.A. land elsewhere. Another 81 tenant farmer families were settled in the two projects sponsored by the Government, the Jenin project for forty families and the Beit-

Shean project that provided for forty-one families. All told, 348 families out of 654 were resettled. The rest refused to accept land, preferring to work for wages in the Jewish citrus groves.[117]

In a survey submitted by the Government to the Anglo-American Committee of Inquiry on the Palestine Problem in 1946, it was found that the land claimed by all the alleged displaced families came to 46,633 dunam.[118]

The P.I.C.A. – Shifts In Its Function as an Agency for Settlement

After the British Mandate over Palestine was ratified by the League of Nations, the status of the Zionist Organization changed. It became an institution whose functions in immigration and settlement were recognized officially by the nations of the world. Thus, the I.C.A. lost its status as the sole agency charged with settlement, a position that it had held unchallenged till the outbreak of World War I. It was replaced by the Jewish National Fund, the Foundation Fund (Keren Hayesod), and the Settlement Department of the Zionist Organization.

In 1924, Baron Edmond Rothschild decided to intensify his activities in Palestine in the areas of settlement and economic development. He founded the P.I.C.A. (Palestine Jewish Colonization Association) as a subsidiary of the I.C .A. and appointed his son James to direct it.

The activities of the P.I.C.A. from this date on were devoted to buying up additional plots of land for existing settlements; to making them economically viable; and to enhancing their capacity to defend themselves. The P.I.C.A.'s main effort lay in extending aid to individual settlers, mostly in the coastal area, where citrus fruit was the main crop. P.I.C.A. lands soon became the private property of the individual settlers.

After the disturbances of 1929, the P.I.C.A. was an important factor in the rehabilitation of the agricultural colonies that had been damaged by the rioters.

In the early 1930's, the P.I.C.A. began allocating land to kibbutzim and *moshavim*. After 1936, when settlement by private individuals became almost impossible because of the Arab revolt, the P.I.C.A. took an active part in the establishment of the "Tower and Stockade" kibbutzim, often in response to pressures exerted by the national institutions. In addition to its settlement activities, the P.I.C.A. also helped finance industrial projects in the country. In the years immediately after the P.I.C.A. was founded, it had reached its peak in land acquisition. But in its later phase, up to 1947, it bought only 50,000 dunam of land. In 1925 the P.I.C.A. owned 467,996 dunam; in 1930 – 519,904 dunam (including 34,911 dunam of concessions granted by the Government).[119]

From 1930 until the Mandate was terminated the P.I.C.A. adopted a policy of transferring title to land to the settlers. It transferred 237,000 dunam to private settlers in 20 *moshavot*, and 35,000 dunam to 15 kibbutzim.[120] It also sold some land to the Jewish National Fund and in 1947 it was left with only 130,000 dunam, which it transferred to the National Land Authority when the State was established.

The I.C.A. and the P.I.C.A. acquired, in all, 293,545 dunam from large land holders, being 68.3% of their total acquisitions.[121] In the course of their activities they reclaimed a total of 125,000 dunam of swamp lands.[122]

The Simpson Report bears witness to the nature of the P.I.C.A.'s relations with its Arab neighbors and the Arabs from whom it bought land: "In so far as the past policy of the P.I.C.A. is concerned, there can be no doubt that the Arab has profited largely by the installation of the colonies. Relations between the colonists and their Arab neighbors are excellent. In many cases, when land was bought by the P.I.C.A. for settlement, they combined with the development of the land for their own settlers similar development for the Arabs who previously occupied the land."[123]

It is true that Simpson's purpose in praising the P.I.C.A. was to denigrate the Zionist agencies by comparison. However, had the P.I.C.A. policy been detrimental to the Arabs, he would not have hesitated to say so.

Simpson's was not the only favorable opinion of the P.I.C.A.'s activities. In a memorandum submitted by the Arab Executive to the Mandatory Government after the publication of the White Paper of October 1930, a similar comment was made: Judging by the policy adopted by the P.I.C.A., no great harm was done to the

Arab interest by the founding of their Jewish villages, and the relations between the settlers and their Arab neighbors were satisfactory; not so in the case of the Zionists, who are denounced in the document for employing Jews only and for displacing the Arab tenant farmers.[124]

In 1946, the Arab Higher Committee, in a memorandum to the Unites Nations Special Committee on Palestine, singled out the P.I.C.A. as having come closest, of all Jewish organizations, to recognizing Arab rights. To a point they tried to be fair in compensating the Arab who had previously held the land; they employed Arabs in Jewish orchards partly out of consideration for Arab rights, partly because Jews were neither suited to nor skilled in agricultural work, and partly because Arab labor was cheaper. The P.I.C.A. also paid some attention to the development needs of the villages. The Jewish National Fund, on the other hand, put an end to the good relations.[125]

The political leadership of the Arabs based itself on the Simpson Report and so tried to lend an air of objectivity to their arguments against Zionism. By commenting favorably on the activities of the P.I.C.A. they were better able to attack the Jewish National Fund and the Zionist settlement policy. (It should be remembered that by this time the P.I.C.A. had ceased functioning). Nevertheless, the Arabs would not have commented favorably on the P.I.C.A. had they had some evidence that it had caused harm to the Arab community or that it had displaced fellaheen or tenant farmers from their land.

CHAPTER SIX

THE STRUGGLE WITH THE MANDATORY
GOVERNMENT OVER STATE LANDS

The granting of the Mandate for Palestine by the League of Natins to Britain was based on the Balfour Declaration, which pledged to assist the Jews in the establishment of their National Home. In the articles of the Mandate, official status was accorded to the Zionist Executive (in official terms, the Jewish Agency for Palestine) to engage in the development of the country, and the Mandatory was obligated to use its best endeavors to facilitate the achievement of this object.

Articel 6 of the Mandate states:

"The Administration of Palestine, while ensuring that the rights and position of other sections of the pupulation are not prejudiced, shall facilitate Jewish immigration under suitable conditions and shall encourage, in co-operation with the Jewish Agency referred to in Article 4, close settlement by Jews on the land, including State lands and waste-lands not required for public purposes."

At the time Britain received the Mandate for Palestine, Jewish settlement had already been going on for forty years. During this period the Jews had used their own resources to purchase land, and they were under no illusion that from now on State lands would be handed over to them free. The Zionist Executive requested "State lands and waste-lands not required for public purposes," referring to lands which, if appropriated, would not lead to the eviction of the Arabs, but to the intensive development of stretches of land where new settlers could find a home and where the existing population could raise its standard of living.

The first experiment in acquiring State lands was made in 1922, when the Society for Demobilized Soldiers, together with the assistance and support of the Zionist Organization, requested land for settlement purposes from the Palestine Government, inasmuch as in Britain special privileges were then being granted to demobilized soldiers. After prolonged negotiations the Government allocated 25,000 dunam in Tel-Arad, north-east of Beer-Sheba, to a group of demobilized soldiers, five hundred of whom were experienced farmers.[1] This group of soldiers asked for a budget in order to drill a well, as there were no springs in this region. The Government performed its duty "to encourage close settlement" with a budget of 500 pounds, which was sufficient for three drillings, all of them failures. Since it was impossible to start an agricultural settlement without water, the pioneers of the Negev were forced to abandon the place.

During the subsequent years further attempts were made on the part of the Zionist Executive to acquire State lands but only a minimum of these requests were complied with, such as the allocation of State lands to Kibbutz Ayelet-Hashahar in Upper Galilee. Most requests were rejected out-of-hand by the Mandatory. The main struggle for State lands was concentrated around the lands of the Valley of Beit-Shean and the acquisition of the Hula Concession.

Valley of Beit-Shean

Wide areas of State lands, eminently suitable for intensive settlement, stretched out all along the Syrian-East-African Rift, from the Hula Valley in the north to the Dead Sea in the south. Settlement of these regions, however, was dependent upon drying the land, drainage and basic soil reclamation. The Mandatory Government, as heir to the Ottoman Empire, had at its disposal 381,906 dunam of land defined as the Valley of Beit-Shean.

How did these lands become the property of the State? In what condition were they when they were transferred to British rule? And why did the first High Commissioner, Sir Herbert Samuel, decide to parcel out these lands amongst the Bedouins of the region?

In 1921, the High Commissioner sent a detailed memorandum on this subject to the Colonial Office in London,[2] stating that in the year 1870 the peasants had ceased to pay taxes, and the Ottoman Government had confiscated the lands. Later, in the year 1920, when the British civil administration in Palestine was established, it

163

made a proposal to the tenant farmers to sign contracts obligating the Government to accord any tenant who cultivated the land for ten consecutive years the right to bequeath this land to his sons and heirs.

In the same document the High Commissioner wrote that even though the Palestine Government, as heir to the Ottoman Empire, held the rights to the lands, it could not ignore the fact that the Sultan had used "a certain amount of compulsion," and consequently he, the High Commissioner, had decided that the holders of the land be allowed to purchase it, under specific conditions. The High Commissioner requested the approval of the Colonial Office considering that he wished to deviate from the principle that State lands were not for sale. He believed that this solution would bring blessing to the land and that it was politically justified.[3]

The Colonial Office approved the High Commissioner's decision, and in November 1921 an agreement was signed between the Mandatory, the representatives of the Bedouin tribes and the heads of the villages of the Valley of Beit-Shean pertaining to the sale of State lands.

The agreement was called the "Ghor-Mudawara Agreement." It determined the conditions under which lands were granted to those who retained it, and the terms of payment:

1 dunam of land (dry farming)........ LP. 1.25
1 dunam of land (under irrigation)... LP. 1.50

payable in instalments over fifteen years. People who did not hold any land or who cultivated less than 150 dunam were allowed to acquire up to 150 dunam; a family of more than five had the right to acquire 50 dunam per additional person.

According to the census taken in 1922 the population of the Valley of Beit-Shean consisted of 2,647 families – 9,277 souls.[4] The Ghor-Mudawara Agreement covered 381,096 dunam; 236,000 dunam were arable and about 145,000 dunam were defined as uncultivable.[5] The calculation was that each family receive approximately one hundred dunam of soil, regardless of whether it was under irrigation or not. However in actual fact the land was allocated in a completely different manner:

164

a) Lands that were not cultivable were still suitable for pasture, and were used by the Bedouins.

b) A family consisting of five people did not manage to cultivate a hundred dunam of arable land, and the sources of spring water were not exploited.

c) The allocation of land was not carried out on an equal basis but according to the principle that whoever occupied a tract of land had the right to acquire it at the nominal price, to be paid in instalments over fifteen years.

Wealthy men, powerful men, the sheikhs and heads of villages – all "proved" that they held large stretches of land, and these they acquired according to the above-mentioned terms. Tenant farmers, of course, were not given the possibility to acquire land, as prior claims and "proof" had already been tendered by the men for whom they were working the land.

In 1932, when Lewis French carried out his research on the situation of the peasants and the tenant farmers in the Valley of Beit-Shean, he found living there 950 families of peasants and 400 families of Bedouins.[6] At the same time absentee landlords who owned these vast stretches of land lived in the towns of Palestine and abroad, while their land was worked by the tenant farmers and was being put up for sale to the highest bidder.

In June 1922 Chaim Margalit-Kalvarisky collected some data on the plots of land that were allocated to wealthy landowners, who declared that they had held these lands before the war. According to his figures eight such landowners acquired 93,867 dunam of land.

In addition, the Government rented out to a British subject named Ross and to Saliman Bey Nassif 6,000 dunam "for the purpose of developing the area for intensive cultivation".[7]

Kalvarisky's data show that, of all the lands parcelled out by the Government to purchasers on extremely good terms, over one-third fell to the lot of the wealthy members of one family. Sir John Hope Simpson maintained in his 1930 Report that a great deal of profiteering flourished around the lands of Beit-Shean: "The custom is that the vendor transfers to the vendee the liability for the price of the land still owing to the Government and in addition takes from him a sum varying from three to four pounds a dunam...''[8]

In fact, in the years following, the men offering land for sale were not those who got the land from the Government, which could only mean that the land had changed hands from time to time. During the years 1929–1930 Zvi Wolff and Joseph Nahmani discovered such new land-owners in the Beit-Shean Valley. Some Germans had also purchased land and attempted to establish a cotton farm.[9]

The land was handed over to wealthy landowners, to peasants and to Bedouins, but the situation in the Valley did not change. The springs continued to flood wide areas, fertile soil rotted and was rendered uncultivable by the penetration of the deep roots of bushes, and the settlers of the Valley fell ill with malaria.

It was hard for the Zionist agencies to accept with equanimity this waste of land, the best and richest in the country. Zionist officials demanded that part of it, which was not in use, be allocated for Jewish settlement, in accordance with Article 6 of the Mandate. To this the Mandatory replied that until such time as the surveyors would complete their survey and the lands could be registered, they would not know whether there was any surplus land. Consequently the Zionist insitutions tried to acquire land by purchase; however one of the articles of the Ghor-Mudawara Agreement stipulated that those who had acquired land could sell it only with the agreement of the Government, which was given only if the purchaser was a public institution, intending to work the land intensively and settle it densely.

In January 1927 the Zionist Executive approached the Colonial Office with the request that it be recognized as a public institution according to the above criteria. The Colonial Office replied that they would consider the request, but the Land Department in Jerusalem had first to receive the agreement of the peasants to sell.[10] The Zionist Executive then requested that the Government agree to the sale of surplus lands, so that the means of livelihood of the seller would not be endangered.[11]

In 1928 a memorandum was presented by the Head of the Political Department of the Zionist Executive, Colonel Frederick Kisch, to the High Commissioner, Lord Plumer, claiming that the

Bedouins and the peasants had received more land than they needed, while the Jews received nothing, in gross violation of Article 6 of the Mandate. In reply the High Commissioner stated that it was impossible to alter a signed agreement; however he would order an investigation and if it turned out that the Zionist claims were justified, the subject of amending agreements could be discussed.[12]

In 1929, at the height of the Shaw Commission investigations, Dr. Weizmann approached the Colonial Office with the demand that the Mandatory allocate State lands for Jewish settlement, as they were committed under the terms of the Mandate. The demand was passed on to the High Commissioner, who gave the same reply as the First Secretary, i.e., until there was a formal Land Register they could not define what was Government property.[13]

On December 13, 1929 Zvi Wolff published an article in the English edition of the newspaper "Davar" on the subject of the lands of Beit-Shean, which aroused great interest and reached as far as the Mandates Commission of the League of Nations.[14] Wolff gave a detailed account of the chain of events in connection with the sale of lands and in his summary presented a list of seven wealthy city-dwellers, some of them foreigners, who together had received 23,690 dunam of land.

At the annual meeting of the Mandates Commission of the League of Nations on the problem of Palestine the Mandatory representative was asked for a reply to Wolff's assertions. The report of the Government to the Mandates Commission for the year 1930 only dealt with part of Wolff's accusations, and in effect the essence of his article was blatantly ignored.[15]

In his evidence before the Royal Commission which visited Palestine in 1936 Berl Katzenelson, testifying on behalf of the General Federation of Labor, asserted that the Mandatory had failed in the obligation imposed upon it to encourage Jewish settlement on State lands. To prove his point he quoted Wolff's article and *inter alia* stated: "Thousands of dunams had been allocated to the wealthy and to citizens of foreign countries..." The Chairman of the Commission, Lord Peel, became very angry:

"If he comes here and says he knows of a man who has

thousands of dunams, cannot he give the name? He is playing with us?"

Berl Katzenelson did not have the article with him and did not remember the details, but he promised the Chairman that within a few days he would send the Committee a letter with all the details. The aged Lord did not calm down and insisted on getting the exact items and dates of sale.[16] The inquiry was continued in an atmosphere of great tension. Within a few days Berl Katzenelson sent a detailed letter to the Commission, meticulously including details from Wolff's article plus some new data, according to which five Arab families received 14,832 dunam of land.[17]

Even the two sets of data together fell short of giving a true picture of the situation. In a memorandum presented to the Jewish Agency by Nahmani, he gave the names of additional land beneficiaries, who had received the land by devious methods and who had never been inhabitants of the Beit-Shean region. Among them were a family from Egypt and privileged urban families, such as Husseini and el-Alami, who received 5,618 dunam.[18] In short, over 43,000 dunam were in the hands of the rich, residents of far-off towns or foreigners, none of whom had the slightest connection with the lands of the region.

The Royal Commission voiced strong criticism of the Palestine Government on the subject of the Beit-Shean lands. In its conclusions it claimed that the original agreement of 1921 had been drawn too precipitately and with insufficient forethought. The Arabs had received very generous terms which they could not put to good use and no provision was made for avoiding abuses.[19]

Until 1936, the year of the Arab riots, the Jews acquired about 25,000 dunam in the Beit-Shean Valley, 22,900 by the Jewish National Fund. The soil was of the poorest quality, in scattered parcels of land, and it was impossible to establish even one settlement on it.

The Jewish purchasers paid the full price for these lands; in addition the Government compelled them to cover all the outstanding debts that the sellers had accumulated. (In most cases not one penny of these bad debts had been paid for years.)

These substantial purchases, the consolidation of the small plots

168

into larger tracts and the establishment of settlements in this Valley
– all took place during the years of the riots (1936–1939) and during
the Second World War. More about this – later.

The Hula Concession

The rich agricultural potential of the Hula Valley did not escape
the keen eyes of the Sursuk family, who had acquired land in the
Valley of Jezreel, the Zebulun Valley and the Jordan Valley. In
June 1911 Mishel Sursuk and Mohammed Omar Behum had signed
an agreement with the Finance Minister of the Ottoman
Government Javid Bey for the acquisition of a concession to the
Hula Valley. The signatories committed themselves to set up within
one year, in accordance with Ottoman law, a public company which
would undertake to carry out the terms of the concession. The
agreement, containing twenty clauses, outlined in detail the terms
of the concession and *inter alia* imposed the following obligations
upon the company-to-be:

A program for drainage and soil reclamation was to be submitted
to offical Government institutions for approval within one year;
work was to commence six months after approval of the plan and to
be completed within six years; the same quantities of water were to
be supplied to the fellaheen as they had used in the past when it
was in free supply, and if this could not be done, compensation
would be paid to them; on completion of the drainage and soil
reclamation, the Company was to purchase the land from the
Government at a cost of two Turkish pounds per dunam; 10,000
dunam was to be *sold* to the fellaheen resident in the concession
area at a price covering the cost of the soil reclamation; up to the
time of the completion of the drainage, the Company was to pay
20% of its income from agricultural produce (most of this derived
from fishing and the harvesting of reeds) to the Government
Treasury – all this in addition to the payment of taxes plus 20,000
Turkish pounds for the concession, payable in instalments over 18
years. Only after fulfilling the above conditions (and others not
specified here) would the Company receive the *qushan* on the
land.[20] At the time of signing the agreement, Sursuk and Behum
paid a deposit of a thousand Turkish pounds.

In 1914, the "Syrian-Ottoman Company for Agriculture" was established; Salim as-Slam was at its head and the main partners were Sursuk and Behum. The Company did not fulfil its obligation to submit a drainage and soil reclamation plan within one year, and after the outbreak of the First World War it stopped functioning altogether.

The Hula Valley passed over to the control of the British civil Government only in 1923, after the borders between the British Mandate over Palestine and the French Mandate over Syria had been defined. In March 1923 the High Commissioner officially endorsed the validity of the former agreement.[21]

On February 29, 1924 an agreement was signed between a representative of the Colonial Office in London and Salim as-Slam, as Chairman of "the Syrian-Ottoman Company for Agriculture," renewing the concession. The amendments in the Agreement dealt mainly with renewed obligations on the part of the Company to give the work out to a contracting firm with capital at its disposal, capable of completing the operation within one year. The renewed agreement was subject to confirmation by the High Commissioner. As-Slam did not carry out his obligation of having the work completed by a contracting firm within one year, and he asked for postponement until 1927.[22]

On May 15, 1925 as-Slam made an offer of the concession simultaneously to Hankin and to the Zionist Executive in London.[23] Negotiations were started with the Zionists, and as-Slam received a 5,000-pound deposit, which he never returned, even though the negotiations came to nought.[24]

At the beginning of 1927 as-Slam once again approached the Palestine Government to renew the concession, promising to find a company capable of carrying out the necessary work. A lively exchange of correspondence took place between the Chief Secretary of the Palestine Government and the Colonial Office in London on the subject of the renewal of the concession. In one letter dated January 28, 1927 the Chief Secretary stated that the validity of the concession had expired and that the Zionists wished to acquire it. The High Commissioner was prepared to renew the concession to the Syrian-Ottoman Company on condition that it would fulfil its obligations; if not, the option would be handed over to the Zionists.

On March 1, 1927 the Colonial Office replied to the Chief Secretary that the High Commissioner would be making an error in allowing the Zionists to obtain the option to the concession. Since this was the only concession held by the Arabs – even though they be Syrian Arabs – the transfer of this concession to the Zionists would arouse waves of protest within the Arab population.[25]

The office of the High Commissioner turned for an opinion to Norman Bentwich, the chief legal officer of the Mandatory. Bentwich examined the clauses of the agreement, scrutinized all the documents which carried proof of all the delays and failures of the Company to carry out the terms of the agreement, and pronounced his verdict: According to the Lausanne Treaty Britain was obligated to honor only agreements that would be of benefit to the country; this agreement was not beneficial to Palestine, and Britain was under no compulsion to renew it.[26]

The Executive of the Jewish Agency followed these prolonged negotiations with great interest. From their own legal experts they knew full well that according to the Lausanne Treaty the Government was under no obligation to renew the concession, and they repeatedly demanded that the concession be handed over to the Jews. On January 29, 1930 the Jewish Agency Executive delivered a protest to the Colonial Office, claiming that the Hula Valley was being left desolate and infested with disease. The Colonial Office responded that the opinion of the Arab public must be taken into consideration and that no pressure should be applied.[27]

On January 17, 1931 the Chief Secretary of the Palestine Government, M.A. Young, confirmed the renewal of the concession to the Syrian-Ottoman Company. Under the amended conditions the Government obligated the company to transfer the drainage work to a contracting firm capable of carrying out the operation within a specified time, but nothing was altered in the clause pertaining to the *sale* of 10,000 dunam to the fellaheen at a price which would cover the cost of drainage and soil reclamation.[28]

In a secret memorandum of February 9, 1931 the High

Commissioner informed the Colonial Office of the signing of the agreement and enumerated the conditions, namely, that the Company was under obligation to commence work immediately and completion was to be within six years, namely by January 16, 1937.[29]

The Syrian-Ottoman Company had no intention of carrying out this new agreement. Its only aim, and in this it succeeded, was to continue to retain the concession in order to sell it to the Jews at an enormous profit. Two years after the Syrian-Ottoman Company signed the new agreement, the option for the concession was offered to Joshua Hankin. In November 1933 a contract was signed between the Syrian-Ottoman Company and the Palestine Land Development Company for the purchase of the concession for LP. 192,000, subject to approval by the Government. Approval was granted, but a basic change was introduced in the terms of the concession: According to the 1931 agreement the Syrian-Ottoman Company was to *sell 10,000 dunam* to the tenant farmers; now the P.L.D.C. was obligated to transfer to the tenant farmers *15,000 dunam free of charge*, and to instal on their land a main irrigation pipeline, so as to facilitate the development of intensive agricultural settlement.

On September 29, 1934 the Palestine Government officially confirmed the transfer of the Hula Concession to the P.L.D.C.[30]

The transfer of the Concession to the Jews aroused strong protests from the Arabs. On May 22, 1935 an article was published in the newspaper "El-Jama'e el-Arabiye" by the "Palestine Arab Party," protesting to the Mandates Commission of the League of Nations against the transfer of the Concession to the Jews. The article was based on Simpson's claim that one family of fellaheen needed forty dunam of land to have a fair means of livelihood. Since 1,500 fellaheen families were living on Concession lands, they should have been allocated 60,000 dunam and not a mere 15,000.[31]

The P.L.D.C. allocated the 15,000 dunam of land to the Arabs immediately upon receipt of the Concession, as promised. The Government Report to the Council of the League of Nations stated that representatives of the Government marked out 15,000 dunam of Concession lands for the fellaheen, according to the agreement,

172

and the next step was to be the payment of compensation to a number of claimants.[32]

The Arab political leadership did not acquiesce in the transfer of the Concession to the Jews and demanded the land for the villages of the region. In March 1935 the Supreme Moslem Council made the following demands of the High Commissioner in the name of the inhabitants:

a) that an agricultural nursery be set up in the Hula region:

b) that schools be established in the villages:

c) that the land around Lake Hula that had been drained be handed over to them, since they were in dire need of additiional land.[33]

As mentioned earlier, the total area of the Concession was 57,000 dunam. After handing over 15,000 dunam to the Arabs (to be exact, 15,772 dunam), less than 42,000 would be left in the hands of Jews. Of this, another 5,000 dunam would be covered by the lake, even after it was partially dried. In all, then, only 37,000 dunam would be available for Jewish settlement.

Draining the swamp and reducing the size of the lake (eventually the whole lake was drained) would still fail to cure the Valley of disease and would not transform it into an area suitable for development under modern civilized conditions. To this end it would be necessary to drain and reclaim the lands of the entire northern Hula Valley. Zionist institutions conducted prolonged negotiations with the Mandatory to achieve this object. Shortly before the outbreak of the Second World War the Government published an official announcement proclaiming a budget of PL. 235,000 for reclamation of the lands of the northern Hula Valley. However with the outbreak of the war the Government reneged on its promise. Eventually all drainage and reclamation projects in the Valley were carried out by Jewish institutions.[34]

THE ACQUISITION OF PRIVATE AGRICULTURAL AND URBAN LANDS BETWEEN THE TWO WORLD WARS

Agricultural Land

In 1945 individual Jews owned 514,000 dunams of agricultural land in Palestine, 340,000 of which were in settlements that had been founded before World War I. The balance were in settlements that were established after Britain had received the Mandate.[1] The land in the older settlements had been acquired in one of three ways: 144,000 dunam had been bought by the founding settlers themselves;[2] after 1930 the P.I.C.A. had transferred many tracts of land to the settlers; and, after World War I, the settlers individually had bought additional plots of land from their Arab neighbors in order to expand their holdings. Between 1939 and 1947 private landowners acquired no significant areas of land. Moreover, it is difficult to estimate how much land was bought by Jews during the period from 1920 to the termination of the Mandate. It may be noted that the Jewish National Fund bought 175,000 dunam of land from Jews. They were tracts that were lying fallow, so that there was a danger that they would not remain in Jewish hands.[3]

Individual purchasers of land had left few legal documents to indicate from whom the purchases were made, and on what terms. Therefore we are able to learn about the relations that existed between the Jews and their Arab neighbors only from the few records that were kept by the public companies, such as the Palestine Land Development Company. Occasionally a well-developed settlement kept records that have proved helpful. A further source of information are interviews with individuals who did the actual negotiating for the purchase of land.

Almost all the new *moshavot* established under the Mandate were located in the coastal strip, from Nahariya in the north to Gan Yavne in the south. The lands in this region were suitable for citriculture and most of the additional acquisitions for purposes of expansion were in the older citrus-growing *moshavot*.

174

The story of the lands acquired by the American Zion Commonwealth in the Jezreel and Zebulun Valleys (much of which was later transferred to the Jewish National Fund) was told in Chapter Five. In 1925 the Palestine Land Development Company bought 18,000 dunam of land for the American Zion Commonwealth near the Arab villages of Qiri and Qamon, situated between the foothills of Mount Carmel and the Kishon River. The purchase had been made from the Sursuk and Touwini families, who had other holdings in the Jezreel Valley. The American Zion Commonwealth was forced to sell a portion of this land to the Jewish National Fund, because it was threatened with bankruptcy.

In 1935 preparations were made to establish an agricultural settlement on this tract of land. Negotiations were initiated with the tenant farmers with a view to compensating them. However just at that time the 1936 riots began, and, in the words of Aminadav Ashbel, "...now there was no possibility of coming to an agreement with the tenant farmers who had been persuaded by agitators not to vacate the land..."[4]

Hankin bought the land on which the Nesher Cement Factory and part of Kibbutz Yagur stand today from a rich Haifa Arab, Naseralla Khuri, who owned large tracts of land in the vicinity. In 1921 the plot had been surveyed and it was found to encompass 8,000 dunam in the plain and 11,000 dunam in the hills, but, as was common practice, the deed described the holding as encompassing only an area of 7,000 dunam. Negotiations were conducted with the Land Department of the Government, which claimed that the hill lands were uncultivated and so belonged to the Government. While these negotiations were in progress Khuri died, his heirs went bankrupt, and the parcel of land was up for sale at public auction. Nationalist Arab organizations, who sought to acquire the land for the purpose of developing an Arab quarter on it, prevented the transfer of title to the purchaser.

Litigation continued until 1937. In the meantime part of the land came into Jewish hands and the remainder awaited judicial determination. The matter was concluded when the receivers in bankruptcy were paid about LP. 87,000 for a valid deed. The nominal owners (the heirs of Khuri) were paid an additional sum in

175

cash and took responsibility for reaching an agreement with the tenant farmers and for settling the boundary disputes.[5]

A Beirut effendi named Omri owned 20,000 dunam of land in the villages of Jelil and el-Haram. In 1925 the Palestine Land Development Company bought 8,760 dunam of that land on behalf of the American Zion Commonwealth, for the purpose of founding the town of Herzliya. In testifying before the Shaw Commission concerning lands in the Jezreel Valley, Charles Passman, the Chairman of the American Zion Commonwealth, was asked about the Herzliya lands. Passman replied that the American Zion Commonwealth had bought 9,000 dunam of land and that the village of Jelil was still in existence, with its fellaheen continuing to cultivate their plots of land. His Company had invested 40,000 pounds sterling in draining the noxious Katurya swamp, which had infested the entire neighborhood.[6] This drainage project had created 14,000 dunam of new arable land.[7]

In a report of an inquiry conducted by the Jewish Agency as to the fate of the tenant farmers who had cultivated the land bought by the Jews, the following statement appears: "As far as el-Haram is concerned, those tenant farmers who were not permanent residents there returned to their former homes and used their indemnity money to make a new start. The tenant farmers who were permanent residents of el-Haram invested the money received from reparations in the village itself."[8]

The ninety families that founded the town of Magdiel bought 4,000 dunam of land in 1924 from an effendi named el-Shanti, formerly of Qalqiliya and, at the time of the sale, a resident of Tel-Aviv. There was one tenant farmer on the land from the vicinity of Ibne (Yavne). He moved to Hirbet Azun near Kefar-Saba. A few fellaheen of the 'Arab el-Jarmile tribe, who had cultivated some of the land, moved to Qalqiliya without being indemnified.[9]

The lands south and east of Herzilya, on which Ramat-Hasharon, Ramatayim, Kefar-Malal, Bnei-Berak and others were later established, were bought from the Bedouin tribal chieftain Abu Kishek,[10] a notorious land speculator. It was his custom to offer to sell a certain parcel of land to a number of real estate agents simultaneously, to get them to bid against one another – to his profit.[11]

In the Jewish Agency investigation mentioned above the following comment was made on Abu Kishek's tribe: "The members of Abu Kishek's family built houses and settled permanently on their land with the cash indemnities that they received from the sale of the lands of Ein-Hai (Kefar-Malal) and Ramatayim."[12]

In 1928, 1,400 dunam of land were bought from Saleh Hamdan, the sheikh of the village of Umm Haled. Netanya was later built on this parcel. Hamdan owned a tract of 20,000 dunam, which twenty families from Umm Haled worked as tenant farmers.[13]

Thereafter the farmers of Netanya continued to buy lands from Hamdan, until they completely surrounded the village of Umm Haled. The Jewish National Fund also bought 2,000 dunam from the sheikh, however the fellaheen of Umm Haled filed a claim on 1,400 dunam of this land. There followed a long drawn-out legal battle, which finally came to an end in 1945 with the land being awarded to the fellaheen.[14] Yet during the time that the case was being adjudicated the Jewish National Fund had possession of the land in question, and the fellaheen were being displaced from their lands. In 1934, the Chairman of the "Sons of Benjamin," Oved Ben-Ami, together with J.L. Magnes, the President of the Hebrew University, suggested to the Government that it settle the tenant farmers of Umm Haled on a 400-dunam tract east of Netanya, belonging to the "Sons of Benjamin." In return the Government would give the "Sons of Benjamin" a franchise on 2,000 dunam of sand dunes along the beach. The High Commissioner gave his consent to the plan, and preparatory work was begun on the beach tract. The 1936 riots broke out, and work on the project came to a stop. The 400 dunam remained Government land.[15]

In 1934, 'Auni Abd el-Hadi met with Ben-Gurion to discuss a possible accord between Jews and Arabs. The meeting was arranged by Professor Magnes. El-Hadi bitterly opposed the sale of land which resulted in the displacement of Arabs. To make his point he cited the land purchase at Umm Haled.[16] As has been stated above, the fellaheen won their case in court in 1945 and were

177

awarded the 1,400 dunam of land that they had claimed.

Saleh Hamdan continued to sell land to the inhabitants of Netanya, until in 1947 he was left with only 4,000 dunam, which he refused to sell, even though he was offered LP. 100,000. After Palestine was invaded by the Arab armies in 1948, Hamdan fled the country and his land was transferred to the care of the Custodian of Abandoned Property.[17]

In 1935 Oved Ben-Ami, one of Netanya's founders, had proposed a plan to the High Commissioner for draining the Ramadan swamp. The Government agreed, and granted a franchise to the Netanya Development Corporation on a 5,000-dunam tract, the Faliq sand dunes (Kafer-Sur). Later the land was given as a gift to the Jewish National Fund, and on it Kiryat Nordau was developed as a suburb of Netanya. The fellaheen and the tenant farmers of Kafer-Sur received an indemnity of LP. 8,000.[18]

The Hanun family of Tulkarem sold a 10,000-dunam tract of land to the "Sons of Benjamin" who in 1932 founded on it the *moshava* Even-Yehuda.[19] There were no tenant farmers on the land, but there were herdsmen. In a clash one of them was injured. Indemnity was paid to him and peace restored.[20]

Kefar-Yona was settled in 1932 on 4,000 dunam of land bought from the Jalud, Abu-Taqa, Mustapha Bushnaq and Khalil Abu-Sha'aban families.[21] In the early 1920's Dr. Mustapha Bushnaq had been a member of the Arab Executive.[22]

In 1928 Lord Melchett (Sir Alfred Mond) bought 3,642 dunam of land to found the *moshava* Tel-Mond. It had been wasteland for the most part.

Ismail Natur sold 4,000 dunam of land on behalf of the fellaheen owners. In 1933 this became the *moshava* of Kadima.[23]

The Nashef family from Taiybe and the Makdadi family from Tulkarem also sold lands in the Sharon Plain, on which Jewish settlements were established.[24]

From 1936 on Arabs sold land only when there were no tenant farmers on it. In 1938 the Palestine Land Development Company wrote to the Political Department of the Jewish Agency: "Some time ago you requested detailed information from us concerning

Arabs living on lands in the Sharon Plain, where new settlements were established. For the last two years it has been our policy to buy lands unencumbered by tenant farmers or by other claimants for indemnity. The Arab owners, aware of this policy, have refrained from engaging tenant farmers to cultivate their lands. Instead they have been hiring agricultural laborers."[25]

In the south the Dajani family sold 3,500 dunam of land, on which the *moshava* Gan-Yavne was founded in 1931.[26]

In 1926 Shukri el-Taji el-Farouqi sold 2,000 dunam of land in Zarnuqa to the American Zion Commonwealth on his own behalf and on behalf of his brother Abdallah.[27] Some time later the Jewish National Fund bought these lands from the American Zion Commonwealth and settled the folowng kibbutzim and *moshavim* on them and on additional tracts of land that it had acquired: Give'at-Brenner (1928), Na'an (1930), Kefar-Marmorek (1931), Kevutzat Schiller (1933) and Gibeton (1933).[28]

In the Negev private individuals acquired lands near Gaza and Beer-Sheba. Most of these lands later came into the hands of the Jewish National Fund, which assumed responsibility for indemnifying the tenant-farmers, as will be described in the next chapter.

Urban Land

The Arab opposition to Zionism was based on two main points:

a) The buying of land by Jews inevitably displaced the fellah and the tenant farmer from the land;

b) *Aliya* was inundating the country with Jews, and as a result the Arabs would become a minority, and would ultimately be ejected from their country.

The Arabs never charged that the Jewish urban community in any way interfered with the development of the Arab towns or that it displaced Arabs from the existing towns. The reason no such charge was made was that the city plots sold to the Jews were sold by rich urban Arabs, who were often themselves the spokesmen of the Arab nationalist movement. Some had even organized the gangs of hoodlums who attacked the Jewish quarters in the cities – the very sections which they themselves had sold to the Jews.

Jews bought property in the major cities – Haifa, Jaffa and Jerusalem – from Arabs, from German Templars, and from church groups, all of whom had acquired their holdings from the Ottoman Government many years previously. The onset of Jewish settlement ventures provided the sellers of the land with a considerable income that was used to further their various purposes.

Jews bought land in Haifa from the German Templars, from churches, and from monasteries.[29] Among the Arabs who sold land to the Jews was As'ad el-Shuqeiri, a Moslem religious scholar and the father of Ahmed Shuqeiri, the founder of the Palestine Liberation Organization (P.L.O.).[30]

In Jerusalem property was acquired from churches and monasteries. Among the Arabs who sold land to the Jews were members of the prominent Nashashibi family.[31]

Among those who sold land to Jews in Jaffa were the Dajani family, which included the Mufti of Jaffa, and Alfred Rock, who was a member of the Arab Higher Committee.[32]

CHAPTER EIGHT

ESTABLISHING THE FUTURE BOUNDARIES OF THE STATE

The British Mandate in Palestine endured for nearly thirty years. The last twelve years, from 1936 to 1947, were fraught with peril to its rule. Both the Arabs and the Jews were engaged in a life-and-death struggle to realize their national aspirations.

The years 1926 to 1929 were a period of economic depression for the Jews in Palestine and for the Zionist movement in general. Politically the publication of the Passfield White Paper of 1930 cast a deep shadow on the relations of the Jews with Great Britain. The following year, 1931, an improvement in the political and economic arenas could be discerned.

That year the anti-Zionist thrust of the White Paper lost much of its intensity. The new High Commissioner, Sir Arthur Wauchope, tried to develop an even-handed policy in the spirit of the Mandate. A new area of Zionist cooperation with the Mandatory Government was inaugurated.

The period from 1931 to 1935 saw the labor movement assume leadership in the *Yishuv* [a term generally used to describe the body of Jews resident in Palestine till the establishment of the State of Israel] and in the Zionist movement. A new momentum was given to the development of the country, to the raising of funds, to the growth of the national financial institutions, to the acquisition of lands, and to pioneering settlement.

A large *aliya* began to stream in to Palestine from Germany and Poland. A real solution was offered to Jews at a time when the Nazis were gaining power. The Jews constituted thirty per cent of the total population of Palestine. Reaching a majority within the decade seemed a real possibility.

April 19, 1936 marked the outbreak of the Arab Revolt against the *Yishuv* and against the Mandatory power. Its purpose was to achieve a speedy decision in favor of Arab nationalist goals.

The fifteen-year political struggle of the Arabs was at a point of crisis. The temporary victory achieved by the publication of the White Paper of 1930 was quickly nullified by Macdonald's February 1931 letter to Weizmann. The Arab attempts to organize riots in 1933 were firmly repressed by the High Commissioner. The Arabs were compelled to stand by helplessly during the years 1931–1935, as immigration doubled the Jewish population and Jewish real property.

Because of the Italian invasion of Ethiopia, the entrenchment of the Nazis in power, and the general awareness of the impotence of the League of Nations as a peace-keeping agency, the outbreak of another world war seemed inevitable. The Jews of Germany sought asylum in Palestine from Nazi rule. The Jews of Eastern Europe emigrated in order to escape the economic, political, and social disabilities under which they labored.

The Arabs concluded that they would be unable to change British policy without resorting to extreme measures. The riots of

April 1936 may have started out as a spontaneous series of acts, but very soon the political leadership assumed control of the Revolt, and gave it political goals to compel Great Britain to put an end to the Mandate and to the Zionist movement, and to hand over the reins of government to the Arab majority.

The defense of the *Yishuv* required tactics other than those employed in the 1929 disturbances, which had been of short duration. At that time the Jews were few in number, and the settlements were scattered over large areas. Concepts of strategy were essentially of a local or at most regional nature. The establishment of a territorial continuity between regions of Jewish settlement was impossible because of the great distances between the settlements and between the regions. The land purchase policy of the Zionist movement did not change after the 1929 riots: Land was purchased wherever possible, irrespective of defense considerations.

The situation in 1936 was quite different. The riots lasted for a long time. They were primarily launched by Arab attack squads against civilians in the cities and in isolated agricultural settlements. In addition the attackers sought to disrupt communications between the settlements. There were now many more Jewish settlements and the establishment of territorial continuity was not only possible but a strategic imperative.

A basic revision of policy planning for land acquisition and settlement became a prime requisite in the development of a defense strategy. It had to be national in scope and it required the reinforcement of underpopulated regions, where isolated settlements could not survive without aid.

In 1936 the British Government appointed a Royal Commission of Inquiry to investigate the causes of the riots and to recommend a solution to the conflict between Jews and Arabs. The Commission was also required to make a determination as to the conflicting interpretations of the terms of the Mandate that were being advanced by the parties to the conflict. It submitted its report and recommended the establishment of two states, one Jewish, one Arab. The British Government, which had previously committed itself to implementing whatever recommendations the Commission

182

would make, retreated from this position.

The political tensions that grew in Europe as a result of Nazi conquest and expansion and the threat of a second world war moved the British Government to seek an accomodation with the Arabs by changing its policy regarding the establishment of a Jewish National Home in Palestine.

On May 17, 1939 it issued a White Paper which provided:

A) Jewish immigration would be permitted only for five more years and would be limited to a maximum total of 75,000 people.

B) Land purchases by Jews were forbidden in large areas of the country and severely limited nearly everywhere else. Only in 5% of the area of the country were Jews permitted to buy land freely.

The Land Laws, based on the White Paper of 1939 which became operative on February 27, 1940, divided the country into three regions:

Region A included the hills of Galilee, Mount Carmel, the hills of Samaria and Judea, the Judean coastal plain and the northern Negev. In this region, which extended over 16,860,000 dunam, the right to acquire land was limited exclusively to Palestine Arabs.

Region B covered 8,348,000 dunam including the Hula and Jezreel Valleys together with connecting corridors through the hills of Galilee; the coastal area between Haifa and Atlit; the coastal strip south of Gedera; and the southern part of the Negev. Here, too, the right to acquire land was open only to Palestinian Arabs, except where special permits were granted by the High Commissioner.

Region C included the lands of the Haifa Bay area and the coastal strip from Atlit to Gedera, which amounted to 1,291,000 dunam. In this region land acquisiton by Jews was unrestricted.

Thus the new land laws forbade land sale to Jews in 95% of the territory of Palestine. The necessary implication was the creation of a Jewish ghetto along the seashore, with no opportunity for any further development.

In publishing the White Paper of 1939 Great Britain in effect admitted her inability to fulfill the terms of the League of Nations Mandate and reneged on her commitment to establish a Jewish National Home in Palestine, as expressed by the Balfour

Declaration. This step was obviously taken to appease the Arabs. The report of the Commission of Inquiry did offer a constructive solution to the Jewish-Arab conflict – it suggested the establishment of a Jewish State in a part of Palestine but this solution was abandoned.

However the Zionists believed that a concerted political effort, coupled with a vigorously implemented program for new settlement, could force a change in British policy. The Jewish Agency and the Zionist Organization launched a political campaign to nullify the White Paper, and at the same time began directing the settlement strategy with an eye to the boundaries of the future Jewish State in a part of Palestine.

This was a time when the despair of Europe's Jewry, especially where the Nazis had established their rule, was increasing in its intensity. Tens of thousands of Jews were seeking asylum. The outbreak of the War turned their despair into terrible tragedy. The Zionist Organization and the *Yishuv* were called upon to provide an economic basis for the absorption of the refugees.

Thus in the period from 1936 to 1947 three factors determined Zionist land-purchasing policy:

A) The establishment of territorial continuity between settlements and between regions to assure minimal defense requirements.

B) The campaign to nullify the restirctions of the White Paper on the acquisition of land.

C) The attempt to harmonize the policy of territorial continuity with the probable boundaries of the future Jewish State.

The Beit-Shean Valley

The map drawn by the Commission of Inquiry left half of the Sea of Galilee and the Beit-Shean Valley outside of the proposed Jewish State.

Even before the publication of the Commission's recommendations, the Arabs had established military control in the Beit-Shean Valley and in the southern part of the Jordan Valley. They had permitted the Arab attack squads stationed in Trans-Jordan to use the fords across the Jordan River at their pleasure. In effect Arab control was so complete that even the British were not allowed a foothold in the region.

Jews had bought 25,418 dunam of land in the Beit-Shean Valley, 90% of which was owned by the Jewish National Fund. Yet there wasn't a single Jewish settlement there until 1936,[1] when a small pioneering group, which later became Kibbutz Tel-Amal, struck root as the first Jewish settlement in the Beit-Shean Valley. The members of the kibbutz built temporary wooden huts of a primitive type and began to cultivate their lands. The Arabs burnt down the wooden huts, seized all the Jewish lands in the Beit-Shean Valley, and seemingly established a boundary beyond which there would be no further Jewish settlement.

The Arab attacks on Jews in general, and especially on settlements, roused the Zionist movement to try to break through the Arab siege by a daring settlement program executed by the settlers themselves. Before launching the program it had to take possession of the lands that the Jews had bought, but that were still in the hands of the defiant Arabs.

The first "Tower and Stockade" settlements – Nir-David (Tel-Amal), Sede-Nahum, Massada, Sha'ar-Hagolan, Beit-Yosef, Tirat-Zevi, and Ma'oz-Hayim – were built in a few months, beginning in December 1936, on land that had previously been purchased by Jewish National Fund.

East of the Sea of Galilee a Jewish company had bought 9,000 dunam of land some years previously, but was unable to take possession because of the problematical security situation. In July 1937 a group of members of Kibbutz Ein-Gev settled on the isolated tract which had no overland connection with any other Jewish settlement. On the northwest shore of the Sea of Galilee members of Genosar established their kibbutz on lands belonging to the P.I.C.A.

The momentum for a policy of increased settlement was dependent on the purchase of additional lands. During the first months of the 1936 riots all land transfers ceased because of the threat of terror. But the Bedouins in the Beit-Shean Valley were relatively safe from terror, because they could sell their lands in the Valley at a premium price and immediately slip over to Trans-

Jordan or to Syria and buy good lands there cheaply. In May of 1937 Joseph Weitz wrote in his diary: "Pevsner advises me of negotiations going on with Arabs to acquire 1,750 dunam of land in Zafa, situated in the southern part of the Beit-Shean Valley. The price is LP. 2.250 per dunam, exclusive of transfer fees payable to the Government. The Arab owners of the land are leaving the country for Syria, where they have acquired land."[2] Thus part of the 'Arab ez-Zafa tribe moved to Syria and the rest remained as neighbors to the new Jewish settlements.

Mehmed Zinati offered to sell 3,500 dunam in Ghasawiya and in Mesil el-Jizil (today the kibbutzim Ma'oz-Hayim and Kefar-Ruppin) and to move to Trans-Jordan. In March of 1938 Zvi Wolff sent a list to Weitz containing the number of tents and the number of people that would be going to Trans-Jordan. He writes: "199 tents, 1,048 souls. The Zinati family agreed to the terms proposed by the Jewish National Fund: LP. 4 per dunam for the land, exclusive of the transfer fee to the Government; for the cost of transfer of population (to Trans-Jordan), LP. 1 per dunam for land acquired from Mesil el-Jizil and LP. 2.5 for land acquired from Ghasewiya."[3]

The Trans-Jordanian Government agreed to absorb the Zinati family, and Zinati found lands which he bought. The Trans-Jordanian seller did not deal directly with Zinati. Instead he arranged the sale through Hankin, and so both the Jewish National Fund and the Trans-Jordanian seller were sure of their money.[4] When the Arab terror gangs learned of the transaction, they burned down Zinati's tent and warned him that much worse awaited him should he sell his land to Jews. But Zinati refused to be intimidated. He sold 1,500 dunam and moved part of his family to Trans-Jordan. He himself remained in the Beit-Shean Valley since he had retained 3,000 dunam of land there.[5]

Part of the Zinati family remained in the Valley till 1947, but when partition of the country became imminent they too moved to Trans-Jordan. A representative of the family applied to King Abdullah for Jordanian citizenship for the family. The King referred him to the Minister of the Interior who hinted that a bribe was needed to facilitate the matter. The family representative turned to the Jewish National Fund and requested LP. 3,000 to consummate the transfer to Trans-Jordan. The Fund gave the family LP.2,000, and the family also sold another 2,000 dunam of its holdings in the Beit-Shean Valley. Another member of the family, one Ahmed Zinati, who was a Trans-Jordanian subject, lived in Palestine and was the owner of 800 dunam of land there. After the entire family moved to Trans-Jordan we find Weitz noting in his diary: "In the end he, too, will go there and leave us his 800 dunam."[6]

The lands of Sakhne (today Nir-David) were Government-owned and had been sold to a well-known land speculator, Sulayman Bey Nassif, who had made a good deal of money in his dealings with the Jews. The Jewish National Fund bought 1,453 dunam from him. For fear of terrorist reprisal he refused to register the land in the name of the Jewish National Fund. When LP. 500 were added to the purchase price he consented to go through with the registration. However the tenant farmers refused to leave the land even though they had been offered land elsewhere.[7]

All land disputes were ultimately resolved by Government officials. Thus the District Commissioner, Alec Kirkbride, determined in October 1938 that since the tenant famers would be amply indemnified by lands elsewhere and since land for new settlement was scarce, the Jewish National Fund was entitled to possession of the Sakhne land.[8]

In May 1938, 1,460 dunam were bought from the Germans in the Beit-Shean Valley. Negotiations were conducted with Gustav Boierle, whose office was in Alexandria, and who represented six additional landowners beside himself.[9] The sale signaled the failure of the Germans to farm the fertile land of the Valley successfully. Effective cultivation of the land was dependent on draining the swamps in the area, and not till the advent of Jewish settlement was this goal achieved. Kibbutz Sede-Eliahu settled on the land of the Germans.

The Arab National Company of Nablus was one of the beneficiaries of the Government's generous land grants in the Beit-Shean Valley. It received a tract of 1,200 dunam for intensive cultivation, to serve as a model for the Bedouins in the Valley. At

187

the same time that the Arab leadership was carrying on its violent struggle against Jews, other Arab leaders sought to evolve a constructive policy, which would not only prevent the sale of land to Jews but would improve the lot of the fellah as well. Thus the Arab People's Fund and the Arab National Company provided the fellaheen with instructors to teach them how to grow bananas. The crops failed. The fellaheen, on the advice of their instructors, uprooted the bananas and planted citrus groves, and also tried to raise vegetables. These projects failed as well. In the end these lands were sold to the Jewish National Fund.[10]

Mussa el-'Alami acquired land in the Valley privately and attempted to establish a farm based on modern principles. He, too, failed and he, too, sold his land to the Jewish National Fund. His land constituted part of the tract on which Kibbutz Tirat-Zevi is now located.[11]

The Government had sold land in Ashrafiya to some prominent Arab families who could prove, as it were, that they has previously owned land in the area. In 1929 the P.I.C.A. bought 2,000 dunam of land from these families. The Jewish National Fund acquired an additional 4,300 dunam. During the period of the riots local Arabs seized these tracts of land and held them. In 1940, after the siege on Jewish settlements had been lifted, the P.I.C.A. and the Jewish National Fund sought to reassert their lawful ownership. The Arab squatters made various claims to title and to alleged rights in the real property. Their claims were heard, as was customary, in the Land Court, and were all disallowed.[12] The Jews, pursuant to the Court's finding, sought to plow the lands, but the Arabs did all they could to hinder them and refused to leave the area in dispute. When the Jews continued with the plowing the situation became tense and violence seemed imminent. The Arabs summoned the British police and then attempted to plow the land which the Jews had previously plowed. Four British policemen appeared on the scene and ordered the settlers not to interfere with the Arabs' plowing. When they refused, the police called for help and twelve mounted policemen appeared. They arrested eighteen Jews, but the other Jews refused to leave until the British police promised that they would prevent the Arabs from plowing. Work came to a standstill pending a decision by the authorities in Jerusalem.[13]

Four weeks passed and no decision from Jerusalem. The Arabs again sought to plow the lands of Ashrafiya. A clash ensued, a few people were injured and the police arrested 83 Jews.[14]

A few days later a consultation was held with Moshe Shertok (Sharett), the Director of the Political Department of the Jewish Agency. The participants included representatives of the Agricultural Center of the Histadrut ("Hamerkaz Hahaklai") and of the Regional Councils of the Harod and Beit-Shean areas. Some of the representatives of the settlements expressed disapproval of the use of violence. The decision was to exhaust first all legal avenues, and to turn to violence only as a last resort.[15]

Negotiations had been carried on for many years between the Government and various Zionist agencies for the acquisition of 2,380 dunam of land in Mesil el-Jizil. This was a tract of swamp land that had never been cultivated. The impartial mosquitoes brought disease to Jews and Arabs alike. The Jewish National Fund had offered the tenant farmers other land in exchange so that it might rid the area of the menace to health by draining the swamp. Of course it also intended to establish new settlements on the reclaimed land. The Director of Development set difficult conditions for the exchange, and the matter dragged on. [16]

At the end of 1946 a solution was found. The Arabs of Ma'alul in the Jezreel Valley laid claims to grazing rights on land that the Jewish National Fund had bought, but the latter was of the opinion that it was not obliged to pay a second time for land which it had purchased at full price. To put an end to the dispute the Government offered alternate land which it was willing to cede. Thus an offer was made to the Jewish National Fund to yield its land to the Arabs in Ma'alul in return for 5,000 dunam in the Beit-Shean Valley, including the swamp area in Mesil el-Jizil.[17]

Up to the establishment of the State, the Jews bought a total of 53,848 dunam of land in the Beit-Shean Valley. This constituted 37.4% of the arable land. The Government held 20.5% and the Arabs held 42.1%.[18]

In accordance with the decision of the Royal Commission on the Partition of Palestine, Galilee was to be included in the future Jewish State, but there was reason to fear that as a result of the ongoing political struggle the decision would be reversed and Galilee separated from the Jewish State. Thus the acquisition of land in Galilee became a prime aim of Jewish National Fund activity.

When Jewish organizations began taking an interest in purchasing land on the Lebanese border, Joseph Fein reported to the Political Department of the Jewish Agency:

"There are lands for sale in Khirbet-Samakh, Jurdi, and Arrubin. Most of the tenant farmers have left to join the terrorist gangs and practically no one is living on these lands. Their owners want to sell, taking advantage of the fact that the tenant farmers are no longer there. They also fear the outbreak of a world war."[19]

Near these lands the 20,000-dunam tract of Khirber-Hanuta was up for sale. Part of this tract was owned by As'ad Zaroub of Beirut, who emigrated to the United States, was living in Washington and changed his name to Richard Zoroub. The attorney, Jemil Abiad, traced the owner's whereabouts and purchased the land from him for the Jewish National Fund. In addition he purchased land from 28 fellaheen in the same vicinity and from eight fellaheen in the Khirber 'Ein-Hur area. After making these purchases he transferred title to the Jewish National Fund.[20]

Elias Effendi Qittayet, a Brazilian citizen resident in Cairo, was the owner of 6,000 dunam in Khirbet-Samakh. Two tenant farmers, originally from Beirut, Mohammed Shouish Qiblawi and Suheil Beidoun, were in possession of the land. At the time of the sale to the Jewish National Fund Qittayet gave assurance that he would compensate the tenant farmers. He even invited them to come to Cairo to negotiate the amount of the indemnity. They, however, preferred to deal with Fein, the "Mayor of Hanita," as they called him.

On February 16, 1939 an agreement was made with the two Beirut Arabs, who were to relinquish their rights as tenant farmers for LP 600. At the last moment another claimant appeared. He was paid an additional LP.75.[21]

Even before the agreement was signed Kibbutz Eilon settled on the land on November 24, 1938. The settling on the land, first of Kibbutz Hanita, and a half year later of Kibbutz Eilon, marked a breakthrough of Jewish settlement in the midst of a completely Arab environment. Naturally considerations of defense and political strategy were dominant in the decisions taken. Two years later these two settlements were reinforced, when Kibbutz Matzuba settled on the nearby land of Mas'ub on February 13, 1940.

The land that was settled by Matzuba was previously owned by the Rock family. Alfred Rock was opposed to the sale of the land because he claimed that it would bring shame on him. However one of the members of his family was paid an additional LP.2.500 and the deal was closed. The few tenant farmers were paid suitable indemnities. Seemingly the family honor was somehow preserved.[22]

It was decided to establish a Jewish settlement in a completely Arab area, and with this in mind land surrounding the fortress of Jiddin was bought from the heirs of Rif'at and Abdul Latif Saleh, members of a Turkish family living in Haifa. The Jewish National Fund bought 3,348 dunam. It engaged the Zur Investment and Building Company to act as an intermediary in negotiating the sale. When the transaction was completed the Zur Company reported to the Jewish National Fund:" There are no difficulties such as the need to reclaim part of the land, and there are no tenant famers. The arrangements for the transfer of the land are proceeding smoothly."[23]

The Jiddin purchase preceded the acquisition of the lands of Hanita and Eilon. The establishment of settlements on the future boundary was given priority in the overall strategy. So one finds that Kibbutz Yehiam settled on the Jiddin lands only after the Second World War, in November 1946.

In addition to land acquisiton for strategic reasons, the necessity of buying lands to strengthen existing settlements was not overlooked. In the vicinity of the town of Nahariya, founded in 1934, the Jewish National Fund bought 1,400 dunam from one of the heirs of Jemal Pasha, a Mrs. Samiha Muheizin Pasha who lived in Alexandria. The Jewish National Fund assumed responsibility for indemnifying the tenant farmers, and it wrote to Mrs. Samiha Muheizin Pasha: "Neither you nor Fahri Bey are responsible for negotiating the withdrawal of the tenant farmers. We will satisfy all their claims."[24] Another 1,569 dunam of land from the same inheritance were acquired from Sa'dat Khanun, the daughter of Sa'id Pasha of Akko.[25]

During the 1936–1939 riots traffic on the Akko-Safed road suffered repeated attacks and yet at the peak of the disturbances the Palestine Land Development Company purchased on behalf of the Jewish National Fund two parcels of land along that road. In June 1938 the P.L.D.C. notified its principal: "We bought 5,000 dunam in the villages of Damun and Birwa... The price is LP. 12 per metric dunam, with necessary repairs to be made to the land (by the seller), and free of tenant farmers..."[26]

The tract of land comprising the Hula Concession was transferred to Jewish hands after the P.L.D.C. had promised to allocate 15,700 dunam to the tenant farmers living in the Concession area. The draining of the Hula swamp and the surrounding area was postponed because of the riots, followed by the outbreak of World War II. At first the delay was attributed to the unsettled security conditions, but later it became clear that the needed heavy equipment was not available. The draining project was carried out only after the establishment of the State of Israel.

Immediately after the Hula Concession was granted, the Jewish National Fund, together with other Jewish agencies, began buying up land to the north of the Concession, realizing that the price of land in the valley would soar once the draining project was completed. The area to be drained was 57,000 dunam, while the whole Hula Valley was 192,000 dunam. The draining of such an area would inevitably lower the water table for the whole valley. Surplus water would be drawn off, thus destroying the sources of malaria. Large tracts of land that were previously uncultivable would become fine agricultural land and its value would increase manifold. The beneficiaries would be the absentee landlords living in foreign lands who would have contributed nothing to the

192

amelioration of the lands.

In 1934, after the Hula Concession was acquired, the Settlement Department of the Jewish Agency surveyed the Valley with an eye to future settlement. The recommendations included a plan for settlement in the Valley, after the draining of the swamps and the melioration of the land were accomplished. They applied to Arabs as well as to Jews. According to the plan 2,715 Arab families would be settled on 54,300 dunam, 20 dunam per family. They would raise cattle and farm the land. 4,250 Jewish families would be settled on 85,000 dunam of land, 20 dunam per family. A total of 139,300 dunam of cultivated land would be assigned to settlers, with the remaining lands being available for roads and other public needs.[27]

The plan was made on the assumption that the Zionist implementing agencies would be empowered to divide the land equitably and would be able to effect a degree of agricultural reform. But such overall powers never devolved on them. They continued to acquire one dunam after the other, and were limited to serving only Jewish settlements.

The emir Sham'un Faghour, the head of the Bedouin tribe el-Fadil, who was a member of the Syrian parliament, controlled 10,000–13,000 dunam of land belonging to his family north of the Concession area. A portion of the land he had seized illegally by force. Three complainants from Lebanon filed charges with the Chief Secretariat of the Mandatory Government, claiming that Sham'un Faghour had stolen from them a tract of 700 dunam located in Mansura.[28] The complainants further charged that the tenant farmers had stolen their lands in Ibl el-Qamh.

In 1936, before the riots broke out, the emir Sham'un Faghour had offered his property for sale, but his price was too high and negotiations were broken off.[29] At the beginning of 1939 the emir made a second offer to Joseph Nahmani, but the price was still high. On February 13, 1940 Nahmani wrote to the Head Office of the Jewish National Fund: "After protracted and wearying negotiations, an agreement has finally been concluded at Metzudat Ussishkin A (later Kibbutz Dafna) with the emir Sham'un Faghour on his own behalf and as the duly constituted agent of his sister, his mother and his niece. The transaction covers all the lands owned by the Faghour Family in the Hula region." In accordance with extant maps the area sold came to about 11,185 dunam in size and the price was LP. 134,205.[30]

Most of the land was *musha'a* (i.e. worked by joint and undivided tenancy, together with fellaheen who owned other land in the area). It was a long and tiresome undertaking to change the status of the land purchased to *mafruz* (i.e. divided land), to exchange parcels of land with some fellaheen, to buy land outright from others and to indemnify tenant farmers resident on the land bought.

In the following years Faghour transferred all the lands to which he could establish title. The agreement also required Faghour, who owned land in Syria and Lebanon, to indemnify the tenant farmers. Some of his land holdings were in Betteiha, on the banks of the Lake Kinneret, which was Syrian territory. Faghour employed tenant farmers to cultivate these lands, and he could have easily found room for displaced tenant farmers in his other estates, but he did not do so with the tenant farmers on the land sold to the Jewish National Fund.

In December of 1940 Nahmani noted in his diary: "In Halsa I came upon tens of tenant farmers from 'Azaziat (today Kibbutz Kefar-Szold) who were physically prevented from plowing their lands by the emir's Syrian horsemen. Evidently he does not agree with my policy of paying off the tenant farmers. He seems to prefer the Turkish method of applying the lash."[31]

The emir owned land in Khisas jointly with the fellaheen of the village as *musha'a*, and tenant farmers cultivated his land. Despite the agreement with Faghour that he would indemnify the tenant farmers, the Jewish National Fund paid them their indemnities. In his quarterly report to the Head Office of the Jewish National Fund for the months of February to April 1940 Nahmani listed the following item: "Indemnities to tenant farmers and compensation for Khisas – LP. 1,600."[32]

Faghour met with difficulties when he sought to have the transfer of the real property recorded in the Land Register. According to Nahum Hurwitz, Selim Faghour, the father of the emir, had stolen most of the lands of the fellaheen of Khisas.[33] They now opposed

194

the proposed sale of the land to the Jewish National Fund. The land transfer could not be recorded in the Land Register without it being converted from *musha'a* to *mafruz* land, but the conversion could not be effected without the consent of the fellaheen.

Nahmani, the representative of the Jewish National Fund, negotiated with the fellaheen of Khisas as to the amount of indemnity they would receive and also to get their consent to register the land as *mafruz*. In December 1940 he noted in his diary: "As agreed with the emir, I traveled to Khisas to meet him there. I consulted with the fellaheen and suggested that they appoint three representatives to negotiate the matter of registering the land as *mafruz*. The emir does not behave as we do. He comes, he destroys, and he uproots trees. He doesn't pay reparations, neither to the tenant farmer nor to the owner of the land. As far as he is concerned there is no law and there are no rights."[34]

Faghour was unrestrainedly violent not only in dealing with his tenant farmers but also in his relations with his neighbors. The Francis family owned 5,700 dunam in Kafer-Difnah (Dafna). The family lived in Hazbiyah in Lebanon, while tenant farmers cultivated the estate.

At the beginning of 1939 the el-Fadil Bedouins fell upon the village of Difnah and pillaged it in the best Bedouin tradition. The emir was the chieftain of the tribe. Nahmani wrote to Hankin: "The 'Arab el-Fadil raid on the tenant farmers of Difnah and the ensuing robbery of all their possessions compelled all of them to leave the village and most of them to leave the country. A few settled in the neighboring villages, but most crossed over to Lebanon and rented land in several villages. For more than a year the lands of Difnah have been uncultivated and lie fallow, and there is now an opportunity to buy the land free of tenant farmers. Some influential tenant farmers are ready to secure releases from all the others if indemnities are offered. The Francis family is asking LP. 12.5 per dunam. Of course we have to take in account the additional monies that we will have to pay while settling matters with the tenant farmers."[35]

On April 28 Nahmani wrote to the Jewish National Fund: "After two days of strenuous negotiations I have today reached an agreement with the tenant farmers of Difnah. We met at the home of Milham Francis, one of the former owners, in the town of Qley'a in Lebanon. At first the tenant farmers demanded alternate lands, then they asked outrageous sums of money as indemnity. With the assistance of Kamel Effendi, who had prepared the ground with the tenant farmers in advance of our meetin, and of Abraham Effendi (Durah)* I managed to moderate the tenant farmers' exaggerated ideas of the amounts of money they would receive. In the end we reached an agreement."[36]

The Jewish National Fund's intermediary with the tenant farmers of the Hula Valley was Kamel Hussein of Halsa. The annals of the *Yishuv* refer to him as Kamel Effendi.

In the years 1920–1921, when the Arabs in the northern part of the Hula Valley and in Lebanon rebelled against the French authorities, Kamel Effendi, at the head of an armed force, laid siege to the Tel-Hai courtyard. They wanted to be sure that no French fugitives were hiding there. In the battle that ensued Trumpeldor and his comrades were killed. After British rule had been established and the northern part of the Hula Valley incorporated within Mandated Palestine, Kamel became the intermediary between Jewish buyers of land and the tenant farmers affected by the land transfer. He was the representative of the Arabs of the region in their dealings with the British authorities, and he represented the tenant farmers in their negotiations with the Jewish National Fund. Since he controlled the indemnities that were paid to the tenant farmers, part of the money ended up in his pocket.

Hankin wrote to Nahmani protesting: "I deeply regret that we had to close the deal with Kamel Hussein, the murderer of Trumpeldor of blessed memory..."[37]

When the tractors of Kibbutz Dafna began plowing the land, a few tenant farmers refused to leave. Their women and children lay down in the path of the tractors and prevented them from plowing. A clash developed, the police were summoned and they arrested a

* A Beirut Jew who served as an intermediary in transactions between Arab landowners and Jewish buyers.

few of the demonstrators.[38] Frequently tenant farmers would renege on their agreements and return to the land after they had been indemnified. In the present instance their action was justified. It appears that of the sum of LP. 8,000 agreed on, Kamel Effendi had taken more than half for himself. Weitz commented in a letter to Nahmani: "In the future we must see to it that the tenant farmers receive all the money that is due them. We are not interested in making Kemal rich and powerful at their expense."[39]

Thirty-two tenant farmers occupied a portion of a 5,569-dunam tract of land that comprised the Dauara village (later Kibbutz Amir). The inhabitants were Christians and Druse, originally from Lebanon. When the time came for the representative of the Jewish National Fund to take possession of the purchased land, "the surveyors together with the tenant farmers measured the plot of each tenant farmer separately – 32 separate claims – 1,428 dunam was the sum total." As far as the land to be transferred to the Jewish National Fund was concerned, it was decided at a meeting of the tenant farmers on October 22, 1940 "that a day should be fixed for the receipt of the cash indemnities, because it was the busy season, and they could not afford to lose any time away from work. The tenant farmers will continue to plow all lands that they cultivated in the past and that are not being transferred to the Jewish National Fund. The tenant farmers acquired additional tracts of land in Muftahira and Bureiqat."[40]

The Hula Valley was in the B sector of the country, according to the terms of the 1940 Land Law (based on the White Paper of 1939), which meant that land owned by a foreign subject could be transferred to a Jew only with the prior approval of the High Commissioner. The law that protected the rights of tenant farmers was enforced rigorously. The tenant farmers were aware that even if they agreed to accept a certain sum as indemnity, they were perfectly safe in violating the terms of their agreement. In fact they learned that the courts would uphold their new claims. As a result there was practically no agreement with a tenant farmer that was not subsequently violated.

The tenant farmers of Dauara were no exception – they demanded an additional 200 dunam. The Jewish National Fund countered by offering 100 dunam and it refused to go any higher, whereupon the tenant farmers of Dauara plowed up the lands of Kibbutz Amir by threats and by force.[41] The Jewish national organizations turned to the police and demanded their intervention. Zionist policy was to do everything possible to arrive at an amicable settlement, but to oppose unequivocally any Arab attempt to achieve a goal by force or by threat of force. The firm stand taken by the settlers caused the tenant farmers to withdraw to their lands in their village. Thereafter they maintained neighborly relations with the surrounding Jewish settlements until 1947.

The 2,345 dunam of the village of Khan ed-Duweir (Kibbutz Dan and *moshav* Shear-Yashuv) had originally been the property of fifteen owners, whose twenty-seven heirs all lived in Beirut. In the early part of 1934, when the land was bought, it was said to be free of tenant farmers, but indemnities were nevertheless paid to them,[42] and also to squatters who had recently established themselves on the land for the express purpose of extorting indemnities.[43]

The land of the village of Khiyam el-Walid (later Kibbutz Lahavot-Habashan) belonged to a Kurdish family that lived in Damascus. Nahmani bought it in 1940 and paid the tenant farmers an indemnity of LP. 3,500.[44]

A serious clash took place when the settlers of Kibbutz Neot-Mordekhai attempted to establish their community on land that was bought in the village of Zawiya. Originally part of the land was owned by fellaheen and part by absentee landlords in Lebanon. The land of the absentee landlords had been cultivated by the fellaheen under terms of tenancy. Since during the war years the absentee owners were unable to collect land rents in accordance with the terms of tenancy, the boundaries between their land and those of the fellaheen became blurred and undefined. The absentee owners were Naif and Talib Zuba, and Fawzi Farahat. Farahat had lodged a complaint against the tenants with the Mandatory Government through the French Consul for non-payment of rents, and now he and his co-owners offered to sell the land to the Jewish National Fund. The Arab People's Fund tried to dissuade them from selling the land, but the owners remained impervious to threats and blandishments and went through with the sale.[45]

198

Thereupon emissaries of the Arab People's Fund began inciting the tenant farmers of Zawiya to resist forcibly the impending Jewish settlement on the land. The emissaries promised them that assistance from the neighboring villages would be forthcoming.

On November 3, 1946, as the settlers were setting up tents and beginning to plow the land of their new home, they were attacked by the people of Zawiya with stones and cudgels. The attack was repulsed. The following day another attack was launched after reinforcements had arrived from the neighboring villages. This time firearms were employed. Two Jews and three Zawiya Arabs were killed and eleven Jews were wounded.[46] The police ordered a cessation of work on the land in dispute and the matter was transferred to the Land Court. After a short time a ruling in favor of the Jewish National Fund was handed down.

The settlers again began to plow the land, and again the people of Zawiya opposed them by force. The District Commissioner and the District Officer read the Court Order to the fellaheen, but they would not give in and appealed to the Supreme Court in Jerusalem. In January of 1947 the Court decreed that the fellaheen of Zawiya were entitled to 1,539 dunam of land.[47] Towards the end of 1947 the Government was functioning in a spasmodic and erratic manner. The court files contain no record of further litigation. In any event Zawiya continued to exist as a village until its inhabitants fled the Hula Valley after Safed fell in the Spring of 1948.

The Shahab family, of Kurdish descent and living in Damascus, owned a good deal of land in the Hula Valley. The emir Haled Shahab owned 4,000 dunam in the village of 'Abisiya; Hasiba, the daughter of Mas'ud Shahab, owned 800 dunam in the villages of Qitiya and Lazzaza. The emir Ahmed Abdul Majid Shahab and his family owned 1,020 dunam in en-Na'ama. On July 7, 1937 an agreement was signed between the representatives of the Jewish National Fund and the emir Abdul Majid, Amira Putnah Shahab, and 'Ali 'Omar Shahab for the sale of the foregoing parcels of land. An obligation was attached to the agreement by 'Ali 'Omar Shahab to the following effect: "Inasmuch as the above Sellers have declared that the lands to which the attached Agreement refers are cultivated together with other lands by 35 tenant farmers,

199

individually listed by name in the said Agreement, and that there are no other tenant farmers... we hereby guarantee that there are no other tenant farmers on the land to which the Agreement of April 5, 1937 refers... and I undertake to be solely liable against any claim to the contrary..."[48]

An agreement was signed between the representatives of the Jewish National Fund and Ismail and 'Azziza, the children of Sa'id Khalil, concerning a portion of the land in Lazzaza which they had inherited from the emir Abd-el Kader, together with the emir 'Ali and Haled Shahab, the sons of Mehmed Selim.[49]

Nahmani made the following comment in his diary concerning the payment of indemnities on the above-mentioned parcels of land: "Despite my hesitation and fears the people of Lazzaza gave us a release on 887 dunam west of the Hasbany, waiving all rights... In Halsa the people of en-Na'ama and I came to an agreement about our taking possession of the entire parcel of land... By noon we obtained the signatures of the tenant farmers who had not signed their releases yesterday. Thus the Khiyam el-Walid affair is ended."[50]

Naif and Talib Zuba owned 3,770 dunam of land in Jahula and Buweiziya, of which the Jewish National Fund bought 1,100 dunam. According to the laws of real property in Mandated Palestine first option on the purchase of adjacent land was reserved to the neighboring landholder. At first the neighboring fellaheen had agreed to the transaction, but they later changed their minds and sought an injunction against it. They were prepared to pay LP. 3 per dunam more than the Jewish National Fund had paid. But the seller was a man who honored his own word and he refused the fellaheen offer. Thereupon thirteen of them filed claims as tenant farmers. Five lost their cases and Joseph Weitz noted in his diary: "They tried to influence the people who were ready to come to an agreement with us. They are asking LP. 1,000 as indemnity and wish to retain the village square, which we were to have acquired by the terms of the purchase agreement. I urged Nahmani to accept their offer, just to put an end to the Jahula controversy. When we returned to Yessud-Hama'ala Nahmani awaited us there. He had reached an agreement with the Jahula delegation, to be ratified by the village."[51]

All the Arab villages in the Hula Valley remained in place except two: Khiyam el-Walid and Difnah.[52] Khiyam el-Walid was *Waqf* land held by a family, on which tenant farmers were unable to acquire rights of tenure. The Francis family withdrew all its tenant farmers in Difnah to Lebanon, and Nahmani reached a settlement with the family in Qley'a.

"Tower and Stockade" settlements were established in 1939 and thereafter on the tracts north of the Hula concession. They constituted a crucial element in the struggle of the Zionist Movement against the White Paper.

The tenant farmers living in the area of the Hula Concession were allotted a 15,700-dunam tract of land under the terms of the Agreement. Nevertheless they blithely plowed other areas within the Concession as if the land was ownerless. On July 30, 1935 the Political Department of the Jewish Agency complained in writing to the Secretariat of the Government: "Despite the fact that the fellaheen were given 15,000 dunam they invaded other areas of the Concession..."[53]

At the same time that the Jewish Nationa Fund acquired the Hula Valley it also bought lands west of the Valley, in the Hills of Naftali. These acquisitions were intended to create a territorial continuity of settlemens that would serve two purposes: They would create a safety belt to prevent Arab forces from invading the country from Lebanon, and they would clearly define the northern boundary of the future Jewish State.

In fact territorial continuity of settlement was not achieved. Between the hill lands of Eastern Galilee and the block of kibbutzim – Hanita, Matzuba, and Eilon – in Western Galilee lay a large area clear of Jewish settlement. In general Jewish policy rested on considerations of defense and political strategy. Moreover the policy makers for Jewish settlement came to believe that reclaiming potentially fertile lands in the hill country was no less in the national interest than draining swamps in the valleys or ameliorating marginal lands on the coastal strip.

Most of the land in the Hills of Naftali was the property of absentee owners, residents of Syria and Lebanon. In March 1940

201

Nahmani made a survey of the holdings of landowners who were not Palestinian citizens. He found that they owned a total of 83,467 dunam in the Districts of Safed and Tiberias. 26.000 dunam in the Safed District and 7,000 dunam in the Tiberias District were owned by Circassians, Druse, Iranians and Germans. None of these landowners were citizens of Palestine.

Ahmed Bey, a leader of the Matuala (a Lebanese Shi'ite sect) and a member of the Lebanese Parliament, owned the land of the village of 'Adeisa together with the Nada family and a number of fellaheen. The village was unique in that a part of it was in Lebanon and part in Palestine.

The owners of the 'Adeisa land sold their rights to it to the Jewish National Fund. However the land was registered as *musha'a* and in addition some plots of land were owned by fellaheen from the village of Hunin.

On November 2, 1945, at the height of the struggle with the British authorities against the White Paper, a new settlement was established on the land of 'Adeisa (today Kibbutz Misgav-Am). When actual settlement was begun, the fellaheen of Hunin, who owned parcels of land situated inside the tract, tried to stop the work by force. At the head of the fellaheen was one of the village elders, Abu Rashid, who was accompanied by some younger members of his family. The settlers had put up a few shacks on a portion of his land. The older man protested vocally against the illegal incursion on his property, and the younger ones shouted anti-Zionist slogans of a vitriolic nature. The atmosphere became tense and violence seemed imminent. Nahmani who was in charge of the group of settlers sought a peaceable solution. He turned to Abu Rashid, admitted that the settlers were trespassers, and to show his good faith agreed to pay any price for the land that Abu Rashid would stipulate. The village elder quoted a price of LP. 25 per dunam, much higher than the market value of the land. Nahmani promptly agreed.

The incident occurred on November 2, the anniversary of the proclamation of the Balfour Declaration. There were riots throughout the country. Abu Rashid was reluctant to go to the Notary's office in Tiberias to sign an agreement for the sale and the ceremony was postponed to the following day. When the actual agreement was signed and the notarial seal affixed, Abu Rashid, of his own volition, reduced the price to PL. 20 per dunam.[54]

The Jewish National Fund bought 2,538 dunam from the family of Asa'ad Bey Khuri of Beirut in the village of Khirbet Munara (today Kibbutz Manara), and 5,763 dunam in the village of Hunin (today *moshav* Margaliot).[55] It bought 4,923 dunam in the village of Qedesh (today *moshav* Ramot-Naftali) from a number of families.

Ahmed Mardini, a Kurd from Damascus, owned 2,200 dunam; Hassan Farah, a Christian from Marj Iyun,[56] owned 2,000 dunam; and 520 dunam were owned by Abdallah Khuri and the heirs of Shahadin Khuri, all of whom were from Lebanon.[57]

In July 1938 Weitz reported to the Political Department of the Jewish Agency: "Some of the tenant farmers have been transferred to Lebanon by one of the landowners who sold us more than half of the entire tract. There remain 23 tenant farmers who intend to migrate to Lebanon in the summer."[58]

After the purchase of land from the Khuri family, a report was filed with the Head Office of the Jewish Nationa Fund: "The area in our actual possession is 520 dunam, as recorded in the agreement with joint owners, dated July 12, 1943. This is the net total after we ceded 210 dunam in favor of the tenant farmers. In return they waived all other rights they had in land that we occupied."[59]

A tract of 2,161 dunam in the vicinity of the village of Meiss ej-Jabbal (today Kibbutz Yiftah) was originally settled by Algerians who had accompanied Abd el-Kader into exile (see Chapter One). Over the years the land came into the hands of the Farah family of Marj Iyun. The fields were within the boundaries of Mandated Palestine, whereas the village itself was in Lebanon. The Jewish National Fund bought the tract of land from the Farah family in 1945.[60] The purchase ended all connection between the Farah family and the land within Mandated Palestine – it may be noted that they were not Palestinian citizens. The village remained in the Lebanese domain, as did the village of 'Adeisa.

The village of Malkiya, comprising 765 dunam, was owned by the heirs of Hussein Sulayman Buza, Moslem Kurds living in Damascus, and was sold to the Jewish Natioanl Fund. The

203

regulations of the White Paper of 1939 were in efffect at the time and a compaign of terror was being conducted against Arabs who sold land to the Jews. The heirs gave a fictitious mortgage to one Abd el-Razak el-Daudi el-Dajani. A fictitious foreclosure ensued, followed by a public auction, at which the Jewish National Fund made the successful bid and was awarded the land.[61]

Territorial Continuity Between the Jezreel Valley and Lower Galilee

When settlement began in the Jezreel Valley the problem of malaria was acute. The settlers of the earliest kibbutzim, Ein-Harod and Tel-Yosef, suffered considerably from it. They sought to establish the permanent site of their communities on a hill where the Arab village of Qumia was situated. Their health problem was compounded by considerations of defense. Arab villages looked down on them from the north and from the south, and it was necessary to erect their permanent buildings on a defensible site. Half the land of the village of Qumia, some 3,260 dunam, was owned by the Rais family, an aristocratic Christian family from Haifa; 561 dunam belonged to the Manasse family of the resort town of Aley in Lebanon; 1,310 dunam belonged to the el-Hadi family; and 2,009 dunam were owned and cultivated by fellaheen. The fellaheen also worked the land of the other owners on the basis of tenancy.[62]

In 1929 Hankin conducted negotiations to purchase the land belonging to the fellaheen. He wrote: "In order to buy the land in Qumia we have to offer the fellaheen alternate land for the 2,000 dunam we wish to acquire. In order to close the deal we will have to do the following: a) we will have to buy some other plots of land at a cost as yet unknown; b) we will have to pay extra for about 1,000 dunam that has been sown with green fodder to improve it; c) we will have to give *double the land* that we will receive; d) we will need an additional sum of money – I don't know exactly how much."[63]

Thus the Jewish National Fund bought land in the neighbouring village of Tamra as an exchange for the land of the Qumia fellaheen. At first the fellaheen agreed to the exchange. They were

204

encouraged by the promise of an additional payment of money, and furthermore they were apprehensive about continuing to live alongside the Jewish settlers and preferred to live with their own people. But there was a delay in consummating the exchange: there were tenant farmers on the land in Tamra, and the Jewish National Fund was unable to negotiate a settlement with them. In the meantime the fellaheen found the Jewish settlers to be good neighbors, and they decided not to leave the village. Nevertheless they agreed to sell some of their land to the Jewish National Fund,[64] on condition that the Jewish National Fund erect a water pumping station for the village. During the war years it was difficult to acquire the requisite motors, pipes, and accessories, and the Jewish National Fund made considerable efforts to meet the obligation. Its files contain copies of an extensive correspondence with governmental agencies for the necessary permits and licenses. Ultimately water was supplied to the village.[65]

The Jewish National Fund finally negotiated a settlement with the tenant farmers of Tamra. The Director of Development strictly supervised land transfers to prevent tenant farmers from being deprived of their rights. A report to the Jewish National Fund in September 1940 states: "Because of the Government pressure we were obliged to pay an additional LP. 100 to the Bedouins in return for their leaving the Tamra land. Tomorrow we will be going to Tamra to pay the Arabs half the sum that is due to them. We will pay the other half after plowing the land."[66]

In 1930 a group of German Templars was negotiating with the villagers of Kafer-Shatta (today Kibbutz Beit-Hashita) for the purchase of their land. When the neighboring kibbutzim learned of the negotiations they immediately proposed to the Jewish National Fund that it acquire the land. But the treasury was empty. Zevi Lederer (Dar), a member of Kibbutz Hefzibah, wrote to Richard Steiner, an active Zionist in Czechoslovakia, apprising him of the threat to the territorial continuity of the area should a German colony be interposed. Lederer suggested that Steiner conduct an emergency campaign for funds for this project. The money was raised, the Jewish National Fund bought the land, and the territorial continuity was maintained.[67]

The land in Shatta extended over 14,750 dunam. The Abiad family owned 4,500 dunam; the lawyer Jemil Abiad held one third of the family's share in his own name, the effendi Raja Rais, who owned land in Qumia, was the proprietor of 9,000 dunam; the Manasse family, who also owned land in Qumia, were the owners of 900 dunam; and the balance, 350 dunam, was the property of one Fuad Qasab.[68]

The Political Department of the Jewish Agency was repeatedly called upon to answer accusations that Arabs were being displaced from their lands by Jewish settlers. It scrutinized each sale of land and followed up the fortunes of the tenant farmers whose land had been acquired. On January 28, 1931 the Palestine Land Development Company wrote to Colonel Kisch, the head of the Political Department: "We have no contact with the tenant farmers of the tract acquired. The sellers, Raja Rais and his associates, made all the arrangements with the tenant farmers and therefore we have no particulars concerning them."[69]

The Development Department of the Mandatory Government also regulated the sales of land, in accordance with the provisions of the Tenant Farmer Law. On November 18, 1932 the Political Department of the Jewish Agency advised the Director of Development, Lewis Andrews: "Concerning the Shatta land... the sellers are about to give the tenant farmers other plots of land. There are 24 people on the land, five of whom are annual sharecroppers."[70]

It would seem that Hankin did not trust the sellers to give the tenant farmers alternate land, or to pay adequate indemnities. He therefore paid the indemnities directly, even though according to the agreement of sale the duty to do so devolved on the sellers. Lighter moments were not lacking. In 1937, after the accounts with Raja Rais were closed, Hankin wrote to the Palestine Land Development Company: "When Mr. Rais learned that his share of the cost for indemnifying the tenant farmers amounted to LP. 2,009, he fainted on the spot and while falling hurt his hand."[71]

In addition to the villages of Qumia and Tamra, the villages of Na'ura, Taiyibe and Tira, and the Mugrabi villages of 'Ulam, Ma'ader and Shara separated the Jezreel Valley from the Jewish

206

settlements in Lower Galilee. The fellaheen of Taiyibe, Tira, Tamra and Na'ura had mortgaged their lands to money lenders, mostly the family of Abd el-Hadi. Gradually the mortgagees acquired title to large portions of the land. The situation became critical. The fellaheen were unable to repay their loans and there was an immediate danger that they would lose all their land. In order to get free of the oppressive moneylenders they sought to sell part of their holding, a tract of 50,000 dunam.

They turned to Hankin and offered to sell the land to the Jewish National Fund, if it would undertake to pay their debts. The Jewish National Fund bought these lands during the years 1936–1939.[72] The fellaheen escaped the embrace of the moneylenders and the Zionist movement advanced another step towards its goal.

The following are some of the details of the transaction: Eleven fellaheen in the village of Taiyibe sold 5,967 dunam and kept 3,202 dunam for themselves. Five fellaheen of the same village were so deep in debt, that they sold all their holdings, 1,265 dunam. They received LP. 8,993, paid off their debts and bought land elsewhere.[73]

In Na'ura, the Jewish National Fund bought 7,250 dunam. A report to its Head Office stated: "We paid the sellers all that was due them in accordance with their specific property rights in the land and arranged for the tenant farmers to leave. We also took into consideration that there might be some small additional claims, amounting to about LP. 150."[74]

The Sursuk family owned some lands in the area, but they themselves did not know exactly how far their holdings extended. They owned a tract of 7,000–8,000 dunam in the village of Tira which they sold in 1936 to the Jewish National Fund for LP. 4.75 per dunam, "free of tenant farmers." Joseph Weitz recorded in his diary: "The land is hilly, but beautiful and it connects with the Jezreel Valley."[75] This land purchase emphasises the paramountcy in the minds of the buyers of strategic considerations above economic ones.

The P.I.C.A. owned 2,354 dunam in the village of Tira. It had bought the land many years previously, but had never established a Jewish settlement there, and it was being worked by tenant farmers. In 1946 the Jewish National Fund bought the land and undertook to indemnify the tenant farmers. It paid them LP. 6,097 as a compensation and also bought their houses and adjoining gardens for an additional LP. 9,548.[76] The fellaheen who remained in Tira as neighbors to the Jewish settlers gained a further major benefit when malaria was eradicated from the area. Two years before the land was bought in Tira, Dr. Sliternik, the head of the Jewish Agency's Health Department, visited the village with a view to planning for the eradication of the disease. He found that "... almost all the villagers suffered from malaria... The probability of our settlers being stricken is close to 100%. The danger is redoubled because of the many swamps in the area, over which we have no control or supervision..."[77] Once the tract was bought the swamps were drained, and the Jewish and Arab settlements were freed from the disease.

The fellaheen of the above-mentioned villages had lived on the land for many generations and had struck roots in their villages. Not so with the fellaheen of the Mugrabi villages. Half their lands were owned by emirs, descendants of exiles who had accompanied Abd el-Kader, who for the most part were living in Syria.

In the village of 'Ulam there were 11,035 dunam; in the village of Ma'ader – 6,235 dunam. Half the area was owned by the heirs of 'Ali Pasha, known as "Aljesiri" or "the Algerian" and part of it was sold to "Yavne," a private Jewish company. Unable to put them to use, the company sold its holdings to the Jewish National Fund, with the proviso that it would be responsible for indemnifying the tenant holders. In Ma'ader there were 57 tenant farmers, and in 'Ulam – 53. In the same year the emir Sa'id Aljesiri, a resident of Damascus, sold 1,100 dunam, representing his portion of the family holdings. The property was mortgaged and the Jewish National Fund paid off the mortgage and acquired title.[78]

The tenant farmers in the Mugrabi villages wanted to get their indemnities and to return to their places of origin, but the negotiations were prolonged. In May of 1946 Nahmani notified Weitz that he took possession of "... 21 wooded groves. Their owners have left for Trans-Jordan. I wish the other villagers would follow in their footsteps so that we would be able to buy all the lands in the village."[79]

The Egyptian nobleman Shedid was awarded tracts of land in Kafer-Miser at the time of the Egyptian conquest of Palestine and Syria. His heirs – 85 in number – sold them to the Jewish National Fund in 1939.[80] The tenant farmers who were in possession of 1,661 dunam carried on prolonged negotiations over the amount of indemnity, until finally in January 1945 an agreement was signed on the following terms: LP. 3 per dunam for unirrigated agricultural land;LP. 15 per dunam for land suitable for building; and LP. 30 for irrigated agricultural land. Each house was evaluated separately and compensation was paid. Aaron Danin signed the agreement on behalf of the Jewish National Fund, and there were eight signatories on belhalf of the tenant farmers. The agreement was witnessed by Mas'ud Ya'ish and by David Baum.[81]

In 1944, the Jewish National Fund bought 1,800 dunam in the village of Umm el-Ghanan, near Mount Tabor, from the Metropolitan Hakim, subsequently the Chief Patriarch of the Greek-Catholic community. The sale was rescinded because of the pressure of the Arab People's Fund.[82] The Metropolitan himself had no scruples about the transaction.

The heirs of Wadiye Beshara el-Ghazzi, a resident of Egypt, owned a 572-dunam piece of land in the village of Daburiya (today Kibbutz Dovrat). During the Second World War the heirs sold the land to the Jewish National Fund.[83] The Fahum family of Nazareth sold the Fund a 3,000-dunam tract of land "in fee simple and free of tenant farmers."[84] The head of the family, Yussuf Fahum, who was Mayor of Nazareth for a time, sold his land despite terrorist threats. According to the Jewish National Fund functionaries who dealt with him, he was a proud man and he despised the hypocritical Arab public figures who sold land to Jews in secret and then gave vent to extreme nationalist utterances. He effected the sale openly and publicly without resorting to intermediaries or fictive owners.[85]

Between Mishmar-Haemek and Yokne'am to the northeast and Giv'at-Ada and Karkur to the southwest there was not a single Jewish settlement. Many tracts of land had been bought before the 1936 riots by the Palestine Land Development Company, by the P.I.C.A. and by private investors, but no settlements were established on them. When the riots of 1936 began, the Jewish owners of the land feared that they would lose their property and they offered to sell their holdings to the Jewish National Fund, which agreed to buy them. Toward the latter part of 1936 the Jewish National Fund bought 4,540 dunam in the village of Ju'ara and 5,460 dunam in Reihaniya.in July 1937 Kibbutz Ein-Hashofet settled on half of the Ju'ara land that was free of tenant farmers. Striking root in the midst of a concentration of Arab population expressed the determination of the Jewish settlers not to yield to Arab terror. In addition it furthered the strategy of establishing settlements with an eye to the boundaries of the future Jewish portion of a partitioned Palestine.

The building and loan company "Zur" of Haifa was commissioned to negotiate with the tenant farmers concerning the other half of the Ju'ara tract. On June 26, 1939 the company submitted a report and a bill for its services. The report stated that the land in Ju'ara was owned by the heirs of one Abdul Latif Saleh, a Turkish family that made its home in Haifa. They also owned land in Jiddin, 'Ein Ghasal, Tira (near Haifa) and other localities. There were eighteen tenant farmers in Ju'ara who worked an area of about 2,500 dunam. Most of them were from the village of Kaferein, where they also cultivated land. The report states: "Some of the tenant farmers own houses and land in Kaferein. One of them is the village chief of Ju'ara, who also owns a house in Haifa. He lives off the rent from it and works as a watchman."[86]

Ju'ara made its historical mark as a training site for the Haganah underground.

In 1936 the P.I.C.A. bought 10,073 dunam in Daliyat el-Ruha and Umm ed-Dafuf (today Kibbutz Daliya).[87] Because of the disturbances it was unable to establish settlements on the land, and, as in many similar situations, in 1937 it sold the tract to the Jewish National Fund. In order to expand its holdings in the Hills of Menashe area and ultimately to link up with the Giv'at-Ada-Karkur region, the Jewish National Fund made a special effort to acquire additional lands to the south, in the villages of Khubeize and Buteimat. There was a well-grounded fear that in the existing political climate the tenant farmers would refuse to accept indemnities. Dr. Aaron Ben-Shemesh, the attorney for the Jewish National Fund, suggested that the police be persuaded to establish a police station in the area, so that they would be in a position to facilitate the take-over of the purchased tracts. Weitz and Ben-Shemesh toured the region looking for a likely site for a police station. As they approached one of the villages all the men came out of the community barn and confronted them. As it turned out Weitz was right when he suspected that they had been undergoing illegal military training. The villagers realized why two Jews were wandering about in a purely Arab area and said to their visitors emphatically: "... no police station or Jewish settlement will be established here as long as there is one live Arab among us. A police station will be built over our dead bodies. It would just be a forerunner of a Jewish settlement."[88]

So long as the terror reigned the young Arab nationalists were successful in preventing any amicable arrangements with the tenant farmers. On August 29, 1938 the "Zur" Company advised the Jewish National Fund that it had reached an agreement with the tenant farmers of the villages Sab'ein and Kaferein. However when the time neared for the tenant farmers to leave, the person who represented them in the negotiations was murdered. It was impossible to make contact with the tenant farmers because "most of them are under the supervision of the police and the rest are afraid of having any connection with us."[89]

In October 1939, when the violence waned, the "Zur" Company reported to the Jewish National Fund: "On October 4 our representative in Ein-Hashofet informed Kibbutz Bamifne (later Kibbutz Daliya) that the land was good as theirs, since an agreement was reached with the tenant farmers. Most of them have already signed the necessary papers and the rest will sign in the near future."[90]

At the height of the terror the Jewish National Fund bought 7,600 dunam in the villages of Khubeize and Buteimat (today Kibbutz Gal'ed) on March 24, 1938. There were 124 deeds of sale for the land in Khubeize and a mere 6 for the land in Buteimat. No claims on behalf of tenant farmers and no claims for rights in the property were filed. However four Arabs from neighboring villages filed claims under the provisions of the law which gave first option to purchase to adjoining property owners. The claims were heard by the Land Court on April 10, 1941 and were all denied.[91]

The Judean Hills and Judean Plain

The acquisition of strategic footholds in the Judean Hills was not a first priority during the period 1936–1947. Not even the purchase of land along the avenues of communication between Jerusalem and the Judean Plain was considered a prime necessity.

Until 1936 there were only a few Jewish settlements near Jerusalem: Kiryat-Anavim, Neve-Ya'akov and Atarot. Two small, isolated *moshavot*, Hartuv and Kefar-Uriya, nestled at the foot of the hills in the Judean Plain. During the 1929 riots both settlements were attacked. Kefar-Uriya was destroyed and its residents abandoned it, while Hartuv was rebuilt and its residents returned, but it remained a lone outpost. Private investors did buy some plots of land in the vicinity of Jerusalem and west of the city in the Judean Hills. In the area that was later known as the Etzion District a Rehovot Jewish citrus grower bought 5,200 dunam of land and on one part of the plot he planted an orchard. A Zionist club in England, "The Ancient Maccabees," together with some private investors, bought a 5,000-dunam tract in Gezer, a village near Ramle.[92] During the 1936 disturbances Arabs uprooted the orchard of the Rehovot citrus grower and seized the land. The land in Gezer was worked by tenant farmers and a Jewish settlement was not established there.

In 1942 the Jewish National Fund bought a piece of land from the Arabs of the village of Nahalin. Joseph Weitz recorded in his diary: "Yesterday the village chief of Nahalin, together with the

212

elders, signed the map that indicates the changed ownership of the land, in the presence of the District Commissioner. Thus one more step was taken in the process of acquiring title. Now we have to wait until the Land Department approves the amended map – only then will the land be ours. We have finished plowing 1,700 dunam of the Etzion land. The problem of the tenant farmers has been settled."[93] Two years later Kibbutz Kefar-Etzion settled on the site.

The tenant farmers were indemnified, but there were some fellaheen from the village of Nahalin who refused to come to terms with the Jewish National Fund. Fruitless negotiations dragged on for five years. In February 1947, when the settlers of the future Kibbutz Revadim were about to go on the land, the Arabs made preparations to resist by violence. The village chieftains and the Jewish National Fund agreed on an indemnity of LP. 6,000 that would be used to erect a school in Nahalin.[94] After the agreement was concluded the settlers of the Etzion region plowed up a tract of 2,800 dunam. A relieved Weitz confided to his diary: "So has ended one of the most complicated transactions in the history of soil redemption."[95]

After the land purchases were made, four Jewish settlements were established. During the War of Independence they were conquered by the Jordanian Arab Legion and their defenders taken prisoner. (See Chapter 13)

Few of the proposals to buy land in the Judean Hills and Plain bore fruit. Early in 1940 negotiations were conducted with Ragheb Nashashibi, the Mayor of Jerusalem, for the purchase of lands in the village of Yalo, near the Valley of Ayalon. He offered to sell his land at that time in anticipation of the prohibition of land sales following the White Paper of 1939. However the price was exorbitant, as Weitz remarked in his diary: "He wants a political bribe, not the price of the land."[96]

The Greek-Orthodox Patriarchate Monastery owned a 20,000-dunam parcel of land in Burj, a village northeast of Beit-Guvrin, near the Jaffa-Jerusalem railroad. In 1946 2,500 dunam were acquired from the Monastery. Half the tract was situated in the village of Sura. On this site Kibbutz Tzor'a was later established.[97]

After the Land Transfers Regulations based on the 1939 White

Paper had been promulgated the Jewish National Fund decided to purchase the lands of Gezer. As mentioned above, the 3,400 dunam tract was acquired some years previously by the English Zionist club "The Ancient Maccabees" on behalf of some private investors. The Jewish National Fund planned to pay tenant farmers an indemnity of LP. 5,000.[98]

The Sharon Valley

From 1937 on there were no pressing reasons of political strategy to acquire land in the Sharon Valley. Since the White Paper of 1939 there were no restrictions on the purchase of land there. Despite the urgent need to buy elsewhere for political and defense reasons, it was nevertheless the policy of the Jewish National Fund to buy whatever lands were being offered for sale in the Sharon Valley.

The largest tract purchased was 10,000 dunam in Wadi Kabani, a continutation of Wadi Hawarith. This created a territorial continuity between Hadera and Natanya over a 40,000-dunam stretch.

This land was originally acquired in the middle of the nineteenth century by Mustafa Aga Kabani, a Moslem minor official in Beirut. He registered it in 1877 in the Land Register, as required by Ottoman law, in the name of his son Sa'ad ed-Din Kabani, and in the names of Sa'ad's sons. Some time later Sa'ad's sister filed an appeal claiming that her father had intended to leave her a one-seventh interest in the land. The appeal was sustained and one-seventh of the land was registered in her name. One of Sa'ad's sons sold his share – one-seventh of the total property – to one Abu Hantash, a Tulkarem Arab. Matters became involved when the transfer to Abu Hantash was recorded in the Land Register by mistake as a one-sixth interest, and not a one-seventh interest.[99]

In September 1928 Hankin managed to identify the heirs of the Kabani estate and executed an agreement of sale with them. The Political Department of the Jewish Agency inquired of Hankin as to the provisions for the tenant farmers, and he replied: "The whole matter of the tenant farmers is the responsibility of the sellers."[100]

In the meantime the massive immigration of 1932 began, land

214

prices rose, and the sellers changed their mind about the deal. New negotiations began and they were completed shortly before the outbreak of World War II in 1939, when agreements of sale were executed in Beirut with the heirs for five-sevenths of the tract. The agreement provided for the sale of 7,000 dunam at a price of LP. 13.5 per dunam, totaling LP. 94,500. It stipulated an initial payment of LP. 45,150 which was to be made at the time of the transfer of title and possession of at least 2,000 dunam, free of tenant farmers and free of any other claims. Upon transfer of possession of additional parts of the tract, free of tenant farmers and all other claims, further proportionate payments of the total sum would be made.[101] The agreement was signed in the presence of the British Consul in Beirut on February 5, 1940.[102]

The settlers did not regard the provision to transfer possession of the land "free of tenant farmers" as binding, nor did Hankin, who was aware that in the final analysis the purchasers would have to pay an indemnity. Hankin wrote in his diary even before the agreement of sale was formally executed: "We hope that we will be able to conclude matters with the tenant farmers who occupy about 3,100 dunam of Wadi Kabani. I'll need about LP. 7,000 for the deal. We have prepared all the necessary documents and have arranged to receive the tenant farmers' declarations of waiver of rights in the presence of a Government official of the Netanya District."[103]

The Jewish National Fund continued to maintain that the agreement of sale obligated the sellers to indemnify the tenant farmers, but in practice, whenever the tenant farmers were ready to vacate land, the Jewish National Fund paid out the necessary sums for their indemnification.[104]

When Abu Hantash learned of the negotiations for the sale of the land in Wadi Kabani, he recruited some of Mustafa Kabani's offspring and together with them filed claim to the property in the Land Court.

The hearing was held on May 1, 1939 before an official of the Government Land Department, who disallowed the claim in its entirety, finding the arguments of the claimants unfounded.[105]

After the verdict was rendered Abu Hantash sold his portion of the land to the Jewish National Fund on May 20, 1940. Soon after, the heirs of Amina, the daughter of Mustafa Kabani and the sister of Sa'ad ed-Din Kabani, sold their portion of the land, 1,400 dunam, and so the land in Wadi Kabani was finally acquired.[106]

There were 150 fellaheen and Bedouins who occupied the land in Wadi Kabani in 1932 when the first agreement of sale was signed.[107] One hundred received indemnities and moved elsewhere, while fifty remained on 600 dunam of the land until 1947. Weitz noted in his diary: "Matters reached a point where the Jewish National Fund offered them LP. 8–10 per dunam, but they remained adamant. In the meantime the United Nations decided to establish a Jewish state in a part of Palestine, and the Arab attack on the *Yishuv* began. The position of the Arab tenant farmers in the midst of a concentrated Jewish population became precarious, for them as well as for their neighbors. The representatives of the Jewish National Fund again offered them indemnities. At first they put on a brave front, claiming that they would get larger indemnities in the future Jewish state, but when the Arab attacks increased in severity they lost courage and fled to the hills."[108]

In 1939 the Jewish National Fund bought 2,800 dunam of land northwest of Wadi Hawarith from the Samara family, one of whose heads, Abdallah Samara, had been a vociferous advocate of the rights of the tenant farmers in Wadi Hawarith and Wadi Kabani. Most of the tract consisted of sandy soil unsuited for agriculture. While the riots were going on the family hesitated to sell the land because of the bad name it would give them as collaborators with the Jews and because of the fear of Arab terrorist reprisals. After the Second World War broke out and the tension between Jews and Arabs waned the Samara clan sold the land for LP. 30,000.[109] The *moshav* Mikhmoret was established on it.

As mentioned before, private investors stopped acquiring land in the war years so that the Jewish National Fund was no longer hampered by the activities of unscrupulous speculators.

Some of the fellaheen sold portions of their land to the Fund, so that they might devote themselves to growing vegetables intensively and planting gardens on the land they retained. The British Army stationed in Palestine was a lucrative market, and consumption

216

increased and prices soared.

The fellaheen in the villages of 'Atil and Zeita, situated just east of Netanya, sold 4,000 dunam to the Jewish National Fund. The villagers of Qalansawa, who had been notorious for their savage attacks on the settlements and their lines of communication, did not hesitate to sell 4,000 dunam to the Jewish National Fund.[110] The Mayor of Tulkarem, Salim Abd el-Rahman Hajj Ibrahim, sold the Jews 1,200 dunam of land south of Netanya.[111] The Shanti family, owners of many parcels of land in the Qalqiliya area and large-scale entrepreneurs in Jaffa, also sold land to the Jewish National Fund. Kamel el-Shanti sold 190 dunam "free of all encumbrances and occupier or owner claims to the whole domain or to part of it..."[112] Mehmed el-Shanti sold 623 dunam of "land free as to encumbrance, ownership, tenancy, right of hire, or any other right..."[113] Rashid Hanun of the Hanun family of Tulkarem, who had sold land to private investors in Netanya, sold land to the Jewish National Fund in the village of Zur in 1939. Rashid lived in Beirut, apparently for fear of the Arab terror.[114]

In this period the Jewish National Fund lost a court case on a first option claim filed by the fellaheen of Umm Khaled. They opposed the sale by Saleh Hamdan to the Jewish National Fund of 1,400 dunam of land adjacent to theirs. After prolonged litigation the King's Council in London rendered a verdict in favor of the fellaheen.[115]

In the same decade the P.I.C.A. increased its holdings by about 30,000 dunam. Most of this land had been awarded to the P.I.C.A. many years previously as concessions, but many claims were filed against the awards, and until they were adjudicated and final judgment rendered much time elapsed. It was only at the end of the decade that the P.I.C.A. established clear title to these areas. (Among the tracts of land involved were the sand dunes of Caesarea).

The kibbutzim and the *moshavim* that had founded tens of "Tower and Stockade" settlements during this period, often at great risk and with much hardship, found themselves stymied in their efforts to settle on P.I.C.A. lands. It was only after considerable pressure that the P.I.C.A. officialdom was persuaded to participate in the national effort, and an allocation of 20,000 dunam of land was made for the "Tower and Stockade" type of settlement.

The South and the Negev

The southernmost settlement of the Jewish State as proposed by the Royal Commission in 1937 was Beer-Tuvya, which had been founded as a *moshava* by Baron Rothschild in 1887, destroyed in the riots of 1929, and reestablished in 1930 as a *moshav*. Ruhama, south of Beer-Tuvya, was founded in 1911 and was destroyed after the First World War. It was rebuilt in the twenties, but Arab marauders destroyed it again in 1929. In 1932 attempts were made to restore the settlement, but it was once more completely destroyed in the 1936 riots and remained in a desolate state until 1944. So it is accurate to consider Beer-Tuvya the southernmost point of Jewish settlement around 1936.

Jewish investors did sporadically acquire land in the South and the Negev prior to 1936. Attempts were even made to plant citrus groves in the South and plans were drawn up to search for sources of water and to establish settlements based on citriculture, as in the Sharon Plain. The disturbances of 1936 put an end to these plans. Part of the Jewish land was cultivated by tenant farmers and the rest lay fallow. No settlements were established and the Jewish ownership of the land was in jeopardy.

The proposal of the Royal Commission was a clear warning to the Zionist movement that the boundaries of the future Jewish State would not extend beyond existing Jewish settlement. Furthermore manpower and funds were insufficient to establish more "Tower and Stockade" settlements in the South and in the Negev at the same pace as the settlement efforts in the North. It was only towards the end of World War II, when Zionist policy crystallized into a demand for the termination of the Mandate and the establishment of a Jewish state, that the main settlement effort was concentrated in the South and the Negev.

At the beginning of the period under discussion Jews owned 28,100 dunam in the South and 41,400 dunam in the Negev.[116] Zionist groups in the United States and some new immigrants with

218

capital bought some parcels of land from a few villages. Moshe Smilanski, representing some private investors, bought 36,424 dunam in the Negev.[117] Most of the land purchases were based on agreements between the individual sellers and buyers and were not registered in the Land Register as required by law. The reason for this was that the sheikhs and village chiefs were in possession of the lands they sold, but they did not have clear title.

When the 1936 riots broke out the private investors found themselves unable to take possession of their property and offered to sell it to the Jewish National Fund. The purchase was still legally feasible because, while the South and the Northern Negev were areas where land transfer would be forbidden to Jews, the Land Transfers Regulations were to come into force only in February 1940. The Jewish National Fund would have to indemnify the few tenant farmers on the land and would also have to pay additional sums to earlier Arab owners for their releases. In short the price was not going to be low. Furthermore most of the land in question was barren and unfit for cultivation without major expenditures for land amelioration.

Part of the land of the present-day Kibbutz Yavne was purchased in 1931 from Abdel el-Rahman el-Taji el-Farouqi, a member of the Moslem Supreme Council, and from Mustafa el-Surani.[118] In 1937, when plans were being made to establish a settlement, fourteen tenant farmers filed claims for their rights and the Palestine Land Development Company paid them an indemnity of LP. 290.[119]

Some years later, in 1947, when the Arab Higher Committee lodged repeated protests against continued purchase of land by Jews, it pointed out that some of the Yavne land that had been registered as uncultivated Government land was actually covered with cultivated vines and fig trees. It went on to claim that the destruction of villages like Sheikh-Muwanis, Jeljuliya, Sumeil, Jamassin and Jarishe undermined the status of the Arabs and exposed them to the perils of discrimination and extermination. Their only alternative would be to leave their homes as did the Arabs of the Jezreel Valley. The protest was signed by Hussein Fahri el-Khalidi.[120]

Kibbutz Kefar-Menahem, the first of the "Tower and Stockade" settlements in the South, was built on part of the land of the village of Idhniba. It had been bought from Jamal el-Husseini, a member of the Gaza branch of the el-Husseini family. On October 14, 1937 he wrote to the Palestine Land Development Company requesting a mortgage release on the part of the property that had not been sold, taking into account the fact that the sellers had fulfilled their part of the contract in full.[121]

Hankin bought another 120 dunam from the el-Husseini family and wrote to Weitz: "I need another LP. 70 for the transaction, so that I can pay off the tenant farmers who are still on the land."[122]

The foregoing purchases were executed before the regulations of the White Paper of 1939 went into effect in February 1940. In 1941 the Jewish National Fund bought a 500 dunam tract in the village of Zaffa from Ismail Khalil el-Ghazzi, a member of a prominent and wealthy Hebron family. The land was given to Kefar-Menahem to supplement its previous land allocation. Since the transaction was executed in a zone where it was forbidden to transfer land to Jews, a fictitious transfer was recorded in the name of Yusef el-Jarusha, who lived in a tent camp near Gedera. He went into a fictitious bankruptcy, the land was put up for sale at public auction and the Jewish National Fund was able to acquire title legally.[123]

Moshe Smilanski had purchased certain lands in 1934, and in 1939 he offered to sell them to the Jewish National Fund. Among these lands were: a 7,000-dunam tract east of Gaza; 5,000 dunam in the village of Hujj (today Kibbutz Dorot); 1.000 dunam in Breir (today Kibbutz Bror-Hayil); and 1,000 dunam that he had bought from Bedouins. Ismail el-Ghazzi and George Sur sold the lands of Hujj and Breir.[124] When the sale of the lands was proposed Smilanski wrote: "The transfer can be made only after all the claims of the tenant farmers have been met. (There are no tenant farmers on these lands)"[125]

The hypocrisy of some of the leaders of the Arab national movement became very apparent in the matter of purchase of lands near the villages of Sumsum, Hirbiya, Barbara, and Deir-Suneid, on which the kibbutzim Yad-Mordekhai and Gevar'am were established in 1947. On the one hand they secretly solds land to Jews, while on the other they were vociferous in their public denunciation of such sales and even organized the tenant farmers to resist the sales violently. The Gaza branch of the el-'Alami family owned 6,000 dunam of land in Barbara abd Deir-Suneid. In 1940 the head of the family offered to sell the land for LP. 6 to 7 per dunam, and he undertook to secure the High Commissioner's permission for the transfer.[126] Hafez el-'Alami sold to the Jewish National Fund 1,700 dunam in the village of Hirbiya.[127]

In view of the increase of land sales in the South, 'Auni Abd el-Hadi tried to incite the tenant farmers of the village of Sumsum, near Hirbiya, to resist the land transfers,[128] but he failed because "the fellaheen know of the existence of the Committee and fear the consequences of its activity."[129]

The fellaheen who sold land in Beit-'Affa were exposed to the vengeance of the terrorist gangs. Kibbutz Negba settled on the land on July 12, 1939. "On that day a large crowd of people gathered and among them were some Arabs who had come to sell watermelon and eggs. Zukerman was busy making final payments of indemnity to the fellaheen of the village..."[130] A few days later a gang attacked the village. There was an exchange of fire and both sides suffered casualties. Despite the defense that the fellaheen put up the gang succeeded in kidnapping the two village chiefs.

The wealthy el-Ghazzi family also sold some land in the village of Iraq el-Manshiya,[131] on which Kibbutz Gat was founded in 1942. The seller, one Abdul Rahman el-Ghazzi, had bought up parcels of land from other Arabs and put together one large tract which he sold to the Jewish National Fund. The sale contravened the Land Transfers Regulations, but they were circumvented with the assistance of el-Ghazzi. He also sold land to the Jewish National Fund in the village of Ra'ana, on which Kibbutz Gal'on was founded in 1946.[132]

A parcel of 623 dunam was purchased from Sidqi el-Dajani,[133] whose family had been selling land to Jews ever since Rishon le-Zion was founded in 1882.

A 306 dunam citrus grove was bought from Ya'akov Ghuzyein, the founder of the Arab Youth League, a member of the Arab Higher Committee, and the heirs of Tawfik Ghuzyein.[134] The grove was part of the area on which Kibbutz Nir'am was founded in 1942.

221

Fahmi el-Husseini, the Mayor of Gaza, asembled and sold large tracts of land to the Jewish National Fund. In July of 1940 Nissan Meirowitz wrote to the Jewish National Fund Head Office: "I managed to assemble a parcel of 3,000 dunam near Gaza. The deed was made out in the name of Fahmi el-Husseini, the Mayor of Gaza. He received LP. 5,500 in cash and a first mortgage on the land. I assumed the obligation of a second mortgage amounting to LP. 4,000."[135] In August of 1940 2,250 dunam were registered in the name of the Jewish National Fund.[136]

Fahmi el-Husseini made a deal with a Jewish convert, the leader of an English Mission, that wished to settle Jewish converts in Palestine. A down-payment was made and the land mortgaged to the Jewish convert. The Jewish National Fund gave him back his money and Fahmi sold the land, a parcel of 5,200 dunam, to the Fund.[137] Kibbutz Beeri was founded on the land the night after Yom Kippur of 1946, a date marked by the founding of eleven settlements all in one night.

Sa'adi el-Shawa sold 1,380 dunam to the Jewish National Fund. Like Fahmi el-Husseini, he had assembled the tract from the holdings of three individual Arabs. He placed fictitious mortgages on the property in the name of one Anton Abdallah Hasbun, and so the restrictions of the White Paper were circumvented. The land was registered in the name of the Jewish National Fund in 1946.[138]

On all the lands that Arab notables sold there were either no tenant farmers to begin with or else the notables saw to it that there were none when transfer of title was made. There was one exception: In the case of the transfer of land in the vicinity of Gaza, which Fahmi el-Husseini had sold, the documents of transfer indicate that tenant farmers were indemnified.[139]

Until 1936 Jewish companies and private investors had bought 41,000 dunam of land in the Negev without ever having founded a settlement. By 1947 the Jewish National Fund had bought 13,500 dunam of those lands, and in addition it had acquired 65,000 dunam from Arabs. When the State was established, 95,000 dunam in the Negev belonged to Jews; two-thirds of that area was owned by national institutions.

The redemption of the land in the Negev did not involve

indemnification of tenant farmers in most cases because the land was desolate and generally unfit for cultivation. The Arabs sold only the poorest land; whatever good soil there was they worked, and it was not for sale.

A map submitted to the Royal Commission, showing the sections of Palestine where more than 10% of the total area was being cultivated, did not include the Negev. A line from Rafah to Beer-Sheba marks off the region to the south, where the annual rainfall is less than 200mm. With rainfall below 200mm. extensive agriculture is not feasible, and in the Mandatory period the millions of dunams of land south of this line were considered uncultivable. All the maps and publications listed them as desert, and of no agricultural value. Even in the areas that Bedouins plowed and sowed the drought seasons outnumbered the rainy ones. In very hot years thousands of Bedouins would migrate northward to escape the famine and drought that threatened them and their flocks.

In consequence there were few tenant farmers on the land. In 1935 preliminary agreement had been reached for the sale of certain lands in Asluj. It was not until 1941 that the final documents of transfer were executed by the owners, Sheikh Salame Ibn Hajj Muslim Ibn Sa'id and Sulayman Ismail el-Sarbawi. In the revised agreement it was stated: "In consideration of the fact that the price is LP. 2.5 per dunam instead of LP. 1.4... the land is hereby transferred... free of tenant farmers and free of claims based on attendant rights. To this end we will obtain and turn over the necessary documents to the Company."[140] Kibbutz Revivim was founded on this land in 1943, the same year in which the three observation points were established in the Negev.

Sheikh Salim, one of the principals of the Arab People's Fund, sold 4,000 dunam in the village of Hasali. Weitz noted in his diary: "We returned to Beit-Eshel and immediately set out for Hasali to see the three parcels that we bought a month ago – 4,000 dunam. What a great disappointment: It is all sand, nothing but drifting sand."[141]

The 1,600 dunam plot in Qeltta (today Kibbutz Hatzerim) was all saline soil. Only after considerable expenditure of money and labor

223

was the land made fit for cultivation. (See Chapter Ten). Nevertheless here and there tenant farmers were to be found. There were even court cases and on occasion the purchaser, the Jewish National Fund, was in the wrong and lost the case. Weitz noted in his diary in 1943: "We lost a tenancy case in Beer-Sheba yesterday. The tenant farmer was awarded 320 dunam."[142]

At the time of the establishment of the State Jewish land holdings in the South and in the Negev came to 170,000 dunam, of which 130,000 dunam were owned by national institutions.[143] In the last decade of the Mandate the Zionist movement established 31 settlements in the South and in the Negev in an effort to reinforce the claim that these regions be included in the Jewish state. The founding of eleven settlements on the evening after Yom Kippur in 1946 was an event of prime political significance. It gave expression to the classical Zionist concept: reclamation of wasteland and prosperity for all inhabitants. When the settlers went on the land, water pipes that began at Nir'am were already in place to bring life to the parched earth. The taps were open to the Bedouins as well as the Jews.

The Zionist settlement agencied had plans to irrigate hundreds of thousands of dunams of land in the Negev; to settle Jews on the reclaimed land; to create permanent villages for the Bedouins. All this was cut short by the Arab attack on the Jewish State.

CHAPTER NINE

THE SELLERS OF LAND

In 1947 Jewish holdings in Palestine amounted to 1,850,000 dunam, owned by national institutions, public companies, or private individuals. The Jewish owners acquired 180,000 dunam from the Mandatory Government in the form of concessions, such as the Hula Concession, the Dead Sea Concession, and the

Caesarea Sand Dune Concession; 120,000 dunam were bought from various churches, and 1,550,000 dunam from Arabs. More than a million dunam, two-thirds of the total of Arab sales, were bought from large-scale landowners, and about 500,000 dunam from fellaheen of moderate or of limited means.[1] Some of the large-scale landowners resided in foreign countries. The rest, who lived in Palestine, were rich in capital and in land.

Material relating to the acquisition of 682,000 dunam during the years 1936–1938 was collated by the Statistical Department of the Jewish Agency. It showed that only 9.4% of the land had been bought from fellaheen.[2] However the proportion of land purchase from the fellaheen during the years 1936 to 1947 grew steadily. A fair judgment for the entire seventy-year period of Jewish settlement (up to 1947) would be that a third of all lands obtained from Arabs was acquired from the fellaheen.[3]

A likely explanation of the shift from large landowners to fellaheen as the major sellers of land after 1936 is that landowners resident in foreign countries ran out of land to sell. But another aspect should not be overlooked. The relatively high prices offered by the Jews were attractive to the fellaheen. From the year 1932, when large numbers of German Jews immigrated to the country, the areas of citrus groves increased enormously and land prices, especially along the coast, soared. Poor, sandy soil which the Arab fellah had held in low esteem became an excellent source of income, after irrigation was introduced and citrus groves planted.

Another reason for the readiness of the fellaheen, the very poor fellaheen, to sell their land was the traditional mode of land use in the Arab village. Land possession and use under the requirements of *musha'a* led to the splitting up of estates into uneconomical small plots and to their cultivation at irregular intervals. The result was that the poor fellah saw no point in being tied to his village and to his land, living constantly in poverty and want.

The demand of the Jews for land gave the impoverished fellah an opportunity to sell his not-so-valuable plot of land, free himself from his economic burdens, and learn a well-paying trade. When a Jewish buyer appeared in the village, the fellah who was the potential seller urged his fellow villagers to consent to register the

225

land as *mafruz* instead of *musha'a* so that he would be able to sell his land free and clear. The eager Jewish land buyer expended considerable sums of money to pursuade the other fellaheen of the village to give their consent to the change in registry. Thus the sale by the individual fellah brought a bit of prosperity to all concerned.

The nationalist Arab leaders fought untiringly against the sale of land to Jews. They opposed the conversion of *musha'a* land to *mafruz* because it would facilitate land transfer to Jews. The battle was waged despite the fact that it was common knowledge that the principal sellers of land were rich Arab families who were often active in the Arab nationalist movement.

In 1946 the Arab nationalist leadership submitted a memorandum to the United Nations Special Committee on Palestine (UNSCOP), in which it declared that of the two million dunam that the Jews had bought, 15% had belonged to fellaheen. (In fact the total area of land bought by Jews was smaller than stated in the memorandum, but the percentage of fellaheen affected was greater. The Arab leadership was lax in verifying the figures that it published).

The memorandum went on to state that the sellers of land were not Palestinians: Sursuk was a Beiruti, Tayan and Kabani also were Lebanese. "They were bereft of nationalistic sentiments and the Arabs of Palestine should not be blamed for these sales. But the rest of the land was bought from Palestinian Arabs and they should not be justified. Perhaps some sold land because of economic difficulties, but others – because they were profiteers".[4]

As for the large landholders living in Palestine, most of them were involved in the Arab nationalist movement. There were families who for three generations had been selling land to Jews, even though the members of the second and third generation were aware of the aims of Zionism and had openly expressed their opposition to them. There were other families where a separation of functions existed: Some of the members of the family were active in political and communal affairs, while others engaged in business which included the management of real property owned jointly by the entire family. In such cases certain nationalist politicians could be as extreme as they pleased in demanding a ban on the sale of

226

land to Jews, while property in which they had interests was being sold to Jews at a profit. Some of these political figures were so skillful in hiding their transactions with Jews, through numerous transfers of title to fictitious intermediaries, that their names are not to be found in any document of record. And yet there are enough well-documented lists of nationalist public figures who sold land to Jews to substantiate the thesis that they wanted to have their cake and eat it too. They wanted the economic benefits that Zionism was bringing to the coutnry, but they also wanted an Arab national state that would have neither Jews nor Zionism.

Below is a list of nationalist public figures some of whom played an active role in the bloody attacks on Jews and Zionists. It does not contain the names of all the land barons living in Palestine. Many of them were apathetic to Arab nationalist aspirations and devoted themselves to their personal affairs. Others secretly condemned the hypocrisy of those communal leaders who demanded standards of others which they were not willing to apply to themselves. Absent from the list are also the names of those resident in foreign countries who sold land to Jews – they have been mentioned in previous chapters.

Abu Hantash Abdul Latif of Qaqun, planned and participated in the attack on Hadera in May, 1921,[5] and brought the Jewish National Fund to trial in an attempt to foil the purchase of land in Wadi Kabani. (All his claims were denied.) He sold 1,400 dunam to the Jewish National Fund.[6]

Nimer Abu Deba of Jaffa belonged to a family that was active in the Arab national movement. Adiv Abu Deba was a member of a mission to Arab countries in 1922 to raise money and to propagandize for the Arab cause.[7] Nimer sold land of Miska in the Sharon Plain which he owned jointly with 'Omar el-Bitar, Hassan el-Jaiyusi, and with the sons of Mussa Khazm el-Husseini.[8]

Sheikh Shakr Abu Kishek of the Abu Kishek tribe led the attack on Petah-Tikva in the 1921 riots. He was arrested and sentenced to fifteen years imprisonment. In 1923 the Jews of Petah-Tikva made a peace pact with their neighbors and as a result Sheikh Shakr was pardoned.[9] The Sheikh sold the land on which later Magdiel, Ramatayim, Kefar-Malal (Ein-Hai), Benei-Berak, and other

227

settlements were founded.[10]

Hajj Hamed Abu Leben, Mahmud Salim Abu Leben, and *Ahmed Abu Leben* of the Abu Leben family of Jaffa were among the organizers of the 1936–1939 riots.[11] The family sold lands on which the Pardes-Katz section of Benei-Berak was later founded.[12]

Dr. Mustafa Bushnaq, a member of the Arab Executive,[13] and his partners sold land on which Kefar-Yona was later settled.[14]

'Omar el-Bitar was at various times Mayor of Jaffa, head of the Jaffa Moslem-Christian League, a member of the Arab Executive, and one of the fomenters of the 1921 riots in Jaffa.[15] He sold the land on which a section of Benei-Berak was settled and part of the Miska land that he owned in partnership with Abu Deba. (See above).

Hassan el-Jaiyusi, of Tulkarem, belonged to a family that was very active in the Arab nationalist movement in that town.[16] He was a joint owner of the land that Abu Deba and 'Omar el-Bitar sold.

Ya'akov Ghuzyein of Ramle was the Chairman of the Arab Youth Conference. He participated in the 1929 disturbances and was subsequently arrested. In 1936 he was a member of the Arab Higher Committee and was exiled to the Seychelles Islands in 1937. He returned to Palestine in 1942.[17] The Jewish National Fund bought 300 dunam of a citrus grove that he owned in Beit Hanun.[18]

The Dajani family of Jaffa:

Sheikh Mohammed Tawfik el-Dajani, the Mufti of Jaffa, and Alfred Rock sold the land in Jabaliya (today the city of Bat-Yam) to the Palestine Land Development Company.[19]

The brothers *Salim and Abdallah el-Dajani* sold 750 dunam of land adjacent to Jabaliya to the Palestine Land Development Company.[20] Abdallah el-Dajani was a member of the Supreme Moslem Council.[21] *Sidqi el-Dajani* sold land in Sumeil to the Jewish National Fund in 1942.[22] Prior to World War I, the Dajani family sold land on which Rishon-le-Zion was founded. (See Chapter Four).

Abdul Rahman el-Hajj Ibrahim was a judge of the Religious Court and Mayor of Tulkarem until 1938. In 1928 he and his son Salameh began trading in real estate. Another son, Salim, was a member of the Arab Executive, one of the outstanding leaders of the Arab national movement, and one of the chief organizers of the riots of 1921 and 1936.[23] Salim let his brother Salameh handle all his real estate affairs. Salameh conducted an export business in oranges and cooperated with the Pardess Syndicate (a Jewish firm) in preparing shipments. In the 1936 riots he contributed money to the terrorist leader 'Aref Abdul Razak, one of Kaukji's lieutenants. Among his other activities Salameh assembled single plots of land into unified tracts and sold them to Jews. Shortly after he sold the land for the settlement of Ma'ale-Hahamisha an attempt was made on his life on November 8, 1946.[24]

Subhi el-Hadra of Safed was a member of the Arab Executive and was active in the riots of 1936. He propagandized against selling land on Mt. Canaan to Jews, but himself sold land to Jews in Safed.[25]

The Hanun family of Tulkarem were avid supporters of the Moslem Youth League and of the Nashashibi political party.[26] They sold 10,000 dunam of land to the "Sons of Benjamin," who founded on it the *moshava* Even-Yehuda.[27]

The Jerusalem el-Husseini Family:

Ismail Bey el-Husseini was nominated by the Mandatory Government in 1923 to be a member of the Legislative Council but he declined.[28] He sold his land holdings in Nazle, near Petah-Tikva (today Kibbutz Giv'at-Hashlosha), to the Jewish National Fund.[29]

Tawfik el-Husseini, the brother of Jamal el-Husseini, was one of the founders of the Arab nationalist youth organization "el-Nadi el-Arabi," and also the Director of the Moslem orphanage in Jerusalem.[30] He sold his share in land that he owned jointly with Mussa el-'Alami and Dr. Tawfik Canaan (see below). Tawfik el-Husseini and his son, Ya'akov, sold part of their citrus groves in Wadi Hanin (today Nes-Ziona).[31]

Jamil el-Husseini was another of the prominent organizers of "el-Nadi el-Arabi" and was active in the Moslem-Christian League. He sold land to Jews in Deir-'Amar.[32]

The sons of *Mussa Khasem el-Husseini*, who was the Chairman of the Arab Executive, sold their share of the Miska land to Jews. They were joint owners of the land together with Abu Deba and el-Bitar, who have been mentioned above.

The *el-Husseini Family of Gaza:*

Jamal el-Husseini sold land in Idhniba to Jews.[33]

Fahmi el-Husseini, the Mayor of Gaza, sold 5,200 dunam of land to Jews in Nakhabir.[34]

The Arab National Company of Nablus established a model farm in the Beit-Shean Valley for the instruction of fellaheen and Bedouins in methods of modern agriculture. It failed to achieve its aims and sold the land to Jews.[35]

Dr. Tawfik Canaan was active in the national Arab movement and wrote anti-Zionist articles and pamphlets. He owned land in the Beit Shean Valley jointly with Mussa el-'Alami and Tawfik el-Husseini. The land was sold to the Jewish National Fund. Kibbutz Tirat-Zevi was founded on this land.[36]

Mu'in el-Ma'adi, a member of the Arab Executive of Haifa,[37] who was an active participant in the 1936 riots, sold land to Jews in the vicinity of Atlit.[38]

Amin M'rad, a prominent leader of the "Arab People's Fund" in Safed, cooperated with Nahmani in his efforts to acquire land.[39]

Sulayman Bey Nassif was a very wealthy moneylender in Haifa. He was considered a moderate who stood for cooperation with the British rule and with the Jews. At one time he favored Arab participation in the proposed Legislative Council.[40] He sold his land in the Beit-Shean Valley to the Jewish National Fund. (See Chapter Eight)

The Nashashibi Family of Jerusalem:

Judath Nashashibi, a member of the Arab Executive, sold land in the village of Dileb (today Kibbutz Kiryat-Anavim) to the Jewish National Fund prior to World War I.[41]

Ragheb Nashashibi was the Mayor of Jerusalem, a founder of the "National Defense Party" and a member of the Arab Higher Committee since 1936. He sold land on Mount Scopus to the Hebrew University.[42] During World War II he negotiated for the sale of his land in the village of Yalo, but because of the high price he asked the sale did not materialize.[43]

Fahmi Nashashibi, the brother of Ragheb, sold land indirectly to Jews. He encouraged the Government to confiscate his land for public use, to wit: for the erection of the Hebrew University on

230

Mount Scopus.[44]

Nusseiba Zaki of Jerusalem, a member of the Arab Executive, was a partner in the sale of land in Dileb by Judath Nashashibi.[45]

Fuad Sa'ad of Haifa, a Greek-Catholic member of the Arab Executive,[46] sold land to Jews on which Giv'at-Ada was later founded.[47]

A'asem el-Said, the Mayor of Jaffa, was an active member of the Moslem-Christian League. Together with Taji el-Farouqi and other partners he sold a part of the land of the village of Qubeiba.[48]

The two branches of the *Abd el-Hadi Family in Nablus and Jenin:*

Qasem Abd el-Hadi, in 1912, sold to Jews the land on which the *moshava* Karkur was built.[49] He was the father of 'Auni, Fuad, Nismi and 'Afif Abd el-Hadi.

Nismi Abd el-Hadi sold 1,620 dunam to the Palestine Land Development Company. On this land Kefar-Pinnes was later founded. Part of the land also belonged to Qasem Abd el-Hadi as *musha'a*. When he refused to implement the terms of the sale, Amin Abd el-Hadi interceded and an agreement was reached.[50]

'Auni Abd el-Hadi, one of the founders of the "Istiqlal" Party and a member of the Arab Higher Committee, led the legal battle against the Jewish National Fund to thwart the purchase of Wadi Hawarith. He assisted Hankin in assembling large tracts of land which the Jewish National Fund later acquired. (See Chapter Five)

Fuad Abd el-Hadi openly assisted in assembling the large tracts of land for the Wadi Hawarith purchase.

Amin Abd el-Hadi was a member of the Supreme Moslem Council. He helped Hankin settle boundary and land disputes.[51] Amin sold 2,000 dunam to the Jewish National Fund in the village of Mukbeile, situated in the Jezreel Valley.[52] Land owned by the family in the village of Qumia and another parcel of 6,000 dunam in Kafer-Zar'in were sold to the Jewish National Fund.[53]

Fahri Abd el-Hadi of Jenin was one of the leaders of the terror squads of 1937.[54] With his friend Farid Irshed he organized the "Peace Squads" that opposed the terror imposed on the Arab populace and sought to end the Arab Revolt. On August 2, 1939 the two met with representatives of the Jewish Agency in Jenin and offered to sell land for a Jewish settlement. The reasons for the failure of the negotiations are unknown.[55]

Abdul Rahman el-Ghazzi sold family property to the Jewish National Fund. He also put together individual plots of land belonging to fellaheen into large tracts and sold them to the Jewish National Fund. The kibbutzim of Gat and Gal'on were later built on these lands.[56] Abdul Rahman was among the more prominent Arab terror squad commanders in 1938.[57]

The el-'Alami Family of Jerusalem:

Mussa el-'Alami was Government Advocate of the Palestine Government and a member of the Arab Higher Committee. At the height of the 1936 riots he and his joint owners, Tawfik Canaan and Tawfik el-Husseini, sold their land in the Beit-Shean Valley to Jews.[58] (See above)

In 1940 a member of the *el-'Alami Family in Gaza* offered to sell to Jews 6,000 dunam of land in Barbara, located in the southern part of the Judean Plain.[59]

Hafez el-'Alami sold to Jews 1,700 dunam of land in Hirbiya in the South.[60]

Sidqi el-'Alami sold to Jews 1,600 dunam of land in Khirbet Buza, near Migdal.[61]

Yusef Fahum, the Mayor of Nazareth, sold land to Jews openly, despite terrorist threats. At the beginning of the century the heads of the family sold land to Jews in Upper Galilee. (See Chapter Four)

The el-Surani Family of Gaza was well represented in the Arab nationalist cause. Mussa el-Surani was a member of the Secretariat of the Husseini Party in Gaza.[62] Mahmud el-Surani was a member of the Arab Executive.[63] In 1935 the family sold land in Yavne to the Jewish National Fund.[64] The el-Surani family was among the first to sell the land on which Rishon-le-Zion was later founded. (See Chapter Four)

Alfred Rock, a Jaffa Christian and a member of the Arab Executive and later a member of the Arab Higher Committee, sold land in Jabaliya jointly with the Mufti of Jaffa, Tawfik el-Dajani, to the Palestine Land Development Company.[65]

Arthur Rock, the brother of Alfred, sold land to the Jewish

National Fund in Beit-Dajan.[66]

Alfred Rock's nephew sold land in Mas'ub (today Kibbutz Matzuba) to the Jewish National Fund. (See Chapter Eight)

The *el-Shawa Family of Gaza:* Said el-Shawa was a member of the Moslem Supreme Council. His brother, Rushdi el-Shawa, was the Mayor of Gaza.[67] Another brother, Sa'adi el-Shawa, and other members of the clan handled the business affairs of the family. Their holdings in real property in the Gaza area were considerable. Sa'adi el-Shawa sold 1,380 dunam of land to the Jewish National Fund in Majdal.[68]

As'ad el-Shuqairi of Akko (the father of Ahmed Shuqairi, a member of the Arab Higher Committee and the first Chairman of the Palestine Liberation Organization) was a highly respected Moslem religious figure in the country and a leader of the Nashashibi Party.[69] In 1921 he was considered for the office of Mufti of Jerusalem.[70] The same year he sold 702 dunam of land to the P.L.D.C. Later the Neve-Shanan quarter of Haifa was built on this land.[71]

The el-Shanti Family of Qalqiliya and Jaffa: Ahmed el-Shanti was in the twenties an extremist in the ranks of the Arab nationalist movement.[72] Ibrahim el-Shanti was one of the principal fomenters of the 1936 riots.[73] Members of their family sold land in Taiyiba to the Jewish National Fund.[74]

Shukri el-Taji el-Farouqi of Ramle was a member of the Arab Executive. His brother Abdul Rahman el-Taji el-Farouqi was a member of the Moslem Supreme Council.[75] The two brothers sold to Jews their share of a 13,000-dunam tract of land in Qubeiba.[76] In the 1930's Shukri sold 2,000 dunam in Zarnuqa to the American Zion Commonwealth.[77]

To sum up: the fact that Arab leaders of the nationalist movement sold land to Jews was well-known in the Arab community. The political leadership tried unsuccessfully to suppress this information. The subject came alive when Lewis French stated in a memorandum to the Government that certain members of the Moslem Supreme Council had sold land to Jews and that the Arab leadership had no objection to such sales of surplus land. This comment caused more than a ripple among the Arabs. The Arab

233

Executive called a special meeting to consider the demand of the Arab press to publish the names of the sellers of land. Many members failed to attend the meeting and finally the Executive ceased to function altogether.[78] Only at the outbreak of the 1936 riots was the Arab political leadership reorganized into the Arab Higher Committee.

CHAPTER TEN

REHABILITATION OF THE LAND

The Jewish settlement effort in the country caused radical changes in the landscape. Swamps were drained; the blocked channels of rivers and streams that caused extensive flooding were cleared and the resulting free flow allowed drainage of adjoining lowlands; waste-land was reclaimed and cleared of wild vegetation; bare hills were afforested; the encroachment of sands along the coast was halted by the planting of trees and bushes. Rocky soil was cleared and made fertile; excessively salty soil was treated and made suitable for farming.

Swamp Drainage

In 1936 Abraham Granott, who was then a member of the Jewish National Fund Directorate and later its Chairman, summed up the Jewish efforts at drying the swamps and enriching the land. According to his book, "Land and Waterways," 32,500 dunam of swampland was dried by 1936 and as a result 453,000 dunam of land were developed to a state satisfactory for agriculture.[1]

A summary of swamp drainage and land enrichment up to and through 1947 appears in the table ont the next page:

234

	Actual Swamp Area (Dunam)	Total Area Drained (Dunam)
From the beginning of Jewish Settlement to 1936	32,500	453,000
Swamps in Beit-Shean	28,000	53,000[2]
Hula Valley (Lake included)	44,800	95,000[3]
Rubin Brook	1,500	3,300[4]
Wadi Kabani	1,500	1,500[5]
Total	108,300	605,800

In addition to the above, swamp drainage was also undertaken by private landowners and municipal bodies, e.g. drying of the Nahariya swamp and others. These projects actually created land for town development in Nahariya and elsewhere. Nor did Granott include in his accounting the drainage of the Petah-Tikva swamp which comprised 1,500 dunam and was accomplished at the very beginning of Jewish settlement. In the area of the Kishon River 70,000 dunam of Arab land that adjoined Jewish land was improved.[6] Jewish swamp drainage added a total of 700,000 dunam to the available agricultural land.

The Arabs initiated practically no work of this kind. The Concession over the Hula swamp area was in their hands for twenty years, during fourteen of which there were civil government and peace – from 1920 to 1934. In 1934 the Concession was handed over to Jewish settlement agencies. The Arab political leadership protested against the transfer vigorously, and although the British Administration was clearly inclined against giving the Concession to the Jews, no Arab public body and no non-Jewish investment group could be found that would assume the obligation of draining the Hula swamp. The Jewish State began the drainage work in 1951.

Characteristic of the Arab attitude to restoring the soil to health is the incident of the Ramadan Pool. This was a swamp in the central Sharon, entirely in the possession of the Waqf, a nationalist-religious Arab organization. The Waqf was governed by the Moslem Supreme Council and so the issue of the Ramadan

Pool was a local one. Despite the fact that the swamp was a breeding place for the malarial mosquito and all the villages of the area, Arab and Jewish, suffered from it in consequence, the Moslem Supreme Council did not undertake to drain it. The cost of that project, LP. 18,000, was subsequently divided between the Netanya Beach Development Company (LP. 6,000), the Mandatory Government (LP. 7,500) and the Moslem Supreme Council (LP. 4,500). When the work was completed, the Waqf was left with 4,500 dunam of fertile land, the value of which was increased immeasurably.[7]

Another similar case is that of the Rubin Brook. On a sandy site near the mouth of the brook stood a mosque that attracted thousands of worshippers. Not far from it there was a malarial swamp created by the brook's blocked estuary. In 1926 a Jewish National Fund representative attempted to obtain a lease on the land near the Rubin Brook which was Waqf property, and therefore not for sale. In a report to the Head Office Ettinger wrote: "The mosque stands on sandy ground south of the Rubin Brook, and the great throngs of people who attend prayers there would not be inconvenienced by the drainage of the swamp nearby. On the contrary, they would benefit greatly by the work done by us."[8] The Jews did not get the lease. The swamp was eventually dried by the Mandatory Government at the expense of the tax-payer. Years later, when its drainage ditches were blocked up with silt and again caused malaria in the district, the task of eliminating that problem was performed by Kibbutz Palmahim. That was in 1949.

The Mandatory Government did not do much swamp drying. Whatever they did in the Sharon and Beit-Shean Valleys was done for the re-settlement of tenant farmers who had left land bought by Jews and were re-established on Government land.

Ravaged Lands

Even after the investment of money and work at a risk to health and sometimes to life in drying the swamps, the soil in the nearby areas did not reach a standard adequate for agriculture without further treatment. This kind of land was termed ravaged land. A

236

description of ravaged land was given by Joseph Weitz: "It is land on which wild brush of various kinds grows, jujube and Zizipheae. These entangled thorny bushes spread across the face of the soil and prevent cultivation. This type of barren soil is found in valleys with an abundance of water, that were at one time closely settled by man. At a later period they were occupied by herdsmen who had come from the desert and did not till the land. The land fell to waste and the wild brush took over. Such land, extending over thousands of dunam, was to be found in the Jericho and Beit-Shean regions, and also in the northern plain of the Hula".[9]

The Jewish settlement agencies and the settlers themselves did not maintain accurate records of ravaged land that was restored to use. Reference to the Palestine Exploration Fund maps will illustrate how extensive the ravaged lands were throughout the country.

A map of the Zebulun Valley, dated 1878, shows that 61,800 dunam out of a total 96,500 dunam was ravaged land.[10] A map of Beit-Shean marks 128,000 dunam of ravaged land out of a total of 190,000 dunam.[11] A large part of these lands was designated by the Mandatory Government as uncultivable. When it divided the Beit-Shean territory among the Bedouins and landowners, it classified 137,910 dunam as ravaged land which was not to be allocated.[12] Though to a lesser extent, the situation was similar in the Jezreel Valley, the northern part of the Hula Valley (the section north of the swamp area) and the flatlands alongside the swamps.

The Arab plowman never worked the ravaged lands and never attempted to improve them, consequently they increased from year to year. It was the Jewish settler who restored the ravaged land to a cultivable state.

The records of the first settlers speak frequently of uprooting the wild vegetation as a chief occupation in the early stages of settlement. The plowing of virgin soil was commemorated in many of the early photographs. They took photographs of teams of 10–12 horses hitched to a giant plow, with tens of plowmen working alongside.

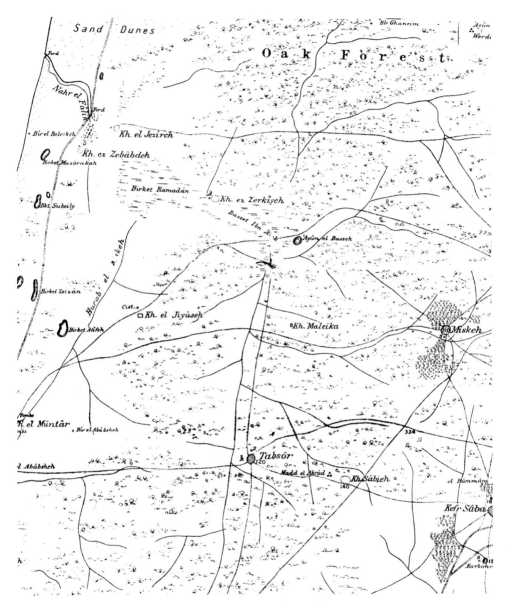

The Plain of Sharon, P.E.F. 1878, Sheet X.
An oak forest covers thousands of dunams.

Afforestation

At the beginning of modern Jewish settlement there were still remnants of forests in the country. A map of the Palestine Exploration Fund indicates wide areas of forest in the Galilee and Samaria regions. However Arab flocks and the widespread use of charcoal by the Arabs substantially reduced these afforested areas from year to year. Final destruction occurred during the First World War, when the Turks took wood wherever they could find it as fuel for their locomotives.

In the first Jewish colonies only garden and decorative trees were planted, and then eucalyptus groves were planted to absort excessive soil dampness in the vicinity of swamps. The first planting of a projected forest was that of the olive trees at Hulda, undertaken by the Jewish National Fund before the First World War as a memorial to Herzl. During the war these olive trees were neglected and destroyed by Arabs. Right after the war the afforestation of Hulda was renewed. Instead of olive trees, forest trees were planted there and at Ben-Shemen. Following this successful attempt at afforestation the Forestry Department of the Jewish National Fund was established and became responsible for the planting of millions of trees in many parts of the country.

Afforestation was a novelty to the Arabs. In 1878 C.R. Conder wrote that in Gaza local people said not a single olive trees had been planted there since the Moslem conquest. According to the local tradition the olive trees in the Gaza district were planted by Alexander the Great.[13]

The Jewish National Fund saw the massive tree planting projects primarily as an endeavor to halt soil erosion and to improve the climate and beauty of the country. To achieve this aim it was prepared to invest heavily in labor and in research to achieve the proper acclimatization of the saplings. The economic prospects of lumbering for construction and industry were hardly considered when this work was begun. Weitz was the moving spirit behind the afforestation activities of the Jewish National Fund. The forests were planted on bare, desolate slopes of mountains and along the banks of rivers and streams, and where it was thought that they would impede encroaching sand. Until 1948 the Jewish National Fund planted 23,000 dunam of forests and groves that contained 5,000,000 trees.[14] Hundreds of additional dunams were afforested by the P.I.C.A. and municipal bodies.

In addition to new planting, a great deal was done – primarily by the Jewish National Fund – to renew ancient woods that had degenerated over the centuries. Through these efforts 350,000 dunam of ancient woods were saved from destruction by herds of Arab cattle, sheep, and goats, most of them after the establishment of the State of Israel.

Mountain Land

After 1936 serious efforts were made at making mountainous areas suitable for farming and a great deal of work was done in stone clearing, levelling and initial groundbreaking to uncover fertile layers. During the following ten years, up to 1947, 15,423 dunam of mountain land was made cultivable, with an investment of 168,746 work days, 30,987 work days of draught animals, and 2,713 work hours of heavy tractors, aside from the work of a variety of earth-moving machiners.[15]

Saline Soil

The Jewish settler was not deterred by excessively salty soil, even if its salinity reached as high as 17%. In Kibbutz Beit-Ha'arava, in the Jericho Valley, 370 meters below sea level, a successful attempt was made to turn over-salty soil into fertile land by washing the salt out with sweet water. Two to three thousand cubic meters of water were used per dunam, until the excess salt was washed out and fertility higher than in many other places was attained.[16] The members of the kibbutz managed to improve 200 dunam before they were compelled to abandon their site because of the invasion by the Trans-Jordan Army in 1948. The Jordanians later neglected the project, and the soil returned to its former saline state.

Kibbutz Hatzerim, which settled in 1946 west of Beer-Sheba, was also allocated very salty soil. After the War of Independence, when the kibbutz began to develop in earnest, it was found that the yields on the saline soil were too poor to make working it economically feasible. After long deliberation, and with the financial support of the Israel Government and the assistance of a Government experimental station, starting in 1960 the first 500 dunam were washed out. The yields on the washed out soil were good, especially in flowers and various other irrigated crops.[17]

The Beit-Ha'arava experiment was a trailblazer for many successful desalination projects after the War of Independence in the Negev and in the Arava, in desert areas which even the Bedouins found no use for. In the twenty years following, more than ten settlements were established in such desert areas. In the Arava alone 11,500 dunam of saline soil was washed out and ameliorated to produce record crops. This work of reclamation is continuing.

So the Jewish settler has not only worked the land, but has actually created it.

CHAPTER ELEVEN

ZIONIST LAND POLICY

The fundamental aims of the movement of Jewish national rebirth – the Hovevei Zion, followed by the World Zionist Organization – were to return to the Land of Israel and to strike root in its soil as of right and not by anyone's leave. The right to the Land was interpreted to mean an obligation to develop it and the assumption of responsibility for the new settlers and for the people living on it. The conception was of all-embracing sovereignty: Just as a legal government is authorized and obligated to plan for the full utilization of the potential in water, land and other natural resources for the benefit of all the inhabitants, so the Zionist movement is entitled and is obligated to plan and to execute a program designed to achieve this aim. The term "the inhabitants of the country" was interpreted to refer to the actual inhabitants,

241

both Jews and Arabs, and to the potential inhabitants, namely the future Jewish settlers who were to return to their Homeland.

The Arabs regarded Palestine as part of the broader Arab domain, and they denied the right of a foreign people to change the character and the demographic make-up of the country by an active program of development, accompanied by the influx of immigrants from the outside. They rejected the Zionist contention that without Jewish effort, ability and money the land would remain neglected. In 1933 Mussa el-'Alami told Ben-Gurion[1] that he preferred that the land remain poor and desolate, even for a hundred years, until the Arabs had the strength and ability to revive and develop it.

These opposing views were impossible to bridge. The Zionist movement refused to consider Arab agreement as a necessary condition for its activities, but it did assume an unwritten but deeply rooted obligation to prevent injustice to the individual Arabs living in the country. The Labor movement in Zionism went even further – it was committed to the belief that development of the country for the benefit of the entire population was bound to bring about a change in the social and economic relations within the Arab community, and as a result there would come an end to Arab opposition to the Zionist endeavor. The common prosperity and a recognition of the true common interests of the two peoples would bring about an understanding between them, and the joint concern for the future of the country would put an end to Arab refusal to accept the establishment of the Jewish National Home.

In later years, with the growth of Arab opposition, despite the economic prosperity and the improvement in the position of the lower Arab classes, a change occurred in the Zionist conception of the future relations between the two peoples. It was then thought that when the Jewish settlers grew in numbers and in strength, the Arabs would be bound to reach the conclusion that the *Yishuv* could not be liquidated, and they would acquiesce in their activities. But this new conception did not take away from the strict obligation of the Zionist movement not to do harm or perform any injustice to the individual Arabs as a consequence of Jewish settlement.

The first to implement this principle in practice – as described

242

earlier – was Chaim Margalit-Kalvarisky, the I.C.A. director in Upper Galilee at the beginning of the century. In his footsteps followed the heads of the Palestine Land Development Company and of the Jewish National Fund, and all those who were involved in land purchase and settlement – Ruppin, Ussishkin, Hankin, Granovsky (Granott), Weitz, Moshe Smilanski, Kisch and others. This was the line followed by the Zionist Organization from the beginning of its organized settlement activity in 1908.

Arthur Ruppin, the man who guided the settlement program with a clear view in sight of the national aim of Zionist realization, said at the Eleventh Zionist Congress in 1913:

"We have before us the task, which can in no wise be evaded, of creating peaceful and friendly relations between the Jews and the Arabs. In this respect we have to catch up a great deal that we have neglected, and to rectify the errors that we have committed... A proper regard for the Arabs must teach us to proceed with the utmost tact in our land purchases, and to make certain that no harsh results ensue from our actions. We have in fact so guided ourselves until now, having for by far the largest part bought such lands as were not fit for grain cultivation, and were therefore practically useless to the Arabs. In the few cases of grain land purchases we have been careful to indemnify the tenants till then in occupation, so that they bore us no grudge."[2]

After the First World War the purchasers required of the Arab sellers to set aside land for the tenant farmers, as was the case in Nuris (Ein Harod) and in Ma'alul (Nahalal). But the sellers often failed to live up to their obligations. Some landowners would dismiss the tenant farmers before the sale.[3] The responsibility for resettling the tenants or for compensating them devolved on the Zionist institutions. Aside from the moral obligation which they took upon themselves, they were also obligated to abide by the Mandatory laws for the protection of the tenant farmers. These were based on Article 6 of the Mandate, which stipulated that the Mandatory was to "encourage... close settlement by Jews on the land" (which was not done) while "ensuring that the rights and position of other sections of the population are not prejudiced."

One of the stipulations of the law protecting the rights of the tenant farmers was that they were to be given alternate land or a portion of the land about to be sold. But in many cases the tenants preferred a cash settlement, which gave them the opportunity to make a fresh start elsewhere, free of obligations to the effendi, or to move on to some non-agricultural occupation. The Director of Land Department of the Mandatory testified before the Shaw Commission that the law stipulating that alternate land be given to the tenant could not be implemented, because the tenants received a cash indemnity, moved on elsewhere and could not be located.[4]

The Zionist agencies rejected the solution offered by the Commissions of Inquiry and incorporated in the White Papers of 1930 and 1939, because these meant in effect that Jewish settlement activity would come to a halt. Instead they looked for constructive solutions in the spirit of the principles of Zionism: continued development of the country and settlement on the land, making sure that no injury was caused to the individual Arab.

At the beginning of 1931 the head of the Jewish Agency's Political Department, Col. Fred Kisch, sponsored a consultation with all the settlement agencies concerning the tenant farmers. He put in writing a series of proposals, intended primarily for Dr. Chaim Weizmann, the President of the World Zionist Organization, and he sent copies to the Jewish National Fund, to the Palestine Land Development Company, to the P.I.C.A., to the Histadrut (General Federation of Labor), to the Farmers' Association and to a number of influential personalities of the *Yishuv*. In the letter outlining his proposals he stated: "It is clear that we cannot evade the issue of the tenant farmers by expecting the sellers to remove them from the purchased tracts. The problem must be solved, and we must not seek ways of evading responsibility for its solution."

Kisch raised a number of possible alternatives and asked the recipients of the letter for their opinion as to the most desirable course:

a) To enable the tenant farmers to settle on part of the land which will remain in their hands, adjacent to the plots purchased by the Zionist agencies, and to give them, in addition to the land, sums of money to develop intensive agriculture;

244

b) To buy other land in the same general area and lease it to the tenant farmers for an indefinite period (in effect – in perpetuity);

c) To buy land in other regions and turn it over to the tenants;

d) To purchase land in Trans-Jordan and reach a political agreement with the Emir Abdallah about absorbing the tenants:

e) To pay a certain sum to the Government, so that it should assume responsibility for resettling the tenants on land.[5]

The reaction of the Zionist agencies and of the individuals Kisch turned to was not single-minded. Only on two points was there general agreement – one in favor, and one against. Everyone opposed the suggestion of a transfer to Trans-Jordan, first because it was considered impractical and secondly because a program of this sort was bound to be interpreted as a Zionist attempt to deport the Arab population, or at least part of it, from the country. On the other hand everyone agreed that whatever policy was followed the tenants were entitled to full compensation. But there was no agreement as to whether they were to be compensated by other land, and if so – where.

Col. Kisch's initiative did not lead to a full-scale debate on the subject or to definite conclusions. At the Seventeenth Zionist Congress in Basle (1931) Kisch was replaced by Chaim Arlosoroff as head of the Jewish Agency's Political Department. Arlosoroff aimed at reaching a long-range agreement with the Mandatory on the questions of *aliya,* settlement on the land, and the development of agriculture, industry and the public services, an agreement which would take into full account the aims of Zionist realization and the needs of the local population. He was convinced that if such an agreement were reached it would be possible to come to an understanding with the Arabs, once they realized that the Mandatory Government had a fixed policy from which it could not be moved by protests and propaganda. Should the Arabs refuse to accept the policy, the Government would have no choice but to carry it out regardless, because of its obligation toward the Jewish side in the dispute. Progress in implementing Arlosoroff's political program was interrupted in a tragic fashion – he was murdered two years after he was elected to his new post.

In 1933 Arthur Ruppin published a paper entitled "A

245

Development Scheme for Palestine," in which he refuted the negative findings of Simpson and French, and presented a broad plan for agricultural development that would release the Arab peasant from his debts and would enable him to engage in intensive agriculture, while at the same time making large areas of land available for new Jewish settlement. To illustrate his idea Ruppin went into great detail about the application of his plan to the Coastal Plain. According to his calculations at the end of 1932, the Coastal Plain contained a total of 2.5 million dunam of arable land, of which 400,000 were in Jewish hands and the remaining 2.1 million dunam were worked by 22,000 fellaheen, so that the average holding of a fellah family came to 95 dunam. Ruppin proposed that, on the average, the fellah would sell 32 dunam of his land, in return for LP. 150, a sum which would enable him to do the following:

a) to pay up his debts, amounting on the average to LP. 30, on which he was now paying LP. 6–9 annually in interest;

b) to invest LP. 30 as his share in an irrigation system for the village, which would enable him to put 6 dunam under intensive cultivation;

c) to invest LP. 30 in 3 dunam citrus plantation;

d) to invest LP. 15 in improving his livestock;

e) to keep LP. 45 as a reserve toward his living expenses during the first three years, before the new plantation began to bear fruit. In the course of time he would add at least another 3 dunam to his citrus grove, and would end up with 12–15 dunam of intensively cultivated land, with the rest of the land used for dry farming, as heretofore.

Ruppin went on to say that in the event the land did not belong to the fellah but to a large landowner and "the large landowner is willing to sell his estate, the Government may, by invoking the law defending the rights of tenants, frequently compel him to leave part of the irrigated land (10 to 15 dunam per family) in lease to the fellaheen who have hitherto worked it, or to sell it to them on long-term arrangements."

The plan would enable the settlement of thousands of Jewish settlers on the 700,000 dunam that would be bought from the

Arabs, once the lands were meliorated and irrigation facilities installed.[6]

Ruppin proposed that similar plans be worked out for the Jordan and Beit-Shean Valley. "The proposals submitted above," he went on to say, "are not based on pure theory; on the contrary, there is a whole series of cases in which the process described had taken place, and Arabs who have sold land to the Jews in the Coastal Plain have used the money to introduce intensive agriculture on their farms. A not inconsiderable proportion of the orange plantations which are today owned by Arabs in the vicinity of the Jewish colonies of Rishon-le-Zion, Petah-Tikva and Rehovot were planted with money which the Arabs received from the Jews in return for part of their land. For the Arabs it was an excellent stroke of business, for the sandy soil which they sold to the Jews had, until that time, brought in practically nothing, whereas today they derive from the plantations started with Jewish money very large incomes."[7]

A comprehensive program such as Ruppin prescribed required, first and foremost, Arab agreement. Not only great political differences precluded this, but also the contrasting outlook of Jews and Arabs on social and economic matters. The Zionist movement stood for the dynamic development of the country. This meant an energetic, rational exploitation of all natural resources that were available or could be uncovered by technology and science; developing new water sources, preparing for cultivation of areas not used hitherto, meliorating cultivated land, improving the quality of livestock and the strains of the various crops by scientific breeding methods aiming at getting maximum yields in all agricultural pursuits. The Mandatory's agricultural experts, on the other hand, viewed the position of the fellah and the agricultural activity he pursued as something fixed and stationary, which, if it were ever to change, would do so only slowly and grudgingly. If Government experts on agriculture and development took this view, the Arab leaders certainly did. The Government officials acted as colonial officals did everywhere, aiming at the preservation of the *status quo* in order to protect the Imperial interests. The Arab leadership, too, was interested in the preservation of the *status quo*, out of political as well as social considerations. In this respect their views coincided with those of the Mandatory. In the paper mentioned above Ruppin observed: "An important Arab newspaper recently expressed the liveliest objection to the action of the Government when the latter tried to discover water that would have enabled the fellah to live on a smaller farm."[8]

The Arab leadership knowingly ignored the fact that the situation of the fellah and of the tenant farmer was bound to improve through the sale of some of the land, for this would put an end to the state of exploitation by the landowner and bondage to the moneylender. To them the source of the evil was the Jewish buyer, not the property relations which brought the Arab peasant to his sorry lot.

In a memorandum to the Mandatory which 'Auni Abd el-Hadi submitted in the name of the Arab Executive in reaction to the Passfield White Paper of 1930 – which did not satisfy all the Arab demands – he argued that the fellah could free himself from economic oppression only by selling his land to the Jews, the only interested buyers, below the market value.[9]

Eventually the Arabs set up an organization, the Arab People's Fund, with the aim of buying land from Arabs who were about to sell it to Jews. The Fund had little money and it bought altogether about a thousand dunam in the Gaza area, which it sold to fellaheen in plots of 25 to 100 dunam.[10] Its main activity was to persuade rich Arabs to buy land which was offered for sale to Jews, an activity which benefitted the wealthy Arabs but did nothing to help the poor out of their economic straits.

A thorough and detailed study of land worth irrigating was made by the Jewish National Fund in 1936. At the same time it investigated the country's water resources. It was found that about 3,950,000 dunam of level land could gainfully be irrigated and that there were 2.75 billion cubic meters of water to be tapped. According to the formula used to determine the quantity of water required for irrigating a dunam of land, it was ascertained that 2,143,000 dunam could be irrigated."[14]*

* It was found some years later that the estimate of available water was

248

Abraham Granott wrote in 1937: "The irrigated land in all of Palestine comes to 350,000 dunam. Another 1,180,000 dunam is unirrigated and gives a poor yield. By intensive cultivation with irrigation the yield can be increased five-fold... The Arabs come with maximalist political demands, claiming that Palestine belongs to them and they will not tolerate Jewish immigration because it threatens their future. But these claims are balanced by the right of the Jewish people to its ancient homeland, a right which they will not give up because their entire national existence depends on it. And there is no need for them to give it up, for their work of reconstruction will do no harm to the local population. On the contrary, it will gain from it greatly. In fact it is probably the only way to improve the lot of the Arabs."[12]

In October 1934 Joshua Hankin presented a memorandum to the Palestine Land Development Company concerning the Negev lands. "We have reached the conclusion," Hankin wrote, "together with Dr. Ruppin, that we ought to initiate negotiations with the Government [all Negev land officially belonged to the Government] and propose an arrangement that will solve our problem and will also benefit the Arabs... We should negotiate about a large area that will provide us with a broad expanse of land and will also solve the problem of settling the Negev Bedouins, about whom the Government is very much concerned. I believe there are some 4,000,000 dunam which can be considered suitable for cultivation. Concerning the number of Bedouin candidates for settlement (10,000 families), half the area should suffice for them once the water problem has been solved. This would leave 2,000,000 dunam for Jewish settlement, and at the same time the Bedouins, too, will become established farmers thanks to the development projects which will come into being through the influx of Jewish capital."[13]

The Hankin-Ruppin plan was similar in outline to the one that was implemented for the tenant farmers in the Hula Concession. By the terms of the Concession, the Jewish National Fund set aside 15,722 dunam for the tenants who had occupied the area before,

exaggerated. On the other hand better results in the utilization of water were achieved, so that altogether the estimate turned out to be quite accurate.

while the expense of drying this area was to be covered by the Jewish National Fund. (Unlike what was to be the case with the previous, Arab concessionaires, who were to have *sold* 10,000 dunam to the tenants). Granott wrote in July 1938 to the Vaad Leumi (the National Council): "The terms of the concession specify that we are to give the Arabs 15,722 dunam free of charge. Furthermore we are obligated to carry through the full amelioration for this area as well – drainage, irrigation installations, etc., again free of charge to the Arabs. The amelioration costs are estimated at LP. 15 per dunam, so that the Arabs will be receiving a gift of LP. 236,580."[14]

Even though setting aside a large area for the tenants placed a heavy burden on the Zionist financial institutions, they thought that a fair deal had been struck. Weizmann proposed at a meeting with the High Commissioner, in the presence of Moshe Shertok (Sharett), that the Hula model be applied to the Negev as well. Sharett noted in his diary: "There is the problem of the Negev... We are about to present our proposals, including the plan to carry out some test drilling for water. But we must get a commitment from the Government that the irrigation possibilities which may be uncovered will be placed at the disposal of Jewish settlement, subject to the setting aside of sufficient land for the Arabs, more or less along the lines of the Hula Concession. Secondly there is the problem of Beit-Shean, where we seek a clear determination of the areas that will be made available to us. Again the Hula arrangement can serve as a precedent."[15]

Hankin's plan was near realization, when the outbreak of the 1936 distrubances deterred the Negev sheikhs from reaching an agreement with the Jewish buyers.

The Zionist movement followed a consistent land policy from the early days until the termination of the Mandate. The realization of the policy often encountered opposition on the part of those whose accustomed way of life would be disturbed by the development program – as often happens with governmental development projects. But unlike government officials who, as a rule, do their work without much personal involvement, the Zionist leaders, planners and settlers were possessed by a sense of mission and devotion to the job at hand, which left little room for compromise. The aim they set for themselves, for which they were ready to give their lives, was sometimes opposed by just claims of the tenant farmers which the Zionists did their best to satisfy, while sometimes the claims were clearly invented to serve hostile political ends, and this provoked a sharp reaction from the settlement agencies. We note, beside examples of compromise and even acts of magnanimity towards the tenants, also cases of neglect, lack of consideration and occasional violence in the encounters between Jews and Arabs. The clashes caused ever more extreme reactions on the part of the Arabs, such as the reaction of the Arab Executive to the feud over Wadi Hawarith, which blamed on the sale of land to the Jews the turning of the fellaheen into paupers.[16]

The Zionist leadership would review the problem of the Arab tenants from time to time with a view to avoiding injustice, violent clashes and the intervention of security forces, whether British units or units of the "Hagana." In the final analysis the intentions and the acts of the Zionists did not bring the desired results. Zionist settlement was carried out with a minimun of infringement of the individual Arab's rights, but it provoked stiff political opposition on the part of the Arab leadership, which argued that dispossession of the fellaheen and the tenant farmers was bound to lead to the loss of the natural rights of the Arab community and to its eventual uprooting from its homeland. The fear lest this come to pass is what motivated the Arab community to take up arms against the *Yishuv* toward the end of 1947.

How small was the damage and how few the cases of injustice toward the fellaheen and tenants was related in the previous chapters. Did the Zionist movement aim to remove the Arab community from its economic, social and cultural positions? Was the Arab community toward the end of 1947 in danger of being uprooted from its homeland? We shall deal with these questions in our next chapter.

CHAPTER TWELVE

THE ARAB COMMUNITY IN PALESTINE, LATE 1947

The Demographic Growth

In 1947 the Mandatory Government submitted a report on the economic, social and political condition of the country to the United Nations Special Committee on Palestine (UNSCOP). The report was accompanied by a good deal of statistical data. As the Committee was finishing its work, the Government submitted a pamphlet containing up-to-date figures on the permanent population of Palestine as of December 31, 1946:[1]

Moslems	1,076,780
Christians	145,060
Others (mainly Druse)	15,490
Jews	608,230
Total permanent population	1,845,560

In its summary the Mandatory Government divided the population into religious categories rather than those of national origin. As a result non-Arabs were included among the Christians, and the Druse were listed under the heading of "Others." At the end of 1946 there were about 30,000 non-Arab Christians.[2] Therefore the figures for the permanent Arab residents really read as follows:

Moslems	1,076,780
Christian Arabs	115,060
Druse	15,490

giving a total of 1,207,330 permanent Arab residents. The natural increase of the Arab population (estimated at 3%) for the eleven months up to November 30, 1947 was 33,220 souls.* Therefore on the day that the United Nations proclaimed the establishment of the State of Israel the estimated number of permanent Arab

---

* The rate of natural increase among Moslem Arabs was 30.7 per thousand; among the Christians 18 per thousand; among the Christian Arabs more than 18. Therefore we took a mean of 30 per thousand.

residents, including Druse, was 1,240,550. The number of Bedouins who lived in the country should be added to this figure.

The Mandatory Government statistics on the Bedouins were full of errors and miscalculations, and corrections were made. All in all the data available on the subject were far from accurate. The 1922 Census reported more than 103,000 Bedouins in the country. Thereafter a correction was made by subtracting 17,000 from the number of Bedouins and adding them to the permanent Arab population. The 1931 Census reported 66,553 Bedouins. This figure was repeated annually by the Census without change. Professor Bacchi estimated the number of Bedouins in the country at the end of 1947 at about 80,000.[3]

In estimating the rate of growth of the Arab population between the years 1922 and 1947 a comparison can be made only between the permanent population that was reported in the first Census and the estimated permanent population of 1947. In the Census of 1922 and 1931 and thereafter in the annual census estimates of the Office of Statistics of the Mandatory Government the statistician divided the map of the country into Districts. This was done to keep track of the population movement in accordance with the specific conditions obtaining in each region. The editors of the Israel Atlas divided the map of Palestine into 48 "natural regions for statistical purposes"[4] that are correlated with the boundaries separating the State of Israel from the West Bank and the Gaza Strip, as demarcated in the Armistice Agreements of 1949.

The population figures for each "natural region" were indicated on the above-mentioned map. The figures were derived from the 1922 Census, and the estimate made by the Mandatory Government at the end of 1946. It is in this manner that one is able to compare the rate of natural increase of the permanent Arab population living within the regions of Jewish settlement as opposed to those outside these regions.

In the Israel Atlas, the figure for the permanent Arab population in Palestine in 1922 is given as 554,500. This is very close to the 1922 Census which reported 565,317 including the Druse. A certain difficulty arises in comparing the figures as of December 1947. According to the updated pamphlet issued by the Mandatory

Government under the date of December 31, 1946 there were 1,240,000 permanent Arab (Druse included) residents in Palestine, after taking into account the natural increase for eleven months. The figure given in the Israel Atlas is however, 1,207,000, including the Druse. Professor Bacchi investigated the errors and distortions that marked the statistics of the Mandatory Government and concluded that at the end of 1947 there were 1,200,000 permanent Arab residents, exclusive of the Druse.[5] If one adds the 17,000 Druse then living permanently in the country, the figures of the Israel Atlas and of Professor Bacchi practically coincide. Therefore the data of the Israel Atlas will be used in estimating the permanent Arab population between the years 1922 and 1947.

During the years 1922 to 1947 the permanent Arab population increased from 554,500 to 1,207,600. This represents an increase of approximately 120%, but the rate of increase varied in the different regions. In the areas heavily populated by Jews the rate of growth of the permanent Arab poplation was much above the national average. On the other hand in the sectors where Jews were not present the rate of growth was low, and there were a few regions where the rate was zero or even negative.

In 1922 there were 324,000 permanent Arab residents in the 35 regions within the boundaries of the State of Israel as established by the 1949 Armistice. On December 1, 1947 there were 756,600 permanent Arab residents in these regions – an increase of 134%; whereas in the thirteen regions where there was no Jewish settlement the permanent Arab population in 1922 was 229,600 and on November 30, 1947 it was 451,000 – an increase of only 98%. Even the rate of 98% can be explained in part by the fact that it includes the Arabs of Jerusalem. Their rate of increase was much greater than that in the other Arab regions, probably because of the existence of close economic ties with the Jewish community.

Parenthetically it may be pointed out that despite the rapid growth of the Arab population in Jerusalem, there is no basis for the allegation that Jerusalem was ever an "Arab city," let alone a "Moslem city." From 1880 to the present writing the Jews have been an absolute majority in the population of Jerusalem.

254

Population of Jerusalem 1800–1946[6]

Year	Jews	%	Moslems	%	Christians	%	Total
1800	2,000	23	4,000	46	2,750	31	8,570
1850	6,000	40	5,400	36	3,600	24	15,000
1870	11,000	50	6,500	30	4,500	20	22,000
1880	17,000	55	8,000	26	6,000	19	31,000
1900	35,000	64	10,000	18	10,000	18	55,000
1922	33,971	55	13,403	22	14,699	23	62,073
1946	99,400	60	33,700	21	31,300	19	164,400

Over a 25-year period the Moslem population of Jerusalem grew by more than 150%, while the Christian population increased by 115%. Of course a portion of the Christian group was not Arab. At all events, of the three cities (Jaffa, Haifa and Jerusalem) with a mixed Jewish-Arab population, only in Haifa was the rate of increase in the Arab population higher than in Jerusalem.

Non-Jewish Population – Moslems and Christians in the Cities in the Years 1922 and 1947.[7]

City	October 1922	January 1, 1947	Percentage of Increase
Safed	5,774	10,210	77
Akko	6,227	13,420	115
Tiberias	3,570[8]	5,780	62
Beit-Shean	1,900	5,520	190
Nazareth	7,371	15,540	111
Haifa	18,240	70,910	290
Jenin	2,415	4,310	78
Nablus	15,782	24,660	56
Tulkarem	3,317	8,860	168
Jerusalem	28,102	65,010	131
Bethlehem	6,656	9,140	37
Hebron	16,147	26,380	64
Jaffa	27,429	70,730	158
Ramle	7,277	16,380	126
Lydda	8,092	18,220	125
Gaza	17,423	37,820	117
Jericho	1,209	3,010	150

Haifa, which was a shabby town at the beginning of the present century, underwent tremendous expansion, once the port was built, the agricultural hinterland of Jewish settlement in the Jezreel Valley was developed and industry began to flourish in the Zebulun Valley. Commensurate with the population increase in the Jewish sector the Arab population quadrupled between the years 1922 to 1946.

Despite the fact that it was in the interest of Jaffa's Arabs to develop close reciprocal relations with the Jewish community, no way was found to restrain the extremists from attacking the Jews in 1921, and again in 1929. In 1936 the Arab port workers closed the port to Jews and laid siege to neighboring Tel-Aviv. Despite the distrubances Jaffa remained a mixed city of Jews and Arabs, and benefited from its relations with the Jews of the city and of the agricultural hinterland. During the years 1922 to 1947 the Arab population increased by 158%. Ramle and Lydda, where Jewish communities had sprung up on the outskirts, showed a 125% increase for the period. Even Akko and Nazareth, that were outstripped by Haifa, had a greater increase in population than the Arab towns that had little contact with Jews. Nablus, Hebron and Gaza, so-called "pure" Arab cities, declined in their population figures until 1920. Only when Jewish settlement developed significantly did they recover somewhat, but their rate of population increase was smaller than it would have been had they grown at the rate of natural increase for the Arabs of Palestine.

In 1897 Nablus numbered 21,000 inhabitants. By 1922 the figure had declined to 16,000. In the ensuing 25 years its rate of population increase was 56%, about one-half of the natural rate of increase for the Arabs of Palestine. Hebron's population in 1887 was 15,000, and it remained at that level for 45 years. In the 25 years between 1922 and 1947 it grew at a rate of only 64%. In 1886 there were 20,000 Arabs in Gaza (See Chapter Two) and in 1922 they were fewer. Their number began to grow significantly after the outbreak of World War II, once British army camps were built in the Negev and Jewish settlement began. In 1931 the Census showed that Gaza had a population of only 17,045, no more than nine years previously. But it more than doubled its population in the ensuing fifteen years, due to the presence of the British Army and Jewish settlers in the area.

Bethlehem had only a 37% increase. This would indicate a real decline in population. Jericho is outstanding for its growth. The reason: the erection by Jews of phosphate plants at the northern and southern ends of the Dead Sea. Similarly Beit-Shean came to life with a 190% population increase once Jewish settlement began in the area.

The Arab political leadership and the Mandatory Government's officialdom were hostile to the Zionist effort. The several Commissions of Inquiry argued that the growth of the Arab urban population resulted from the displacement of rural Arabs by Zionist settlement. They allegedly were left no choice but to flock to the towns, there to create a landless proletariat.

This thesis is not tenable in the light of the fact that during the same period (1922–1947) the population in the Arab rural areas displayed the same growth characteristics as the urban areas: In the Arab agricultural areas adjacent to Jewish settlement regions or included within such regions the rate of population increase was much higher than in the "pure" Arab areas. In fact, while the Arab villages close to Jewish settlement enjoyed an unprecedented increase in population, the Arab villages in the "pure" regions suffered a decline. It is reasonable to conclude that a rural Arab population flowed from the "pure" regions to those containing Jewish settlements.

Permanent rural Arab Population (Moslems and Christians) 1922–1947[9]

District	October 1922	January 1, 1947	Percentage of Increase
Safed	12,785	38,730	202
Akko	24,892	49,510	100
Tiberias	11,279	20,640	83
Beit-Shean	8,079	11,820	46
Nazareth	14,608	26,380	80
Haifa	25,509	55,780	119
Jenin	30,897	56,900	85
Nablus	40,747	69,940	72
Tulkarem	31,622	68,180	115
Ramallah	26,928	43,750	63
Jerusalem and Bethlehem	43,088	72,720	69
Hebron	36,994	66,430	80
Jaffa	13,619	42,530	211
Ramle	28,613	67,810	137
Gaza	47,143	85,930	82

The rate of increase of the rural Arab population was 212% in the Jaffa District, a region where Jewish settlement was most dense. In the Districts of Ramle and Tulkarem – a citrus-grove region – the Arab population grew by 137% and 115% respectively. In the Haifa and Akko Districts the fellaheen expanded the areas of vegetable growing and orchards to supply the needs of the developing port city. On the other hand, since Jerusalem's agricultural hinterland was in the Judean Plain, the Arab villages surrounding Jerusalem languished.

A different situation obtained in the Tiberias and Nazareth Districts. These were regions with a high density of Jewish settlement – they included the Jezreel Valley and Lower Galilee – and yet the rural Arab population did not achieve a rate of increase equal to the national average. The reason for this was that many tenant farmers, after having been indemnified, moved to other parts of the country. Large numbers of young men from the villages were drawn to Haifa, as scarcity of water prevented the development of more intensive farming in their home region.

In the Districts of Jenin, Nablus, Ramallah, Hebron and Gaza the rate of increase of the rural Arab population was considerably below the national average, since they were far from the influence of the burgeoning Jewish settlement. The lowest rate of increase was in Beit-Shean District, where the land had been sold to the Jews by nomad Bedouins, who moved on to other tracts of land east of the Jordan River. The money they received enabled them to buy land in Trans-Jordan.(See Chapter Eight) On the other hand in the northern part of the Beit-Shean District, in the vicinity of Degania, where Jewish settlement was dense, the permanent rural Arab population grew from 3,055 in 1922 to 6,000 in 1946.[10]

Thr rural Arab population of the Safed District showed an increase at a rate of 202%. This high figure can be accounted for by two factors: a) Jewish settlement in the area brought in its wake improved health conditions; b) The Hula Valley did not come under civilian rule of the Mandatory Government until 1923, and as a result the residents of the Hula Valley were not counted in the 1922 census.

The rate of increase of the rural Arab population in areas devoted to citriculture can be attributed only in small degree to the employment of Arab labor in the Jewish-owned groves. The total number of hired Arab laborers in Jewish agriculture – including citrus groves – was 7,500. (See below) This number is negligible compared with the total rural Arab population of 800,000 in 1946. The increase in this sector of the Arab population may be ascribed chiefly to the overall expansion of Arab agriculture, more specifically to the more intensive methods used in the cultivation of citrus fruits, vegetables and orchards.

The Growth of the Arab Economy

The most profitable branch in agriculture between the two World Wars was citriculture. In 1913 Arabs owned 20,000 dunam of citrus groves and Jews 10,000.[11] In 1945 Arabs owned 127,333 dunam and Jews 120,897 dunam. Not only did Arabs own greater areas of groves than the Jews, but the quality of their groves was superior. Arabs owned 103,179 dunam and Jews 95,580 dunam of groves

259

classified in the "A" category – – the highest category by quality.[12]

The other branch of intensive agriculture in the expanding economy was the growing of vegetables. In 1922 Arab farmers cultivated 30,000 dunam and produced 20,000 tons of vegetables.[13] In the year 1944/5 Arabs farmed 239,733 dunam and supplied 189,804 tons of vegetables to the market.[14] Of this total, 107,000 dunam were cultivated intensively and produced 121,000 tons, or 1,130 tons per dunam.[15] In the same year Jews cultivated 38,000 dunam intensively and produced 54,000 tons of produce, or 1.450 tons per dunam. The difference was not very great. The remaining 133,000 dunam cultivated extensively yielded the Arab farmer less than one-half ton to the dunam. It can be readily understood why the fellah would be ready to sell part of his land so that he could farm the rest intensively and triple his yield. In addition to citrus fruit and vegetables, the Arab farmer also cultivated a variety of fruit orchards. In the year 1944/5 the total area of fruit orchards, apart from olives, cultivated in the Arab agricultural economy was 355,709 dunam, with a yield of 73,320 tons of fruit. In 1922 the fellaheen had harvested only 13,460 tons.[16]

The cultivation of tobacco in the Arab economy expanded from 9,000 dunam in 1926 to 29,189 dunam in 1942.[17] The yield of water-melons in 1922 was 20,210 tons, and in 1944/5 – 128,441 tons.[18] The raising of livestock in the Arab village was in the ascendant. The fellah raised fewer goats and bought cows instead. Between the years 1922 and 1945 the number of goats herded was reduced by about 40,000 head, while the number of cattle rose from 133,000 to 240,570. The number of fowl raised increased from 310,000 to 1,202,000.[19]

While the intensive Arab agricultural economy grew by a million dunam during the 1922–1947 period, their extensive economy expanded as well. In 1931 the Arabs sowed summer and winter grain crops on an area of 4,600,000 dunam, and in 1940 they cultivated 5,200,000 dunam. The yield increased likewise during the same period from 154,270 tons to 225,771 tons.[20] During the War years the fellaheen sowed cereals on even larger areas, but since price controls had been imposed, Arabs did not always report the true figures for their yields and the areas under cultivation, and the

Department of Agriculture was unable to supply reliable statistics.

The increase in agricultural production paralleled the increase of the Arab population that lived in proximity to the Jewish settlements. In 1947, 30,000 Arabs worked as hired laborers in agriculture, primarily in the citrus groves. About one-quarter of them were employed by Jews.[21]

In 1931 there were 2,239 Arab workers employed in industry and trades.[22] At the end of 1946 there was a total of 14,000 such workers: 11,000 employed by Arabs, 2,500 by Jews, and 500 in miscellaneous small enterprises.[23] Firms that operated as Government concessions had 2,619 Arab employees in 1939, and 4,000 in 1947.[24]

There were 10,721 employees in Government service in 1935,[25] and twelve years later they numbered 24,000.[26]

Among the Government employees in 1947 there were 13,000 officials of all ranks. Apart from the English officials who held all the senior posts, and a handful of Jews, all the other ranks – middle-level management and governmental posts in schools, hospitals and other public institutions – were manned exclusively by Arabs.

According to a survey conducted by the Histadrut, there were 147,000 Arabs in the employ of the Government at the beginning of 1946.[27]

The flourishing Arab economy and the steep rise in income had no parallel in the neighboring Arab countries. The following data give some concept of the rate of growth of the Arab economy in Palestine:

In 1931 there were 339 factories owned by Arabs and in 1942 – 1,558 factories.[28] As mentioned above, the number of their employees increased tenfold between 1931 and 1946. In the year 1944/5 gross production in Arab agriculture came to LP. 17,103,133.[29] In the years of 1933, 1934 and 1935 alone Arab landowners sold land to Jews for LP. 4,202,080.[30] It is true that part of the sum went to absentee landlords, primarily in Syria and Lebanon, but the Palestinian landowners who sold their land invested their money either in agriculture, industry or commerce. According to figures submitted to the Royal Commission in 1936,

261

Arabs had invested LP. 6,500,000 in citriculture up to that year.[31]

Between the years 1921 and 1935, LP. 36,500,000 were invested in the building industry, according to Jewish Agency records. Jews invested LP. 21,000,000 and Arabs – LP. 15,500,000.[32] Records of the Mandatory Government for the period 1933 to 1938 (including the peak years of 1933 to 1936) show that LP. 32,700,000 were invested in building, of which LP. 10,800,000 were invested by Arabs.[33] During the same period Arab investment in building in the "pure" Arab cities and villages amounted to a mere LP. 841,494.[34] In other words, in the five-year period Arabs invested LP. 10,000,000 in building in the three mixed cities of Haifa, Jerusalem and Jaffa. This amounted to one-half of all Jewish investment in building in the entire country at a time when *aliya* was at its peak.

Arab savings accounts rose from LP. 298,000 in 1935 to LP. 6,969,000 in 1945. The initial capital of Arab banks increased from LP. 243,000 in 1939 to LP. 2,393,000 in 1945, a twelve-fold growth, while the economic index rose by only 284 points.[35]

The one-time Director of the Economic Department of the Jewish Agency, David Horowitz, testified before the United Nations Special Committee on Palestine that from 1939 to October 1946 wages in the Arab sector of the building industry rose by 541% and that the wages of the Arab agricultural laborer rose by 524%, even though the economic index for the Arab market had only increased by 284 points.[36]

There was a great difference in the rise of wages of the Arab worker, depending on whether the place of work was near a sector of Jewish settlements or in a "pure" Arab sector. In 1947 the mean wage of the Arab laborer rose to LP. 0.080 per hour, but the rates differed in the different regions:[37]

Region	Average Wage per Hour
Jaffa	LP. 0.094
Haifa	LP. 0.077
Jerusalem	LP. 0.070
Gaza	LP. 0.056
Nablus	LP. 0.049

It follows that the economic pattern that obtained in the agricultural sphere held for the wage structure in the non-agricultural realm as well. In other words, the closer the ties of the Arab worker to the Jewish economy, the better was his economic lot. The farther he was from such influence, and the more he functioned in his "natural" sector, the worse was his condition, and the closer it resembled that of his brethren in neighboring Arab lands.

The impetus provided by the development of Jewish settlement was a major influence in agriculture. In spheres other thant that of agriculture the Histadrut was a major factor in enabling the Arab worker to carry on his struggle for higher wages.

The Histadrut adopted a gradualist policy toward the Arab workers. In the first instance it attempted to organize Arab and Jewish workers in the "League for Palestinian Workers." Its purpose was to deal with those Jewish and Arab workers who worked side by. side in Government service or for foreign employers. In this fashion the Histadrut assisted the Arab worker in his struggle for a fair wage and other rights. The achievements of the Arab workers in the employ of the Government, foreign concessions, the ports and other places of work that employed both Jews and Arabs encouraged the Arab workers in other parts of the economy to fight for their rights. To a limited extent they were successful. Yet the conflict that arose between the Jewish worker and the Jewish employer over the Jewish worker's right to employment within the context of Zionist goals inevitably caused discontent among the Arab workers. It is reasonable to assume that the pursuit of a policy of employing Jewish labor was responsible for the birth of Arab unions inimical to Zionism and to the Jewish worker.

The Improvement in Health Services and the Growth of the Educational Network

The rapid development of the Arab economy, with a concomitant rise in the standard of living, both in the cities and the villages, raised expectations of a better life. They gave rise to demands for a higher quality of health and educational services. For reasons not germane at this point the Jewish community had developed independent networks for its health and educational needs. It turned to the Government only for supplemental budgetary assistance in these fields. The example of Jewish achievement in these areas led the Arab community to demand standards in health and education which were far beyond British colonial practice. They were also far beyond the levels of such services in neighboring Arab countries. It should be added that the example set by the various religious Missions spurred the Government on to improve these services.

As a result health facilities were expanded, and the rate of natural increase rose to be among the highest in the world. The scope and level of educational opportunities were also far beyond those prevailing in the neighboring Arab countries.

The mortality rate of Arab children fell drastically between the years 1927 and 1945. Infant mortality (up to one year of age) was 201 per thousand among the Moslems in 1925, and it fell to 94 per thousand in 1945.[38] The rate of natural increase among Moslems rose from 23.3 per thousand for the years 1922–1925 to 30.7 per thousand for the years 1941–1944.[39]

The Arab educational network that was supported mainly by the Mandatory Government and partly by the municipalities and the Missions increased fourfold between the years 1925 and 1945. In 1925 there were 417 Arab schools with a population of 26,944 pupils.[40] In the year 1944/5, 64,790 Arab children attended Government schools, and 38,828 – private schools, on the primary and secondary levels, making a total of 103,618 pupils.[41] In addition, the Education Department of the Mandatory Government maintained an agricultural school in Tulkarem (a gift of the Jewish philanthropist Elias Kadourie) and a few Arab colleges and teachers' seminaries for men and women.[42] In 1945/6 the Mandatory Government expended 77% of its education budget in the Arab sector (LP. 537,750 out of a total budget of LP. 700,000), while 62.7% of income from all taxes were paid by the Jewish community.[43]

Summary

In 1947, as the country awaited the fateful political decision, the economy of the Arab community was in full swing of development in agriculture, industry and commerce, and other branches of endeavor. Jewish settlement in no way displaced Arabs from the economy. The remarkable progress made by the Arab community proved the opposite. To the extent that Jewish settlement prospered, so did the Arab commuity. In fact the general prosperity attracted Arab immigrants from the neighboring countries, both legal and illegal. Had the Arab leaders accepted the basic Zionist thesis that Palestine was the homeland of the Arabs who lived in it and of the Jews who were returning to it, the Arabs would have achieved long-term social and economic success. But the Arabs were not satisfied with less than a Palestine that was exclusively Arab, with perhaps a small, tolerated Jewish minority in their midst. The Jews, for their part, were unwilling and unable to forego their national aspirations for a homeland and for a place of refuge for millions of persecuted Jews scattered throughout the world.

In view of the unwillingness of the Arabs to live in peace with the Jews in one country, the Zionist leadership agreed to a partition of Palestine into two separate sovereign states, Jewish and Arab, that would live in neighborly harmony. The Arab leadership was not ready for compromise. It called on the Arabs in Palestine, and later on the neighboring countries, to take up arms against the State of Israel, which was about to be born in a part of Palestine.

Jewish resistance to the threat of annihilation and the rout of the several Arab armies turned the myth of Arab displacement, fostered by the Arab leaders, into tragic reality. Hundreds of thousands of Arabs were uprooted from their homes, as the Palestinian irregulars retreated and the regular armies of the Arab states fled. Flight and exile were the bitter fruits of a war that the Arab leadership had initiated, and not the result of a calculated Zionist policy of displacement and uprooting.

The price of the war that the Arabs imposed on Israel was paid by the hundreds of thousands of Arabs made homeless, and by the hundreds of thousands of Jews in Arab lands, who became the victims of Arab vengeance and were expelled from their countries of domicile.

CHAPTER THIRTEEN

PARTITION, WAR AND THEIR AFTERMATH

On November 29, 1947 the General Assembly of the United Nations decided to partition Palestine into two sovereign states, Jewish and Arab. This was the solution it offered to the Arab-Jewish conflict that had festered for thirty years under the rule of the Mandatory Government. The Arabs rejected the proposal and responded by making war on the Jewish community. The Jews for their part prepared to comply with the decision of the United Nations. The war was begun by Palestinian Arabs, aided by volunteers from neighboring Arab countries, from Germany, from Yugoslavia, and from other countries. On May 15, 1948, the official date of the end of the Mandate, the regular armies of Egypt, Syria, Jordan, and Iraq invaded the country.

The War of Independence began on December 1, 1947 and came to an end on March 10, 1949, when Zahal (Defense Army of Israel) entered Eilat. In the war the State of Israel lost the Jewish Quarter of the Old City of Jerusalem, the potash plant at the northern end of the Dead Sea, and the electrical installations at Naharayim. In addition the following agricultural communities were overrun by the enemy: Kefar-Etzion, Masuot-Yitzhak, Revadim, Ein-Tzurim, Atarot, Neve-Ya'akov, all in Judea; Beit-Ha'arava in the valley of Jericho; Kefar-Darom at the gateway to the Negev; and Mishmar-Hayarden in Galilee. After the armistice with Syria was signed, Mishmar-Hayarden was returned to Israel. All the buildings of the settlement had been razed to the ground.

There were two places where the defenders were compelled to surrender, in the Old City of Jerusalem and in the Etzion Region. In the Old City the Arab Legion permitted the transfer of non-combatants to the Jewish part of Jerusalem. The non-combatants in the Etzion Region had been removed several months prior to the decisive battle. After the surviving defenders of the Etzion Region surrendered their arms, the Arabs of the surrounding villages attacked and killed 126 men and one woman.[1]

266

The surviving Jewish combatants in the Old City and in the Etzion Region were taken into captivity.

Non-combatants in the settlements that were taken by the enemy – and held by them until 1967 – were safely evacuated. A similar fate befell the non-combatants in those settlements that were temporarily captured by the enemy and then retaken by Zahal. As to the combat troops, they retreated to the rear. The State of Israel took in some 5,000 war refugees and provided for them, as it did for all citizens who had suffered harm in the war.

The Arab community that had initiated the war and had lost it responded in a different fashion. There were hundreds of thousands of Arabs who fled or were exiled from their homes in the cities and in the villages. The Arab States did not hold themselves responsible for the tragic outcome. The armistice agreements were not forerunners of a peace settlement, as set forth in their preambles. The Arabs demanded that the refugees be returned to their homes, but Israel refused to receive them, arguing that their return would create an unacceptable internal situation and the new State would be broken from within. In consequence the refugees remained in camps supported by the United Nations. The contributions to their support by the rich Arab nations were a good deal less than minimal. During the years 1950 to 1974 six member-nations of the Unites Nations contributed $ 803,000,000 (the United States – $ 577,000,000, the Soviet Union – $ 0.00) to the United Nations Relief and Works Agency for Palestine Refugees (UNRWA). The fifteen Arab nations gave less than $ 27,000,000. To this sum, Algeria contributed $ 0.00.[2]

The first to flee the country right after the United Nations decision were the rich Arabs. They had learned the meaning of armed conflict between Jews and Arabs over the years. They understood that it presaged a cessation of commerce, heavy levies imposed by the rival Arab warring groups, acts of terror in the Arab community, and a breakdown of law and order. Those who had fled from the regime of terror in the 1936–1938 period had reason to fear that their enemies would settle accounts with them in the chaos that would follow the British evacuation of the country. The magnitude of the flight of refugees in the years 1936–1938 affords some understanding of the dimensions of the Arab flight at the end of 1947 and the beginning of 1948.

A secret report submitted to the Director of the Political Department of the Jewish Agency, dated November 7, 1938 stated in part: "All the rich families of Haifa, such as Sahyun, Majdali, Toma, Houri, Abiad, Qarqabi, Bagdash and others, have fled. In the last month middle-class and poor families that have been ruined economically have fled... Reliable sources estimate that they number at least 15,000...[3] Nineteen of the richest Arab families in Jerusalem fled and many rich families and prominent public figures in Jaffa also took to their heels."[4]

A similar phenomenon occurred at the end of 1947 and thereafter. Foreign journalists who followed the course of the war from its start and witnessed the events that led to the creation of the refugee problem reported the flight of the rich families immediately after the U.N. resolution on Palestine. They were frightened by the rapidly escalating violence.

In a collection of articles on the Jewish-Arab conflict which appeared in the Unites States, Marie Syrkin quotes the Arab newspaper As-Shaab which wrote at the time that the major Fifth Columnists in Arab ranks were those who abandoned their homes and businesses and settled outside the country, many of them in ostentatious luxury. At the first sign of strife they fled, in order to avoid participating in the war effort, either directly or indirectly.[5]

An American journalist who was in the country in 1948 reported that about 20,000 rich Arabs fled the country in the first few months following the outbreak of violence. Matters became so bad that the Arab Higher Committee requested the neighboring Arab countries to close their boundaries to these rich refugees.[6]

Dominique Lapierre and Larry Collins, authors of the best-seller "O Jerusalem," who made a detailed study of the history of the War of Independence, and who interviewed many trustworthy sources, stated: "Contributing to the exodus everywhere was the exodus that had already taken place, that of the Arab middle and upper-class leaders. Like their brothers in Jerusalem, most of those who left were convinced that their departure was temporary, that they would soon return in the avenging van of the Arab armies".[7]

The Arab version is that the Arabs began to flee only after April 9, 1948, when the village of Deir-Yassin was attacked by a combined force of "Irgun Zvai Leumi" ("Etzel") an "Lohamei Herut Yisrael" ("Lehi") soldiers, and 245 Arabs, including women and children, were killed.[8] Allegedly the flight began because the Arabs were convinced that Deir-Yassin was a prelude to the extermination of the entire Arab community. Indeed the Arabs had reason to fear the revenge of the Jews in view of the cruel, hostile deeds that were perpetrated on the Jewish community. The wiping out of a group of 35 men on their way to reinforce the Etzion Region, the destruction of the convoy to Yehiam with 42 killed, the planting of a time-bomb in the courtyard of the Jewish Agency, and other such acts left the Jews embittered. Nevertheless the "Hagana" and the organized Jewish community condemned the attack on Deir-Yassin and continued its policy of refraining from harming non-combatants. The Arab leadership, while aware of this policy, gave the occurrence wide publicity. They fostered the feeling of shock among the Arabs in the hope that it would engender a fighting spirit. In retrospect after the debacle the Arab leadership regarded Deir-Yassin as the sole cause for the massive Arab flight.

Official statistics of the Mandatory Government for the period January-March, 1948 show that 14,486 more people left the country than came in.[9] Some of those leaving were non-Arab Christians, mostly English, but undoubtedly there were thousands of Arabs among them. It should also be kept in mind that this was a period of chaos in the country. The northern and eastern boundaries were under the control of Arab fighting units, and so fleeing Arabs did not undergo the formalities of registering as emigrants with the authorities. There is convincing evidence from Arab sources to support the conclusion that the signal for mass flight was given by the rich and respected Arabs, and even by the Arab leaders themselves. A.N. Kossa, a leader of the Arab National Committee in Haifa, stated: "The local chairman and members of th Arab Natinal Committee left after the U.N. decision. Even the leaders of the different Arab communities disappeared. No Arabs with political or social authority remained to lead and guide the masses, who were panic-stricken after the 'Hagana' shelled the city indiscriminately..."[10]

Kossa wrote the above eleven years after the war. Another witness to the events of the period was Hajj Nimer el-Khatib, a leader of the Arab National Committee in Haifa. In discussing the causes for the large number of thefts and robberies that had plagued the Arabs in Haifa, el-Khatib enumerates, among others, the following: "... the headlong flight of Arab residents from their homes, while leaving behind their houses and stores containing all their worldly wealth... the introduction of foreign criminal elements into the city, who enjoyed the patronage of well-known figures in the Arab world. Under cover of their protection, they engaged in robbery and theft..."[11]

There was a clear link between the causes and their effects. The flight of the population stimulated robbery and theft, which in turn induced larger numbers of Arabs to flee, fearing for their lives and property.

Attorney Jacob Salomon of Haifa, who participated in the negotiations between Jews and Arabs before Haifa was conquered by the "Hagana", told a reporter of the London *Jewish Observer and Middle East Review* that at the end of March 1948, before any serious fighting had begun, 25,000 Arabs had left Haifa. Another 20,000 left in the first eighteen days of April, after Kaukji had attacked Mishmar-Ha'emek. Rumors persisted among the Arabs that they should leave Haifa to enable the Arab air force to bomb the city.[12]

What took place in Haifa and Jerusalem was repeated in Jaffa. Nimer el-Khatib relates: "...The situation in Jaffa worsened. The soldiers of Rais Mishel el-'Issa (an officer sent by Kaukji to help the residents of Jaffa) behaved as if they owned the city. They robbed individuals and homes. Life was of little value, and the honor of women was defiled. This state of affairs led many residents to leave the city under the protection of British tanks..."[13]

H. Ben-Zevi of Kefar-Vitkin, who served as the Secretary of the Regional Committee, described the manner in which the Arabs abandoned their homes in Emek Hefer at the beginning of the conflict: "As the War of Independence broke out we learned from

270

our guards that the Arabs were planning to flee for fear of what we would do to them. We of the Regional Committee got in touch with the representatives of the Bedouins as soon as we learned of their fears. We invited them to Kefar-Vitkin and told them that we would be responsible for their safety and asked them not to flee. They said they would consider the matter, and it seemed to us that they would remain, but to our surprise they folded their tents and left..."[14]

M. Ben-Yitzhak, a security officer in Upper Galilee, records the story of the Hula Valley Arabs in his diary: "After the 'Arab Liberation Army' attacked Kefar-Szold (January 16, 1948), the Hula Arabs noticed with concern that groups of Arabs were infiltrating from Syria... Many of those who had believed that they could stay out of the fighting are now going to Lebanon. The villages of Mansura and Shouqa in the Hula Valley have been abondoned by their residents. Also, many from Khisas have crossed the border..."[15]

There was another type of flight whose dimensions are difficult to estimate. During periods of prosperity under the Mandatory Government many Arabs from the neighboring countries immigrated legally and illegally to Palestine. When the conflict broke out they returned to their countries of origin, since they did not wish to get involved in a quarrel that was not theirs. It should be kept in mind that during the period of the Mandate 18,695 Moslems and 18,493 Christians (including non-Arabs) immigrated to Palestine legally.[16] In addition, there were tens of thousands who did so illegally. (See Chapter One) Many of them had never severed their ties with their homelands. An interesting piece of evidence came to light in 1977, when civil war broke out in Lebanon and the "Good Fence" was opened to the Christians living in the villages near the border. The residents of the Lebanese village 'Ein Ibel requested the Israeli authorities to return the property that they had abandoned in 1948. They argued that in 1920 they and their parents had emigrated from 'Ein Ibel and had settled in Haifa. In 1948 they fled and returned to their village.[17]

The English journalists Terence Prittie and Bernard Dinnen were in the country during the war and wrote a book on the problem of the Palestinian refugees and the Jewish refugees from Arab countries. They estimate that 30,000 Arabs, mostly rich, left the country immediately after the U.N. decision on partition, and another 200,000 left the cities of Haifa, Jaffa, Safed and Tiberias by May 15, 1948.[18]

To date no valid investigation has been made of the number of Arabs who left the country immediately after the outbreak of the conflict. Some villages were abandoned by their inhabitants, because they had been involved in the "Transportation War," villages on the road to Jerusalem or strategically located on other critical traffic arteries. After the Jews gained control of these arteries, the villagers fled. Others fled in the wake of the retreat of the Arab armies. For example, large Arab forces had laid siege to the South and the Negev, and had cut them off from the rest of Israel. When Zahal freed the area, the Arab residents along the coast south of Ashkelon fled. Some Arab villages and urban areas were forcibly evacuated by Zahal as it advanced, to avoid leaving a hostile population in its rear. History awaits authoritative research on the causes of Arab flight.

On November 30, 1947, there were 809,100 Arabs within the boundaries of the State of Israel. The boundaries referred to are those that were thereafter fixed by the Armistice Agreements of 1949. The above population figure has been arrived at as follows: There were 756,600 permanent Arab residents on that date. The number of illegal immigrants* from the neighboring countries, 13,500, has been subtracted from the above total[19], and the figure of 66,000 has been added to account for the Negev Bedouins, [20] giving a total of 809,100.

According to a census conducted by the Government of Israel in 1949, there were 111,500 Moslems, including Bedouins, 34,000 Christians and 14,500 Druse in Israel, making a total of 160,000 souls. (The number of non-Arab Christians was very small.[21]) A 1951 census found 14,000 Bedouins[22] and a 1959 census reported 25,000[23], for a population increase of 11,000 (or nearly 80%) over

---

* The reference is to new immigrants who had not yet assimilated with the Arab population. There were tens of thousands of illegal immigrants who had arrived years before.

an eight-year span. It is obvious that such a rapid growth cannot be entirely accounted for by the natural increase; it is reasonable to assume that the figure of 25,000 (Bedouins) includes 8,000 to 9,000 returnees. A figure of 168,000 Arabs in the State of Israel after the War of Independence would seem to be fairly accurate. This would leave 640,000 Arabs unaccounted for. If one subtracts 1% or 2% from the total to account for war casualties, there could not have been more than 627,000–633,000 Arab refugees, at most, since after the War many returned, with the permission of the State of Israel, as part of the program of uniting families, or without such permission.

Professor Bacchi estimates that there were 778,700 Arabs (not counting the Druse) living within the boundaries of Israel in 1947. He subtracts from that figure the 146,000 Arabs (not including the Druse) who were in Israel after the War. This leaves a total of 632,000 Arabs not in the country. If one subtracts 1% or 2% from this total to account for war casualties, the possible number according to Bacchi comes to 620,000 to 626,000.[24]

There is no information available as to the number of refugees who were integrated into the general economy of the neighboring countries, or as to the number of refugees in the camps. It would seem evident that there were tens of thousands of refugees who succeeded in rescuing part or all of their property, and so were not in need of relief. Thousands of Bedouins as well did not reach the camps – they continued with their nomadic lifestyle in Sinai and Jordan. Therefore those in the refugee camps at the beginning of 1949 could not possibly have numbered more than 500,000–550,000.

Jewish Refugees from Arab Countries.

Arab propaganda insists on the legend that before the appearance of Zionism Jews and Arabs lived together in Arab countries in amiable fraternity and prosperity. The history of the Jewish communities in Arab countries reveals a reality that is quite the opposite. Arab apologists attempt to disguise overt acts of anti-Semitism merely as expressions of opposition to Zionism. Albert Memmi, in the introduction to his book, *Jews and Arabs*, writes: "We must explode one more myth: The Moslem Arab propagandists claim that these conflicts are the result of Zionism; ignoramuses and fools repeat the charge. From a historical point of view it is pure nonsense. Zionism was not the source of Arab anti-Semitism. The exact opposite is the truth, as was the case in Europe. Israel is the response to the repression that Jews met with in the whole world, including the repression that we, the Jews in Arab countries, suffered."[25]

Persecution, discrimination, pogroms, exile, forced conversion and blood libels were the lot of the Jews in Arab countries for hundreds of years before Zionism came into being. In the countries under Ottoman rule the Jews suffered a double burden: On the one hand they had to endure the despotism of their rulers and the corruption of Turkish officialdom, and on the other hand they were exposed to cruel persecution by the local Arab population.

In the countries of North Africa that had come under European rule in the nineteenth century, the well-to-do urban Jews received a modicum of protection from their foreign masters. But the Jewish masses in their day-to-day contact with the Arabs underwent degradation and persecution. Often they were the defenseless prey of mob violence. Those who murdered and robbed them had no cause to fear punishment. The Jew was an inferior creature in the eyes of the Arabs.

Between the two World Wars anti-Jewish outbreaks occurred in Arab countries, sometimes in concert with attacks by Palestinian Arabs on Jewish settlements and sometimes independently of any other event. During the period of the Arab Revolt against British rule in the years 1936–1938, anti-Jewish riots broke out in Syria and in Iraq. Jews were robbed and killed. When the Arab countries launched a rebellion against foreign rule, it was accompanied by pogroms. Mobs pillaged Jewish property and murdered innocents. After the failure of the rebellion of Rashid 'Ali Khilani in Iraq (1941) the Arabs carried out a pogrom on the Jews of Baghdad. They killed 180, wounded many and robbed and despoiled much property.[26]

In the wake of the U.N. decision on Partition and the end of the British Mandate on May 15, 1948 anti-Semitic riots occurred in all the Arab countries. When the Arab masses were being incited to mobilize for a *Jihad* against Israel, hundreds of Jews were massacred in Arab countries. After the War of Independence, when the Arab troops returned home and the masses began to realize the dimensions of the defeat, Jews were again attacked. The Arab governments arrested many Jews. They staged trumped-up trials on charges of espionage and treason, Jewish property was confiscated, and the lives of the Jews were made intolerable. (Similar events occurred after 1956 and 1967, but they are beyond the scope of this study)

While the British Mandate was in force, the Arab countries had forbidden Jewish emigration to Palestine, in order to prevent the growth of the Jewish community there. Jews who attempted to leave illegally were punished severely. However when the State was established, these same Arab countries compelled their Jews by direct or indirect means to abandon their homes and to migrate to wherever they pleased. The Arab rulers knew full well that the only country that would accept them was Israel. They were also aware that only the masses of Jews in Arab countries could provide the manpower base for a strong Israel, because emigration from Europe had declined to a trickle. Six million Jews had been killed in the holocaust and the Soviet Union did not permit emigration. Nevertheless these Arab rulers did all in their power to facilitate Jewish immigration to Israel.

Jews in Arab lands were compelled to leave their cities and villages in which their forefathers had lived for 2000 to 2500 years. Jews had resided in Yemen ever since the First Temple. The Jews of Iraq were the descendants of a large and flourishing Jewish community that had existed in the time of the Second Temple and thereafter. It had made great contributions to the crystallization of a unique Jewish culture and spirit. Jews had played a prominent economic and even military role in the history of Iraq. The Jews of North Africa settled along the Mediterranean shore from Egypt to Marocco a thousand years before the Arab conquest. After the conquest Jews made notable contributions to the Arab economy, language and culture, until their land came under Ottoman sway. Despite such a history, the Jews in Arab lands were forced to leave in an almost destitute condition. Their property was confiscated in retaliation for the confiscation by Israel of absentee property.

How many Jews were there in Arab countries in 1948? How many remained after 1974?

In a study made by the World Organization of Jews from Arab countries the number of Jews in Arab lands in 1948 is given as follows:[27]

Country	Estimated Number of Jews in 1948	Immigrants to Israel May 15, 1948 to 1972
Morocco	265,000 ⎤	
Algeria	140,000 ⎬	330,833*
Tunisia	105,000 ⎦	
Libya	38,000	35,666
Egypt	75,000	29,325
Iraq	135,000	129,292
Syria	30,000 ⎤	10,402*
Lebanon	5,000 ⎦	
Yemen	55,000 ⎤	50,552*
Aden	8,000 ⎦	
TOTAL	856,000	586,070

Except for Morocco, there remained only 10,000 Jews in all the Arab countries in 1974. In Morocco the Jewish population that year was 25,000. Those who had not immigrated to Israel left for Europe and the Americas.

To sum up, implacable Arab antagonism to Zionism and the estblishment of a national home for the persecuted Jewish people brought about the partition of the country. It was also the cause of the war that the Arabs imposed on the newly-risen State of Israel. The war bequeathed a refugee problem to both parties: 627,000 to 633,000 Arab refugees in 1948 (in 1967 another 100,000 were added by the Six-Day War), as opposed to the 820,000 Jewish refugees, of whom 586,000 were absorbed in the State of Israel.

* In registering immigrants, the figures for these countries were combined.

Some of the Arab refugees, mainly the wealthy and the educated, were absorbed in the various Arab countries. Another portion were absorbed and rehabilitated in Jordan, where they were settled in new villages and new urban districts and given full civil rights. Their number is unknown, because the absorption and the rehabilitation of refugees is defined in the Arab lexicon as "treason." A large number returned to Israel in accordance with the policy of uniting families.

The refugees who lived in the area conquered by Israel in 1967 are being rehabilitated. Israel expended 120 million dollars on their absorption and housing.[28] Hundreds of thousands of refugees are still in camps. (Again, statistics are not published lest they contradict the exaggerated figures used by Arab propagandists.) While the Arab States have contributed huge sums to the terror organizations, they do less than nothing to absorb refugees or to rescue them from a life of shiftless penury and dependence on the bounty of UNRWA.

The Jewish refugees absorbed by Israel built villages and towns. They found their place in agriculture, industry, commerce, the free professions – in the entire spectrum of the economy of the State of Israel. Their absorption in the social fabric of Israel's society is a complicated matter. They are beginning to leave their impress on the national institutions and their leadership, as well as in the municipal arena. Their involvement in education, in the universities, in the Army, in the intellectual and artistic life of Israel is part of a drawn-out process. Progress, crises, impatience on the part of the newcomers, and anxious attempts to speed-up their absorption on the part of the veterans are all part of this process.

Nevertheless, the State of Israel and its society have clearly taken full responsibility for the complete absorption of those who came from Arab countries. Such is the content and the essence of Zionism.

CHAPTER FOURTEEN

THE SUMMING UP

The birth of modern Jewish settlement in Palestine and of political Zionism occurred during a period characterized by fierce competition between the Powers in establishing colonial rule in Africa and Asia. It was a time when movements of national liberation germinated and became powerful among the oppressed peoples of Europe. The first signs of a similar phenomenon began to appear in Asia and Africa. The goal was to be rid of foreign oppressors and to achieve independence.

The movements for national and social liberation in Europe had a considerable effect on political Zionism, though there were major differences in method. The peoples of Europe resided in their national homelands and constituted cohesive social units, while the Jews were scattered throughout the world. Consequently the methods and tactics that served the other nations well in their struggle for independence were inapplicable in the case of the Jews. Their movement of national liberation, Zionism, perforce had a different agenda.

The dream of a sovereign Jewish nation on its own land seemed unattainable. In order to realize that dream the Jewish masses would have to be motivated to migrate to Palestine, to establish a national economy, to create new social and cultural patterns, and to revive an ancient language – in short, to build a nation from the very foundations. Clearly it would take limitless effort before one could think of national independence and sovereignty.

Even though from the geographical aspect Palestine was accessible to the Jewish immigrant, such was not the case in a juridical and political sense. The crumbling Ottoman Empire ruled the country; the imperialist powers plotted to divide Palestine among themselves; it contained an Arab population, even though sparse; Arab nationalism had already appeared on the horizon.

The Zionist movement sought permission from the Turkish authorities to build a national home in Palestine, and turned to the

278

European powers to assist it in achieving its goal. The movements for national liberation, even the socialist ones, were hostile. They regarded the Zionist efforts as supporting the designs of the imperialist and colonial powers for dismembering the Ottoman Empire.

In part this evaluation resulted from a lack of understanding of the situation of the Jewish people at the end of nineteenth and at the beginning of the twentieth centuries. They could not grasp the complex concept of a dispersed people, driven by national and religious yearnings and by the sufferings under the yoke of social and economic disabilities. The choice of Palestine as the national home of the Jews was not made by chance, nor were the considerations of a pragmatic nature – not because the Ottoman Empire was weak and it might be possible to carve out a territory out of the domains under its control by purchase or by an act of conquest, carried out independently or in concert with one of the Great Powers. The historical connection of the Jewish People with the land of Israel has been one of the crucial elements in its survival as a nation. The Jews in exile regarded the Return as the core of their religious and national aspirations, even though they had been cut off from the land for many generations. Throughout history there had been a Jewish community in Palestine, however small, however poor. Above all, the Jewish people at the end of the nineteenth century and at the beginning of the twentieth needed a territory of its own in order to solve the acute political, social, and economic problems that beset it. The need became acute during the period between the two World Wars. Countries that had been open to immigration closed their portals to Jews. The Nazis came to power, first in Germany, and then, during World War II, in many countries in Europe. The Germans and their allies murdered millions of Jews, For the survivors there was no place in ruined Europe. Some of the socialist movements changed their attitude to Zionism, but the more "leftist" elements continued and continue to brand Zionism as a colonialist movement.

The existence of a liberation movement is not, however, dependent on evaluations by outsiders, who are hostile for reasons of self-interest, or for lack of understanding. A nation's right to

279

exist flows from the historical necessity for the realization of its aspirations. Its moral justification may be tested by the kind of means the nation adopts to achieve its goal. The means employed by the Zionist movement were the antithesis of colonialism. The economic aims of colonialism (not to mention its strategic goals) were to seize control of the resources of the conquered country, of its best agricultural land, of its water sources, and of its mineral wealth. Colonialism sought to exploit these resources by using cheap native labor and funneling the profits to the homeland. Alternatively it established a ruling elite that lived a life of luxury at the expense of the enslaved people.

Zionists did not come to Palestine to rule over its inhabitants. They aspired to settle and work the land that they had bought by themselves. They paid the full price for the land they bought, nor did they buy only high quality land. Very often they bought poor land, ameliorated and cultivated it, raised its productivity, and derived their livelihood from their labor. Those who embodied the Zionist ideal sought to create a new type of society and of a national economy, where Jews would engage in all types of labor, from the meanest to the most exalted, without exploiting anyone.

During the thirty-year period of the British Mandate Zionism was constantly opposed by the Arab political leadership in Palestine. The Arabs argued that the Mandate contradicted the Covenant of the League of Nations which promised the right of self-determination to all peoples. Moreover, the Balfour Declaration and the Mandate were self-contradictory on internal evidence: The promise to safeguard the rights of the inhabitants makes the establishment of a National Home for the Jews impossible. The very presence of the Zionist venture threatens the existence of the Arabs in the country.

The Arab political struggle was attended by attacks on Jewish settlements and rebellions against British rule. The Arabs wished to prove that they were able to prevent the Zionist aims from becoming reality, and could also impair the Government's stability. These violent steps brought in their wake British commissions of inquiry. Most of them recommended that the Arabs be appeased, and that limitations be imposed on the Zionist undertaking. The

280

Zionists fought back politically by marshalling world opinion and calling upon Jews everywhere for assistance. In many instances they succeeded in abrogating hostile edicts. Simultaneously the Zionists expended considerable effort and resources on economic development. They regarded this area of endeavor as the true base for success in the ongoing political conflict.

The Arabs viewed with apprehension the increase in Jewish population from 10% of the general population at the beginning of the Mandate to 30% fifteen years later.

The entrenchment of Nazi rule in Europe and the Italian victory in Ethiopia gave the Arab world hope that British and French influence could be eliminated from the Middle East. A zealous Moslem group, that had committed acts of terror against Jews in 1935, began to incite the Arab masses against the Jews. On April 19, 1936 riots broke out against Jews in Jaffa and soon spread to all parts of the country. At that point the Palestinian Arabs were leaderless in a political sense because of internal squabbling. When the riots broke out the Arabs united and established the Arab Higher Committee which assumed the leadership of the Arab struggle and proclaimed a general strike of the entire Arab community. It threatened to continue the strike indefinitely until the Government would proscribe Jewish immigration and the right of Jews to acquire land. Arab attacks were aimed against the Jewish settlements and against the British rule as well.

The strike lasted six months. It ended with the promise of the British Government to send a committee of inquiry (a Royal Commission) to investigate the causes of the disturbances and to suggest solutions to the problems. The Commission, headed by Lord Peel, claimed that it could not reconcile the contradictory commitments of the Mandate. On the one hand the Mandate undertook to safeguard the rights of the Arabs in the country and on the other – to foster the establishment of a Jewish National Home. Therefore it concluded that the Mandate could not be carried out and recommended that Palestine be partitioned into two states, Jewish and Arab. According to this proposal the Jewish State was to get something less than 20% of the total land area. A small enclave stretching from Jaffa to Jerusalem was to be reserved for British rule, and the balance was to be awarded to the Arabs.

The Arabs opposed the proposal violently and renewed the rebellion against the British and the attacks on Jewish settlements. The Jews as well were not ready to accept the proposal as stated. Yet the shadow of an approaching world war induced the Zionist leadership to enter into negotiations for the establishment of a Jewish State in a part of Palestine, but with wider boundaries than those suggested by the Commission.

The continuing Arab attacks on Jewish settlements and the growing conviction that the British were planning to repudiate their obligations under the Mandate moved the Jewish political leaders to adopt a settlement policy that incorporated both strategic and political elements. From this time on land acquisition and settlement were to be directed to the creation of territorial continuity between the settlements. The intent of this policy was to protect Jews against Arab attacks and also to demarcate unofficially the boundaries of the future State.

The Arab claim that the development of the Jewish national home caused the displacement and uprooting of the Arabs is unfounded. Convincing evidence for this conclusion may be found in a survery made of the Arab community when the Mandate was coming to an end, just prior to the crucial years 1947–1949. At this time the Jewish community had increased to 630,000 souls and constituted 30% of the general population. But the relative size of the Jewish population to the Arab had remained almost unchanged since 1936, despite the stream of legal and illegal Jewish immigrants. The reason for this state of affairs was twofold: a) The natural increase of the Arabs was much higher than that of the Jews; b) during the period of the Mandate the country had absorbed 100,000 legal and illegal Arab immigrants and their offspring.

The Arab economy developed far beyond that of the neighboring countries; the standard of living rose; the birth rate and life expectancy increased. Government health and educational institutions, which served the Arab population primarily, expanded. They were supported by tax money, 70% of which was paid by Jews. Most of the employees of the Government, the police, the courts, the railway and the public works were Arabs. The status of the Palestinian Arab was strong and secure. The Jewish National Home did not displace or uproot the Arab population. To the contrary – it accelerated the rate of progress of those Arabs who maintained a symbiotic relationship with their Jewish neighbors. The Arabs who had no contact with Jews enjoyed a slower rate of development.

The Palestinian Arabs started a war against the Jewish community as it was about to declare its independence. After the declaration of independence the neighboring Arab nations joined in the conflict. The Jews fought against forces superior to them in men and arms. They fought for the physical survival of every Jew in a community that was threatened with extermination. In no lesser degree was it a struggle for the absorption of displaced and persecuted Jews unwanted elsewhere in the world. The motivation of the Arabs to fight was weakened by the conflicting interests of the participating nations. A large part of the Arab civilian population was deluded into believing that it was in its interest to withdraw from the areas of conflict and in this way to enable the Arab armies to wipe out the Jews. They hoped to fall heir to the property of the defeated Jews. At a later stage, when they learned of the defeat of the Arab armies by Zahal, they fled for their lives. In some instances they were evacuated by the advancing Israeli forces, to avoid leaving a hostile population in the rear.

When the war ended, more than 600,000 Arabs were found to have fled or been displaced. They left behind a great deal of property – agricultural lands, urban quarters and abandoned villages. The defeated Arab countries compelled their Jewish citizens, by direct or indirect means, to emigrate from their countries of residence. From among the 850,000 Jews, who had lived in those countries for hundreds of years, and in some instances for more than two thousand years, about 600,000 immigrated to Israel, the rest to other countries. In the Arab world today there remains a small Jewish community in Morocco, and there are a few thousand Jews who live in terror in Syria and Iraq. These serve as hostages for political blackmail against Israel. The Jewish refugees left all their property in their countries of origin.

Israel absorbed them into its economy and society, and is still engaged in trying to integrate them and their children fully into the mosaic of the country. The Arab nations that made war on Israel and encouraged the Palestinian Arabs to reject adamantly all offers of compromise continue to refuse to assume responsibility for the Arab refugees. Apart from Jordan that did make an effort to resettle some of them, all the other Arab countries refuse citizenship and rehabilitation to their unfortunate compatriots.

Zionism as a movement for the renaissance and liberation of the Jewish people sought to achieve its goal by constructive deeds. As a matter of last resort the Jews took to arms to defend their very lives. It may not be too late for the model of constructive deeds to serve as a guide to a better life for the two peoples fated to live in one land.

SOURCES

A. Archives

I. Israel State Archive (ISA)
—— Files of Public Record Office, Colonial Office (PRO, CO 733)
—— Record Group 2, Chief Secretary's Office of Palestine Government (RG2 CSO).
—— Record Group 22, Files of Land Registry Department of Palestine Government (RG22 LRD).

II. Central Zionist Archives (CZA).
—— KKL2, Head Office of Jewish National Fund, Cologne – The Hague, 1907–1922.
—— KKL3, The Palestine Office, the Committee for the Jewish National Fund, Jaffa, Tel-Aviv and Jerusalem, 1908–1922.
—— KKL5, Jewish National Fund Head Office, Jerusalem, 1922–1947.
—— S25, Files of the Political Department of the Zionist Organization and the Jewish Agency for Palestine, 1921–1948.
—— J15, Files of the I.C.A. - P.I.C.A. (including the settlement agencies preceding them in Haifa, Jaffa and Jerusalem and other places), 1885–1950.
—— L18, Files of the Palestine Land Development Company 1908–1924.
—— A238, Archives of Joshua Hankin.

III. Archives of the Jewish National Fund (AKKL).
IV. Archives of "Beit Hashomer," Zahal Museum at Kefar Gil'adi (ABH).
V. Other Archives listed in full in the notes.

B. Government Publications, Reports and Memoranda

Great Britain, Colonial Office Report on the Administration of Palestine and Trans-Jordan for the Year 1920 (London 1921); Idem for the Year 1930 (London 1931).
Palestine, Commission on the Disturbances of August 1929, Minutes of Evidence, London 1930, Vol. I/II.
Great Britain, C.O. Report of the Commission on the Palestine Disturbances of August 1929 (Shaw Commission Report, London, 1930).
Great Britain, C.O. Palestine: Report on Immigration, Land Settlement and Development, by John Hope Simpson (London 1930).
Great Britain, C.O. Palestine: Statement of Policy by His Majesty's Government in the United Kingdom (the 1930 White Paper, London, 1930).
Palestine, Report on Agricultural Development and Land Settlement in Palestine, by Lewis French (December 1931, Supplementary Report April, 1932).
Palestine, Royal Commission – Memoranda Submitted by the Government of Palestine (1937).
Palestine, Royal Commission, Minutes of Evidence, Heard at Public Sessions, London, 1937.
Palestine, Labour's Case before the Royal Commission, London, 1937.
Great Britain, C.O., Palestine Royal Commission Report (London, 1937, Cmd. 3692).
Great Britain, C.O., Palestine, Statement of Policy by H.M. Government (the 1939 White Paper, London, Cmd. 6019).

285

Palestine, Report by H.M. Government to the Council of the League of Nations on the Administration of Palestine and Trans-Jordan for the Year 1930 (London, 1931); Idem for the Year 1935 (London, 1936).

Palestine, Department of Agriculture, Forests and Fisheries. Annual Report for the Year 1945/46.

Palestine, A. Survey of Palestine. Prepared in December 1945 and January 1946 for the Information of the Anglo-American Committee of Inquiry, Vol. I/II/III.

Palestine, Notes Compiled for the U.N.S.C.O.P., June 1947.

Palestine, Office of Statistics. Statistical Abstract of Palestine, 1936; Idem for the Years 1943, 1945.

Palestine, Office of Statistics, Bulletin of Current Statistics, 1936; Idem for the Year 1947.

Palestine, Office of Statistics, Census of Palestine, 1931, Report by E. Mills, Vol. I/II.

Memorandum Submitted to H.M. Government by the Jewish Agency for Palestine. May 1930.

Memorandum Submitted to the Royal Commission on Behalf of the Jewish Agency for Palestine, 1936.

Memorandum Submitted by the Jewish Agency on the Reports of Lewis French on Agricultural Development and Land Settlement in Palestine, 1933.

Memorandum on the Influence of Jewish Colonization on the Arab Development in Palestine. Submitted to the Anglo-American Committee of Inquiry by the Jewish Agency. 1946.

The Jewish Plan for Palestine, Memoranda and Statements. Presented by the Jewish Agency for Palestine to the U.N.S.C.O.P., Jerusalem, 1947.

Memorandum on the Palestine White Paper of October 1930 by the Arab Executive Committee, December, 1930.

Palestine, Department of Agriculture, Forests and Fisheries. Annual Report for the Year 1947.

Annual Report of the Director of the U.N., Relief and Work Agency for Palestine Refugees in the Near East, Covering the Period of 1 July 1951 to 30 June 1952.

—— הרצאת הנציב העליון של ממשלת פלשתינה (א״י) בשנת 1920–1925, ירושלים 1925.
—— תזכיר הוועד הערבי העליון לוועדת U.N.S.C.O.P.

C. Books and Articles (Hebrew)

שאול אוביגור, עם העולים לחניתה, מתוך: עם דור ההגנה, חלק ב׳ מערכות, תשל״ח.

ז. אברמוביץ וי. גלפט, המשק הערבי בארץ ישראל וארצות המזרח התיכון. הקיבוץ המאוחד תש״ד.

אהרן אהרונסון, ״הווידוי״, מתוך: תולדותיה של העזה מדינית, אליעזר לבנה (עורך), שוקן תשכ״א.

מנחם אוסישקין, דברים אחרונים, הלשכה המרכזית של הקהק״ל, ירושלים תשי״ז.

ספר אוסישקין ליובל השבעים, ירושלים תרצ״ד.

אוסישקין באגרותיו, שלום שוורץ (עורך), ראובן מס תשי״א.

אחד העם, כל כתבי, דביר תש״י.

עקיבא אטינגר, עם חקלאים עברים בארצנו, עם עובד תש״ה.

רבקה אלפר, קורות משפחה אחת, ניומן, ירושלים תשכ״ז.

מיכאל אסף, היחסים בין ערבים ויהודים בארץ ישראל, 1860–1948, תרבות וחינוך 1970.

—— התעוררות הערבים בארץ ישראל ובריחתם, תרבות וחינוך 1967.

—— תולדות הערבים בארץ ישראל, הערבים תחת שלטון הצלבנים, הממלוכים והתורכים, דביר ומוסד ביאליק תש״א.

חיים ארלוזורוב, יומן מדיני, מפא״י (בלי ציון שנת ההוצאה).

יובל ארנון, פלאחים במרד הערבי בארץ ישראל, האוניברסיטה העברית ירושלים, (סטנסיל).

ארץ כנרות, ש. ייבין וח.ז. הרשברג (עורכים), קו לקו תשי״א.

עמינדב אשבל, ששים שנות הכשרת הישוב, חברת הכשרת הישוב, ירושלים תש״ל.

—— הכשרת הישוב, פרשיות ומפעלים בערי הארץ, חברת הכשרת הישוב, ירושלים תשל״ו.

אלכס ביין, תולדות ההתישבות הציונית, מסדה תש״ה.

יהושע בן־אריה, עיר בראי תקופה. יד יצחק בן־צבי, ירושלים תשל״ז.

דוד בן־גוריון, פגישות עם מנהיגים ערבים, עם עובד וקרן הנגב, 1975.

יוסף ברסלבסקי, הידעת את הארץ, הקיבוץ המאוחד תשט״ז.

יוסף ברץ, כפר על גדות הירדן, גדיש, תשי״ט.

אסף גור, פירות ארץ־ישראל, תולדות ומקורות, הקיבוץ המאוחד 1974.

אברהם גרנות (גרנובסקי), המשטר הקרקעי בארץ ישראל, דביר תש״ט.

—— נתיבות ומפלסים, דביר תשי״ב.

—— הקרקע והבנין בארץ ישראל, הקה״ל, 1935.

החצר והגבעה, סיפורה של קבוצת כנרת, ברכה חבס (עורכת), עם עובד 1968.

דוד הכהן, עת לספר. עם עובד, תשל״ד.

יעקב הרוזן, ארץ ירדן וחרמונים, טברסקי תשט״ז.

חזון ההתנחלות בגליל, מוסד הרב קוק, ירושלים תשל״א.

קובץ השומר, ארכיון העבודה.

יוסף ואשיץ, הערבים בארץ ישראל, ספריית פועלים 1947

יוסף ויץ, התנחלותנו בתקופת הסער, ספרית פועלים 1947.

—— יומני, ו׳ כרכים, מסדה תשכ״ה.

—— מגמדא לרוחא, מסדה 1972.

—— פירות, חלק ג׳ ממגילת האדמה, הקהק״ל, ירושלים תשי״ב.

זאב וילנאי, חיפה בעבר ובהווה, החברה העברית לחקירת א״י ועתיקותיה חיפה, תל־אביב תרצ״ו.

חברות בקיבוץ, לילית בסביין, יוכבד בת רחל, מ. פוזננסקי, מ. שחורי (כינוס ועריכה), הקיבוץ המאוחד
תש״ד.

אליעזר טרופה, יסודות לתולדות פתח־תקוה, תש״ט.

ש. טולקובסקי, תולדות יפו, דביר תרפ״ו.

זכרונות ארץ־ישראל. אברהם יערי (עורך), ההסתדרות הציונית, ירושלים תש״ז.

אלכס כרמל, התושבים הגרמנים בשלהי התקופה העות׳מנית, האוניברסיטה העברית ירושלים, תשכ״ג.

—— תולדות חיפה בימי התורכים, המכון האוניברסיטאי חיפה, תשכ״ט.

אהרן כהן, העולם הערבי של ימינו, ספריית פועלים 1958

כתבים לתולדות חיבת ציון וישוב ארץ־ישראל, א. דרויאנוב (עורך), אודיסה תרע״ט, אודיסה תרפ״ח – תל־אביב,
תרפ״ה.

ריכרד ליכטהים, שאר ישוב, תל־אביב תשי״ד.

מערבו של הגליל, החוג האזורי לידיעת הארץ, 1961.

ק. נברצקי, המנדט ומשק הארץ, ספרית פועלים 1946.

צבי נדב, בימי שמירה והגנה, מערכות 1954.

—— כך התחלנו, הקיבוץ המאוחד תשי״ז.

יוסף נחמני איש הגליל, מסדה תשכ״ט.

דב ניר, איזור בית־שאן, הקיבוץ המאוחד תשכ״ב.

משה סמילנסקי, משוט בארץ, דביר תשי״ג.

—— משפחת האדמה, עם עובד תש״ד.

—— נס ציונה, המועצה המקומית, 1953.

—— פרקים בתולדות הישוב, דביר תש״ח.

יהושע פורת, צמיחת התנועה הלאומית הערבית הפלסטינאית 1918–1929, עם עובד 1976.

סעדיה פז, זכרונות, חיפה, תשל״ג.

יהודה קרמון, גיאוגרפיה של הארץ ואזוריה, יבנה 1973.

—— עמק החולה הצפוני, האוניברסיטה העברית ירושלים, תשט״ז.

287

יעקב שמעוני, ערבי ארץ ישראל, עם עובד תש"ז.

משה שרת, יומן מדיני, עם עובד והספריה הציונית, כרך א', 1968.

ספר תולדות ההגנה, עורכים: בן ציון די־נור, שאול אביגור, יצחק בן־צבי, אלעזר גלילי, ישראל גלילי,
יהודה סלוצקי: כרכים א ו־ב בהוצ. מערכות, כרך ג בהוצ. עם עובד.

D. Hebrew Translations of Books and Articles.

לורנס אוליפנט, חיפה, מאנגלית יאיר בורלא, יד יצחק בן־צבי ובית ההוצאה כנען, ירושלים תשל"ו.

בעיני אויב, שלושה פרסומים ערביים על מלחמת הקוממיות, תרגם סרן ש׳ סבג, מערכות 1955.

מרטין גילברט, יהודי ארצות ערב, ההיסטוריה שלהם במפות ההתאחדות העולמית של יהודים יוצאי
ארצות ערב, 1975 (לא צוין שם המתרגם).

אלבר ממי, יהודים וערבים, תרגום אהרן אמיר, ספרית פועלים 1975.

עָארֶף אל־עָארֶף, שבטי הבדוים במחוז באר־שבע, מערבית מ. קפליוק, בוסתנאי, (ללא ציון שנת
ההוצאה).

—— תולדות באר־שבע ושבטיה, מערבית מ. קפליוק, תל־אביב תרצ"ז.

ארתור רופין, פרקי חיי, מגרמנית א.ד. שפיר, עם עובד 1968.

בית בין גבולות, 30 שנה להתחלות קיבוץ דן, ערך צ. גולדברג,

עבר הדני, ההתישבות בגליל התחתון, חמישים שנות קורותיה, מסדה.

בגליל העליון, יומן ישוב ספר, מ. בן־יצחק. ועד הגוש לגליל העליון.

גנוסר, 15 שנה להיוסדה, 1949.

גניגר, כ"ה שנים.

אריה ססמונוב, זכרון־יעקב – פרשת דברי ימיה. תרמ"ב־תש"ב.

עבר הדני, חדרה, שישים שנות קורותיה, מסדה תשי"א.

עשרים שנה לקיבוץ חצרים, 1966.

כפר־סבא, 70 שנה לייסדה, 80 שנה לגאולת אדמתה, ערך שלמה אנגל, 1963.

כרכור, תרע"ג־תשכ"ח, ערך עבר הדני, הוצ. אחוזה א לונדון־כרכור.

נחשוני החולה, תולדות יסוד־מעלה 1883–1958, עורכים: א׳ חריזמן ויהודה גרינגר, תש"יח.

עין המפרץ, 30 שנה לעליה על הקרקע, תשט"ז.

עין־חרוד, פרקי יובל, עורכים זרבבל גלעד ונריה ציזלינג, הקיבוץ המאוחד ועין־חרוד, תשל"ג.

פלמחים, יומן קבוצת הצופים, 1.7.1949.

ג. קרסל, אם המושבות פתח־תקוה תרל"ח־תשי"ב, עירית פתח־תקוה תשי"ג.

ראשון לציון – תרמ"ב – תשי"א, עורך דוד יחלביץ, 1951.

משה סמילנסקי, רחובות שישים שנות חייה, דביר תשי"א.

שריד, 20 שנה לקיומה, 1946.

עלון לסטטיסטיקה ואינפורמציה מקצועית של ההסתדרות, חוברת 4, יוני 1947.

סיכומים מטעם המחלקה לסטטיסטיקה ואינפורמציה של ההסתדרות, ספטמבר 1930.

288

E. Books and Articles in English and Other Languages.

Antonius, George, *The Arab Awakening*, Capricorn Press, New York, 1965.

Azouri, Naguib, *Le Reveil de la Nation Arabe dans l'Asie Turque*, Paris, 1905.

Bacchi, Roberto, *The Pupulation of Israel*, The Institute of Contemporary Jewry, Hebrew University, Demographic Center, Prime Minister's Office, 1977.

Baldensperger, Philip G., "The Immovable East," *Palestine Exploration Fund Quarterly*, London, 1917.

Ben-Arieh, Joshua, "The Population of the Large Towns during the Eighty Years of the Nineteenth Century, According to Western Studies," from *Studies on Palestine During the Ottoman Period*, ed. Moshe Maoz, Jerusalem, 1975.

Cnaan, T. *Conflict in the Land of Peace*, Jerusalem, 1936.

Collins, Larry and Lapierre, Dominique, *O Jerusalem*, New York, 1973.

Conder, C.R., *Tentwork in Palestine*, London, 1879.

Finn, James, *Stirring Times*, London, 1878.

Macalister, R.A. Steward, "Occasional Papers on Modern Inhabitants of Palestine", *P.E.F.Q.*, 1906.

Mandel, Neville J., *The Arabs and Zionism before World War I*, University of California Press, 1976.

P.E.F.Q. Statement, Vols. 1917–1971.

Porath, Y., *The Palestine Arab National Movement, 1929–1939*, London, 1977.

Prittie, Terence and Dinnen, Bernard, *The Double Exodus*, London, 1974.

Robinson, E., and Smith, E., *Biblical Researches in Palestine, Sinai and Arabea Petraea*, Volume 3, Boston, 1841.

Roumani, Maurice M. with Deborah Goldman and Helene Korn, *The Case of Jews from Arab Countries – a Neglected Issue*, World Organization of Jews from Arab Countries, 1975.

Ruppin, A., *Syrien als Wirtschaftsgebiet*, Berlin, 1917.

—— *Three Decades of Palestine*, Jerusalem, 1936.

Saboy, M., *L'Empire Egyptien sous Mohamed Ali et la Question d'Orient*, Paris, 1930.

Stanley, A.P., *Sinai and Palestine*, London, 1887.

Syrkin, Marie, "The Palestine Refugees," from *Israel, The Arabs, and The Middle East*, ed. Irving Howe and Carl Gershman, New York, 1972.

Tristram, H.B.,*The Land of Israel*, 3rd ed., London, 1876.

Van De Velde, C.W., *Reise durch Syrien und Palästina*, Gotha, 1861.

F. Commemorative Volumes and Internal Publications of Communities and Public Institutions.

בית בין גבולות, 30 שנה להתחלות קיבוץ דן, ערך צ. גולדברג,

עבר הדני, ההתישבות בגליל התחתון, חמישים שנות קורותיה, מסדה.

בגליל העליון, יומן ישוב ספר, מ. בן־יצחק. ועד הגוש לגליל העליון.

גנוסר, 15 שנה להיווסדה, 1949.

גניגר, כ"ה שנים.

אריה סמסונוב, זכרון־יעקב – פרשת דברי ימיה. תרמ"ב־תש"ב.

עבר הדני, חדרה, שישים שנות קורותיה, מסדה תשי"א.

עשרים שנה לקיבוץ חצרים, 1966.

כפר־סבא, 70 שנה לייסודה, 80 שנה לגאולת אדמתה, ערך שלמה אנגל, 1963.

כרכור, תרע"ג־תשכ"ח, ערך עבר הדני, הוצ. אחוזה א לונדון־כרכור.

נחשוני החולה, תולדות יסוד־מעלה 1883–1958, עורכים: א' חריזמן ויהודה גרינגר, תש"יח.

עין המפרץ, 30 שנה לעליה על הקרקע, תשט"ז.
עין־חרוד, פרקי יובל, עורכים זרבבל גלעד ונריה ציזלינג, הקיבוץ המאוחד ועין־חרוד, תשל"ג.
פלמחים, יומן קבוצת הצופים, 1.7.1949.
ג. קרסל, אם המושבות פתח־תקוה תרל"ח־תשי"ב, עירית פתח־תקוה תשי"ג.
ראשון לציון – תרמ"ב – תשי"א, עורך דוד יודלביץ, 1951.
משה סמילנסקי, רחובות שישים שנות חייה, דביר תשי"א.
שריד, 20 שנה לקיומה, 1946.
עלון לסטטיסטיקה ואינפורמציה מקצועית של ההסתדרות, חוברת 4, יוני 1947.
סיכומים מטעם המחלקה לסטטיסטיקה ואינפורמציה של ההסתדרות, ספטמבר 1930.

G. Periodicals
Davar, Palestine Labour Daily.
Plus Material in Hebrew.

H. Interviews:
Ashbel, Aminadav, August, 1972.
Ben-Ami, Oved, March 9, 1977.
Ben-Shemesh, Aaron, September 28, 1976.
Dannin, Aaron, May 12, 1976.

Halfon, Haim, September 28, 1975.
Hurwitz, Nahum, January 18, 1977.
Palmon, Joshua, October 26, 1976.
Repetur, Berl, September 29, 1975.
Weitz, Joseph, August, 1972.

NOTES

CHAPTER ONE

1. Bacchi, p.5
2. Ibid.
3. Ibid.
4. We have subtracted the nember of non-Arab Christians from the total number of Christians in accordance with two data: a.) The 1931 census (Vol 2, p. 235) lists 18,092 non-Arab Christians. b.) For the year 1947, Bacchi *(The Population of Israel,* p. 398) gives the number of non-Arab Christians as 30,000.
5. Sabry, p.191
6. קרמון, גיאוגרפיה של הארץ ואזוריה, עמ' 179
6. ברסלבסקי, כרך ר', עמ' 360
8. Tristram, p. 495
9. שמעוני, עמ' 106
10. Ibid.
11. ויץ, פירות, עמ' 111
12. נדב, בימי שמירה והגנה, עמ' 51
13. טולקובסקי, עמ' 131
14. טרופה, עמ' 6
15. *P.E.F.Q.,* 1893, p.314
16. Interview with Joshua Palmon
17. Interview with Mohammed Masrawa, an attorney residing in Kafer Qar'a, a member of an Egyptian family, which has preserved a genelogical tree going back one hundred and fifty years.
18. The telephone directories of the cities in Judea and Samaria include hundreds of entries under the name Misri. In the Nablus directory alone we found more than seventy names pointing to Egyptian origins.
19. אלפר, עמ' 20
20. CZA, KKL 5/Box 1346/ File KM/1433
21. עבר הדני, חדרה, עמ' 109
22. נדב, כך התחלנו, עמ' 218
23. עבר הדני, ההתישבות בגליל התחתון, עמ' 72
24. *P.E.F.Q.,* 1893, p.13
25. שמעוני, עמ' 106
26. עבר הדני, ההתישבות בגליל התחתון, עמ' 37
27. Tristram, p. 590
28. *P.E.F.Q.,* 1877, p.70
29. *P.E.F.Q.,* 1914, p. 170
30. שמעוני, עמ' 102
31. אוליפנט, עמ' 128

32. ספר תולדות ההגנה, כרך א', עמ' 208
33. Encyclopedia Judaica, Item "Jerusalem".
34. הרוזן, חזון ההתנחלות בגליל, עמ' 72
35. Finn, Volume 1,pp. 226-7
36. Ibid., p. 238
37. Macalister, *P.E.F.Q.,* 1906, p.40
38. Ibid., p. 45
39. Ibid, p.33
40. Ibid, p. 42
41. Finn. Vol. 1, p. 298
42. Tristram, p. 108
43. אוליפנט, עמ' 53
44. Finn, Vol. 1, p. 244
45. גרנות, המשטר הקרקעי, עמ' 65
46. Tristram, p. 482
47. Ibid.
48. *P.E.F.Q.,* 1972, p. 180
49. Conder, Vol. II, p. 112
50. *P.E.F.Q.,* 1878, p.11
51. Ibid., p.63
52. Ibid., p.13
53. Finn, Vol. I., p.265
54. עארף אל-עארף, באר-שבע ושבטיה, עמ' 166
55. Finn, Vol. I., p.315
56. *P.E.F.Q.,* 1877, p.114
57. Conder, Vol. I, p.172
58. עארף, אל-עראף, באר-שבע ושבטיה, עמ' 143
59. שם, עמ' 160
60. Ruppin, *Syrien als Wirtschaftsgebiet,* pp.14–15
61. Ibid., p.26
62. PRO CO 733/4 /File 3832/166
63. *P.E.F.Q.,* 1914, p.170
64. אברמוביץ-גלפט, עמ' 6
65. עבר הדני, חדרה, ע"ע 108–9
66. כרמל, חיפה, עמ' 149
67. Bacchi, p.375
68. Ibid., p.374
69. Ibid., p.36
70. טולקובסקי, עמ' 135
71. אסף, היחסים בין ערבים ויהודים, עמ' 131
72. כרמל, חיפה, עמ' 173
73. אהרנסון, עמ' 374
74. ספר תולדות ההגנה, כרך א' עמ' 644
75. וילנאי, עמ' 141
76. ארלוזורוב, עמ' 11
77. Interview with Berl Repetur, a member of the Labor and Immigration De-

partment of the Histadrut since its inception.

78. הכהן, עמ' 50
79. Bacchi, p.393
80. Palestine, Office of Current Statistics, 1936
81. Bacchi, p.393
82. Ibid.
83. Ibid., p.394
84. Memorandum to Royal Commission, Jewish Agency, p.109
85. ספר תולדות ההגנה, כרך ב', עמ' 633
86. Royal Commission Report, p.291
87. Survey for the Anglo-American Committee, pp. 212, 213, 221
88. נחמני, עמ' 242
89. Bacchi, p.389
90. Palestine, Office of Statistics, Bulletin 1947
91. Palestine, Office of Statistics, Census 1931, Vol.II, p.130
92. ספר תולדות ההגנה, כרך ב', עמ' 451
93. שם, עמ' 654
94. שם, עמ' 658
95. שם, עמ' 284

CHAPTER TWO

1. אסף, תולדות הערבים תחת הצלבנים הממלוכים והתורכים עמ' 301
2. P.E.F.Q., 1873, p.150
3. Ben-Arieh, p.69
4. Robinson-Smith, Vol. III, p.174
5. Tristram, pp.579–580
6. הרווזן, חזון ההתנחלות בגליל, עמ' 238
7. קרמון, עמק החולה הצפוני, ע"ע 63, 73, 78
8. יוסף בן מתיתיהו, תולדות מלחמת היהודים, עמ' 215
9. Tristram, p.413
10. גנוסר, עמ' 17
11. שם, שם.
12. P.E.F. Map of Western Palestine, Sheet VI
13. ארץ כנרות, מאמרו של ד. עמירם, עמ' 18
14. החצר והגבעה, ע"ע 8–23
15. ניר, עמ' 113
16. Tristram, pp.490-1, 494–5
17. Royal Commission Report, p.259
18. ויץ, מגמדא לרוחא, עמ' 89
19. שם, עמ' 91
20. הרצאת הנציב העליון, עמ' 21
21. Tristram, pp.113, 123
22. עין חרוד, רשימתו של יהודה אלמוג, עמ' 41
23. שם, מיכאל אודם, עמ' 32

24. שם, חיים שטורמן, עמ' 26
25. אטינגר, עמ' 136
26. אוליפנט, עמ' 64
27. Tristram, pp.87–88
28. ויץ, מגמדא לרוחא, עמ' 76
29. פז, עמ' 188
30. עין המפרץ, עמ' 4
31. מערבו של הגליל, עמ' 74
32. Van de Velde, p. 240
33. סמסונוב, עמ' 58
34. אוליפנט, עמ' 4
35. ברץ, עמ' 25
36. P.E.F.Q., 1874, p.12
37. P.E.F.Q., 1887, pp.78–80
38. עבר הדני, חדרה, עמ' 59
39. שם, עמ' 60
40. שם, עמ' 59
41. סמילנסקי, משוט בארץ, עמ' 35
42. ויץ, מגמדא לרוחא, עמ' 137
43. Van de Velde, p.157
44. P.E.F.Q., 1874, p.15
45. CZA, KKL3, File 44
46. סמילנסקי, פרקים בתולדות הישוב, עמ' 12
47. שם, ע"ע 14, 18
48. שם, עמ' 20
49. Royal Commission Report, p.234
50. Robinson-Smith, Vol. III., pp.286, 387
51. P.E.F.Q., 1872, p.86
52. Tristram, p.384
53. Ibid., p.135
54. P.E.F.Q., 1872, p.163
55. P.E.F.Q., 1877, p.122
56. סמילנסקי, משפחת האדמה, ע"ע 257–259
57. ראשון לציון, עמ' 18
58. זכרונות ארץ-ישראל, – חלק א', עמ' 408
59. סמילנסקי, משפחת האדמה, עמ' 270
60. P.E.F.Q., 1871, p.92
61. פלמחים, מספר 2
62. P.E.F.Q., 1878, p.12
63. Ibid., p.156
64. Ibid., p.166
65. P.E.F.Q., 1890, p.219
66. Ibid., p.175 f.
67. Van de Velde, p.258

CHAPTER THREE

1. Robinson-Smith, Vol. II, p.386
2. P.E.F.Q., 1891, p.99
3. אוליפנט, עמ' 126
4. P.E.F.Q., 1891, p.99
5. אוליפנט, עמ' 133
6. Royal Commission Report, p.263
7. עארף אל-עארף, הבדואים במחוז באר-שבע, עמ' 164

8. גרנות, המשטר הקרקעי, עמ' 91
9. Royal Commission Report, p.259
10. ארכיון יד בן־צבי, תעודה מס' 2
11. אטינגר, עמ' 164
12. Azouri, p.19
13. אוליפנט, עמ' 26
14. ויץ, התנחלותנו, עמ' 109
15. Interview with Oved Ben-Ami, one of the founders of Netanya.
16. גרנות, המשטר הקרקעי, עמ' 76
17. שם, עמ' 35
18. שם, שם
19. שמעוני, עמ' 40 ואילך; גרנות, המשטר הקרקעי, עמ' 123
20. צבי אילן, "דבר", 17/10/1975
21. סמילנסקי, פרקים בתולדות הישוב, חלק א', עמ' 12
22. "הצפירה" מס' 13, 1885
23. אוליפנט, עמ' 122
24. ברסלבסקי, חלק ב', עמ' 6
25. אסף, התעוררות הערבים, עמ' 37
26. ספר אוסישקין, עמ' 280
27. ששים שנות הכשרת הישוב, ע"ע 142–3
28. CZA S25/ File 6565/ 87/8919

CHAPTER FOUR

1. ביין, עמ' 10
   The author notes that the Baron invested a total of 1,600,000 pounds sterling in settlement, as against 87,000 pounds sterling invested by the Hovevei Zion.
2. ויץ, פירות, עמ' 12
3. Mandel, p.8
4. אלפר, עמ' 30
5. ספר תולדות ההגנה, כרך א', עמ' 75
6. P.E.F.Q., 1872, p.78
7. טרופה, עמ' 19
8. קרסל, עמ' 52
9. שם, עמ' 59
10. זכרונות ארץ־ישראל, חלק א', עמ' 249
11. אלעזר רוקח לפינסקר, כתבים לתולדות חיבת ציון, חלק א', עמ' 762
12. שם, עמ' 358
13. שם, עמ' 768
14. אסף, היחסים בין יהודים וערבים, עמ' 12
15. קרסל, עמ' 356
16. CZA J15/File 3285/584
17. ראשון־לציון, עמ' 30
18. CZA S25/File 7446
19. זכרונות ארץ ישראל, חלק א', עמ' 436 ואילך
20. CZA S25/File 7446
21. ראשון לציון, עמ' 172
22. ISA, RG2, CSO, L 163/37

23. סמילנסקי, נס ציונה, עמ' 18
24. CZA S25/File 7446
25. סמילנסקי, נס ציונה, עמ' 89
26. הרוזן, חזון ההתנחלות בגליל, עמ' 40
27. CZA S25/File 7446
28. אחד העם, עמ' 224
29. הרוזן, חזון ההתנחלות בגליל, עמ' 110
30. זכרונות ארץ־ישראל, חלק א', עמ' 510 ואילך
31. נחשוני החולה, עמ' 11
32. הרוזן, חזון ההתנחלות בגליל, עמ' 237
33. נחשוני החולה, עמ' 54
34. הרוזן, ארץ ירדן וחרמונים, עמ' 160
35. סמסונוב, עמ' 57
36. כתבים לתולדות חיבת ציון, כרך ב', ע"ע 123, 443
37. גרנות, המשטר הקרקעי, עמ' 70
38. ספר תולדות ההגנה, כרך א', עמ' 76
39. CZA A238/File 9/ 5/1800
40. P.E.F. Map, 1878, Sheet No. XIII
41. ספר תולדות ההגנה, כרך א', עמ' 98
42. סמילנסקי, רחובות, עמ' 31
43. שם, עמ' 32
44. סמילנסקי, משוט בארץ, עמ' 35
45. עבר הדני, חדרה, עמ' 59
46. שם, עמ' 109
47. שם, עמ' 184 ואילך
48. ספר תולדות ההגנה, כרך א', עמ' 230
49. שם, עמ' 66
50. CZA S25/File 7621
51. כפר סבא, עמ' 81, 270 ואילך
52. הרוזן, חזון ההתנחלות בגליל, עמ' 376 ואילך
53. השילוח, כרך י"ז, תרס"ז־ח, עמ' 193
54. אחד העם, עמ' 228
55. ספר תולדות ההגנה, כרך א' עמ' 691
56. שם, עמ' 109
57. שאיפותינו, חוברת ב', עמ' 54
58. ספר תולדות ההגנה, כרך א', עמ' 99 ואילך
59. גרנות, המשטר הקרקעי, עמ' 273
60. עבר הדני, ההתישבות בגליל התחתון, עמ' 18
61. David Ben-Gurion wrote about the Circassians as follows (Hashomer Anthology, p. 265): "Our neighbors from Kafer-Kamma, the Circassians who settled in Palestine at the invitation of the Turkish Government, enjoy special privileges. The Government favors and defends them above other sections of the population. Their sheikhs are appointed to do important tasks, and their families reach considerable influence with official circles."

62. עבר הדני, ההתישבות בגליל התחתון, עמ'
67 ואילך
63. CZA S25/File 7446
64. Mandel, p.22 (JCA 258/57)
65. שאיפותינו, חוברת ב', עמ' 53
66. Mandel, p.22 (JCA 262/No 56)
67. Ibid. (JCA 264/75)
68. שאיפותינו, עמ' 54
69. Mandel, p. 67 (JCA 255)
70. Ibid., p.68 (JCA 271/290)
71. עבר הדני, ההתישבות בגליל התחתון, עמ'
69:
Report of Shabtai Levi, land purchasing agent for the I.C.A.
72. CZA S25/File 7446
73. נדב, כך התחלנו, עמ' 231
74. קובץ השומר, "בכנרת", ש.ד. יפה, עמ'
251
75. נדב, כך התחלנו, עמ' 214
76. עבר הדני, ההתישבות בגליל התחתון, עמ'
70 ואילך
77. ברץ, עמ' 48
78. CZA J15/File 1646/ Exhibits 2, 8
79. ביין, עמ' 95
80. CZA J15/File 618/Exhibit 3
81. CZA S25/File 7446
82. Ibid.
83. גרנות, נתיבות ומפלסים, עמ' 18
84. CZA J15/File 106
85. Ibid.
86. ISA, RG2, CSO, L24/34 DHAI,
11,108
87. גרנות, המשטר הקרקעי, עמ' 107
88. CZA S25/File 7621/ 9663-1-1 AD
89. כרכור, עמ' 27
90. קובץ השומר, "בימי כיבוש", יגאל, עמ' 78
91. גרנות, המשטר הקרקעי, עמ' 273
92. CZA J15/File 622
Nine contracts approved by the Land
Registry in Tiberias.
93. Ibid, File 4174
94. Ibid, File 2754
95. Ibid, certifications by the Land Registry in Tiberias.
96. אחד העם, עמ' 24
97. Azouri, p.5
98. רופין, חלק ב', עמ' 123
99. CZA L18/File 275
100. פז, עמ' 57
101. CZA L18/File 275
102. Ibid.
103. Mandel, p.84
104. קובץ השומר, "בימי כיבוש", יגאל, עמ'
124
105. Mandel, p.104

106. פורת, עמ' 21
107. Mandel, 46 עמ' אסף, התעוררות הערבים,
p.85;
108. ליכטהיים, עמ' 192
109. Mandel, p. 183
110. פורת, עמ' 121

CHAPTER FIVE
1. פורת, עמ' 72
2. Ruppin, pp.182-3
3. CZA A238/File 1/M
4. CZA, KKL 3/File 53 B
5. Ibid.
6. Ibid.
7. Ibid.
8. CZA S25/File 6958
9. CZA, KKL 3/File 59
10. CZA S25/File 6958
11. CZA S25/File 6958/ Land File 22/14/32
of the Nablus District Court
12. CZA S25/File 6958
13. CZA KKL 3/File 59/ 6/18/17-9
14. Ibid., Document No. 6/18-12
15. CZA A238/File 16
16. פז, עמ' 178
17. Commission on the Disturbances, Vol.
II. p. 1110, Exhibit 129A.
18. Ibid., pp. 729 ff.
19. CZA A238/File 16
20. CZA S25/File 7621
21. Ibid.
22. Ibid.
23. CZA A238/File 16
24. Commission on the Disturbances, Vol.
II., p. 732 ff.
25. CZA S25/File 7621
26. CZA, KKL 5/Box 365/ Haifa Bay File
27. גרנות, הקרקע והבניך, עמ' 74
28. Royal Comission Report, p.68
29. רופין, חלק ב', עמ' 179
30. Commission on the Disturbances, Vol.
II., p. 1074, Exhibit 71.
31. Shaw Report, p.118
32. Ibid., p. 152 ff.
33. Ibid., p.121
34. רופין, חלק ג', עמ' 185
35. Memoradum, Jewish Agency, May
1930
36. Ibid., p.42
37. גרנות, הקרקע והבנין, עמ' 74
38. Simpson Report, p.65
39. Ibid., p.51
40. Memorandum, Jewish Agency, May
1930, p.43

294

41. Simpson Report, p.51
42. Ibid., p.116
43. Ibid.
44. Ibid., p.26
45. Ibid., p.24. The Geographical Review estimate was:
Hill Country   – 2,450,000 dunam
Valleys and Plains – 4,094,000 dunam
Total   6,544,000 dunam
1,500,000 dunam in the Beer-Sheba District were not taken into account.
46. Ibid., pp. 141 ff.
47. White Paper, October 1930
48. Ibid., p.116
49. Ibid., p.17
50. Ibid., p.18
51. Ibid.
52. Antonius, p.406
53. ארלוזורוב, עמ' 85
54. רופין, חלק ב', עמ' 126
55. CZA J15/File 3312
56. ויץ, פירות, עמ' 109
57. Ibid.
58. Ibid., p.113
59. AKKL/Files 311/315/Exhibits 69, 73-79
60. ISA, R G 22, LRO, G568/File 3522
61. Ibid.
62. Ibid.
63. Ibid.
64. Ibid.
65. ויץ, פירות, עמ' 118
66. ISA, R G22, LRO, G568/File 3522
67. Ibid.
68. Ibid., Document NL/4/910
69. Ibid., File 3522
70. PRO, CO 733, Vol. 190/File 77182/190/112
71. ויץ, פירות, עמ' 111
72. PRO, CO 733/ 190/File 77182/NL-4-911
73. ויץ, פירות, עמ' 123
74. PRO, CO 733/ 190/File 77182 /1077/2
75. Ibid., File 77182
76. AKKL, Files 311/315, Exhibit 76
77. ויץ, פירות, עמ' 126
78. Ibid., p.128
79. Shaw Report, p.119
80. ספר תולדות ההגנה, כרך ב', עמ' 455
81. ארלוזורוב, עמ' 133
82. AKKL, File 311/315, Exhibit 43. Interview was held with Dr. Ben-Shemesh concerning the incident.
83. PRO, CO 733/File 97082. High Commissioner's letter to the Colonial Office, dated Sept. 2, 1933

84. העולם, 31/3/30
85. AKKL, Files 311/315, Exhibit 80.
86. CZA S25/File 9835
87. Ibid.
88. PRO, CO 773/234/File 17282/ 141/33
89. Ibid., Document V/66/33
90. ISA, RG 22, LRO, G 568/File 5522/200/4
91. PRO, CO733/234/File 17282/E/42/76/93
92. AKKL, Files 311/315
93. Cnaan, p.50
94. ארלוזורוב, עמ' 49
95. CZA A238/File 11/5/2001
96. French Reports, p.60
97. PRO, CO733/214/File 97049/V/4/31
98. French Reports, p.20
99. Memorandum on White Paper, October 1930, Arab Executive
100. ארלוזורוב, עמ' 287
101. Ruppin, p.144
102. PRO, CO 733/214/File 97049/1020
103. Memorandum by the Jewish Agency on the Report of Lewis French, 1933, p.6
The memorandum was written by H. Arlosoroff
104. Ibid., p.29
105. Ibid.
106. נחמני, עמ' 79
107. Cnaan, p.50
108. עבר הדני, חדרה, עמ' 336
109. PRO, CO 733/202/File 87109
110. CZA S25/File 6954
111. CZA J15/File 6962/879
112. CZA A238/File 11
113. ספר תולדות הגנה, כרך ב', עמ' 454
Yitzhak Hankin, the son of the Shomer Yeheskel Hankin, was the one who was arrested and tried. Since it wasn't clear who had shot the Arab, Hankin volunteered to confess that he had done so in order to keep another Shomer, who was a family man, from standing trial.
114. CZA S25/File 6547
115. PRO, CO 733/251/File 37249
116. PRO, CO 733/260/File 75049/1/36
117. Royal Commission Memoranda, p.37 ff.
118. A survey for the Anglo-American Commitee, Vol. III., p.1214
119. גרנות, המשטר הקרקעי, עמ' 273
120. סמילנסקי, קמה, ספר השנה של הקהק"ל, תש"ח

121. גרנות, פרשת הקרקע בא״י, עמ׳ 37
122. גרנות, נתיבות ומפלסים, עמ׳ 36
123. Simpson Report p.50
124. Memorandum, Arab Executive Committee, December 1930
125. CZA S25/File 6492, Memorandum to U.N.S.C.O.P by the Arab Higher Committee.

CHAPTER SIX

1. Ben-Zevi Archive ,השאיפה אל הנגב
2. PRO, CO 733/4 /File 38832/249
3. Ibid.
4. CZA S25/File 9847
5. ניר, עמ׳ 118
6. French Reports, p.34 ff.
7. CZA S25/File 10/314
8. Simpson Report p.85
9. ניר, עמ׳ 127
10. PRO, CO 733/133/File 44072/1
11. Ibid., File 44072/17199
12. PRO, CO 733/155/File 57312
13. PRO, CO 733,170/File 207/ 5843/29
14. "The Ever-Present Absentee Landlords," **Davar,"** 13/12/29
15. Report to the Council of the League of Nations for the Year 1930, p.244
16. Royal Commission, Minutes of Evidence, p.227 ff.
17. Labour's Case Before the Royal Commission, London, 1937
    The letter of Mr. Berl Katzenelson on the Beit-Shean Lands.
18. ABH, personal archives of Manya Shohat, D/File 2
19. Royal Commission Report, p. 262
20. PRO, CO 733/203/File 87144/14/8
21. High Commissioner to the Colonial Office, 29/6/27, PRO, CO 733/137/ 44252/9837/27
22. Ibid, Vol. 137/File 44252
23. CZA, A238 /File 9
24. אשבל, ששים שנות הכשרת הישוב, עמ׳ 105
25. PRO, CO 733/137/File 44252
26. Ibid., Vol. 150/File 57149/ 15648/49
27. Ibid., Vol. 157/File 6710/
28. Ibid., Vol. 203/File 87144
29. Ibid./File 77169 (Secret)
30. CZA A238 /File 11/48/1721
31. Ibid., S25/ File 9846
32. Report to the Council of League of Nations for the Year 1935, p.27
33. CZA, S25 /File 3445

34. אשבל, ששים שנות הכשרת הישוב, עמ׳ 107

CHAPTER SEVEN

1. בייגן, עמ׳ 405 ואילך
2. ויץ, פירות, עמ׳ 12
3. ויץ, התנחלונו, עמ׳ 23
   אשבל, ששים שנות הכשרת הישוב, עמ׳ 126
5. פז, עמ׳ 222
6. Commission on the Disturbances, Vol. II. p. 732
7. גרנות, נתיבות ומפלסים, עמ׳ 36
8. CZA S25/File 7621
9. גנזך הוד השרון, מזכרונותיו של השומר אברהם דרויאן
10. Interview with Joshua Palmon, after 1948 adviser to Prime Minister Ben Gurion on Arab affairs; CZA, KKL5 /Box 1579/ File Ein-Hai.
11. תולדות אחת הכניות בא״י בימי הספפסרות של שנת תרפ״ה, ירושלים תרפ״ה
12. CZA S25/File 7621
13. Oved Ben-Ami in letter to author.
14. ויץ, התנחלותנו, עמ׳ 112
15. Oved Ben-Ami in letter to author.
16. דוד בן־גוריון, עמ׳ 23
17. Oved Ben-Ami in letter to author.
18. Ibid.
19. Ibid.
20. Mordecai Peled (one of the founders of Even Yehuda), letter to author.
21. Oved Ben-Ami in letter to author.
22. פורת, עמ׳ 251
23. Interview with Aharon Dannin.
24. Ibid.
25. CZA S25/File 6553
26. סמילנסקי, רחובות, עמ׳ 110
27. CZA, KKL 5 File 1580
28. סמילנסקי, רחובות, עמ׳ 110
29. פז, עמ׳ 239
30. אשבל, פרשיות ומפעלים, עמ׳ 215
31. Ibid., p.46
32. CZA L18/File 141/2 b/9/6

CHAPTER EIGHT

1. ויץ, התנחלותנו, עמ׳ 77
2. ויץ, יומני, חלק א׳, עמ׳ 222
3. CZA, KKL5 /Box 1189/ File Beit-Shean
4. ויץ, יומני, חלק א׳, עמ׳ 331
5. CZA, KKL5 /Box 1189/ File Biet-Shean
6. ויץ, יומני, חלק ג׳, עמ׳ 155

7. CZA, KKL5/ Box 1313/ File Sahne
8. Ibid.
9. Ibid./ Box 1189/ File Beit-Shean
10. ויץ, יומני, חלק א', עמ' 267; חלק ב' עמ' 115
11. ABH, Symbol D/ File 2 (See below chapter Nine, note 58)
12. CZA, KKL5/ Box 1189/ File Beit-Shean
13. ויץ, יומני, חלק ב', עמ' 176
14. Ibid., p/181
15. Ibid., p.182
16. CZA, KKL5, Box 1350/ File Mesil-Jizil; Box 1501/File Mesil-Jizil
17. ויץ, התנחלותנו, עמ' 85
18. Ibid.
19. CZA S25/ File 9838
20. CZA, KKL5/ Box 1198/ File Hanita
21. Ibid./Box 1186/File Hirbet Samah
22. Ibid./ Box 1349/File Mas'ub
23. Ibid./ Bo 1192/File Jidin
24. Ibid./Box 1187/File el Mihmesh
25. Ibid.
26. Ibid. /Box 1194/ File Daman
27. CZA S25/File 9846
28. ISA, RG2, CSO /File L 188/46
29. נחמני, עמ' 15
30. CZA, KKL5/ Box 1339/ File Hula
31. נחמני, עמ' 187
32. ABH, D/File 18/36
33. Interview with Nahum Hurwitz
34. נחמני, עמ' 230
35. ABH, D/ File 11/11
36. CZA, KKL5, /Box 1196/ File Hula
37. Ibid., letter, Hankin to Nahmani
38. נחמני, עמ' 179
39. ויץ, יומני, חלק ב', עמ' 55
40. ABH, D/File 12/43
41. Ibid.
42. Ibid. /Files 10, 18
43. ויץ, יומני, חלק ב', עמ' 115
44. ABH, D/ File 18/ 36
45. CZA, KKL5 /Box 1568/ File Hula/ 412 ZW
46. ספר תולדות ההגנה, כרך ג', עמ' 972
47. ויץ, יומני, חלק ג', עמ' 123, 125, 137
48. CZA, KKL5 /Box 1196/ File Hula
49. Ibid.
50. נחמני, עמ' 3-182
51. ויץ, יומני, חלק ב' עמ' 298
52. קרמון, עמק החולה הצפוני, עמ' 82
53. CZA S25 /File 6965
54. נחמני, ע"ע 117, 288 ואילך
55. ABH, D/File 18/ 84
56. Ibid./ File 18

57. CZA, KKL5 /Box 1776/ File Qedesh/ 1154 Q
58. Ibid. /Box 1189/ File Qedesh
59. Ibid./ Box 1776/ File Qedesh
60. Ibid. /Box 1759/ File Mesil Jizil/ 535M
61. Ibid. /Box 1769 /File Malkiya /66 ML
62. Beit Sturman Archive, File Sturman No. 2
63. CZA, KKL5 /File 1693, 9/6/29
64. Ibid./Box 1370/ File Tamra, Box 1362/ File Qumia
65. Ibid./Box 1460/ File Qumia /404/3
66. Ibid. /Box 1370/ File Tamra
67. Beit Sturman Archive /File 6
68. CZA A238 /File 10 /16/592
69. CZA S25 /File 6552
70. Ibid./Document No. 5721
71. CZA A238 /File 10/ 16/1383
72. Interview with Aharon Dannin
73. Beit Sturman Archive /File 5
74. Zevi Wolff, in the name of the Palestine Land Development Company to the Jewish National Fund, CZA, KKL5, Box 1453 /File Na'ura
75. ויץ, יומני, חלק א', עמ' 149
76. CZA, KKL5 /Box 1748 /File Tira/ 4370
77. Ibid./Box 1577/ File Tira
78. Ibid./ Box 1454 /Files 'Ulam, Ma'ader
79. ויץ, יומני חלק ג' עמ' 94
80. CZA, KKL5 /Box 1346 /File Kafer-Miser/ 1433
81. Ibid./Box 1577 /File Kafar-Miser /181/ Sh KM
82. Ibid./ Box 1555/ File Umm el Ranem
83. Ibid./ Box 1565/ File Daburiya; 268
84. Ibid./Box 1438/ File Daburiya; ויץ, יומני, חלק ב', עמ' 268
85. Interview with Aharon Dannin
86. Report of Zur Company to Jewish National Fund, CZA, KKL5 /Box 1192/ File Ju'ara
87. Ibid. J15 /File 319
88. ויץ, יומני, חלק א', עמ' 263
89. CZA, KKL5 /Box 1192/ File Umm Dafuf /Envelope 1
90. Ibid.
91. Ibid./Box 1196/ File Hubeize–Buteimat
92. ויץ, התנחלותנו, ע"ע 3-152
93. ויץ, יומני, חלק ב', עמ' 272
94. ספר תולדות ההגנה, כרך ג', עמ' 971
95. ויץ, יומני, חלק ג', עמ' 178
96. שם, חלק ב', עמ' 148
97. שם, חלק ג', עמ' 95
98. שם, חלק ב', עמ' 164

297

99. CZA, KKL5 /Box 1195/ File Wadi Qabani

100. CZA S25 /File 6552, 21/1/31

101. CZA KKL5 /Box 1195/ File Wadi Qabani/ 32/9, 26/6/39

102. Ibid.,/Box 1388/ 64/204

103. Ibid./Document 64/465

104. Ibid./Documents 64/1107, 211/18432

105. AKKL/ File 311/315 /Exhibit 50, Judgment 1/5/39/ Document JAO/ASH

106. ויץ, פירות, עמ' 164 ואילך

107. CZA S25 /File 9835

108. ויץ, פירות, עמ' 171

109. Ibid., p. 172 ff.

110. ויץ, התנחלותנו, עמ' 112

111. CZA, KKL5 /Box 1199 /File Taiyibe

112. Ibid., 8/3/37

113. Ibid.

114. Ibid./Box 1198/ Files Even-Yehuda, Tel Zur

115. ויץ, התנחלותנו, עמ' 112

116. Ibid., pp. 131, 141

117. Report of Hiram Donnin to Jewish National Fund, 31/3/42 CZA, KKL5 /Box 1432/ File Negev

118. Ibid./Box 1200 /File Yavne

119. Ibid.-List of Indemnification payments 3/12/37

120. ISA, RG2, CSO, L28/40A, 12/3/47

121. Letter of Jamal el-Husseini. CZA, KKL5/ Box 1205/ File Idhniba

122. Ibid., 27/4/38

123. Ibid., Box 1369/ File as-Safi, 22/4/41

124. Ibid./ Box 1194/ File Negev

125. Ibid.,/ File Huj

126. ויץ, יומני, חלק ב', עמ' 151

127. CZA, KKL5 /Box 1454/ File Sumsum/ 320/43

128. Dr. Ben-Shemesh in letter to Jewish National Fund. CZA, KKL5/ File Sumsum

129. Ibid.

130. ויץ, יומני, חלק ב', ע"ע 4‾83

131. CZA, KKL5 /Box 1456/ File iraq el-Manshiya

132. Ibid./Box 1568/ File Rena

133. ויץ, יומני, חלק ב' עמ' 252

134. CZA, KKL5 /Box 1433/ File Beit-Hanun

135. Ibid./Box 1337/ File Negev

136. ויץ, יומני, חלק ב' עמ' 167

137. Ibid., p.248

138. CZA, KKL5 /Boxes 1575, 1758/ File Majdal

139. Ibid./ Box 1454/ File Negev

140. Ibid./Box 1459/ File Negev

141. ויץ, יומני, חלק ג', עמ' 167

142. ויץ, יומני, חלק ב', עמ' 307

143. ויץ, התנחלותנו, ע"ע 143‾141, 196–195

CHAPTER NINE

1. גרנות, המשטר הקרקעי, עמ' 271

2. Ibid., p.270

3. Ibid., p.271

4. CZA S25/File 6482, Memorandum of Arab Higher Committee to U.N-.S.C.O.P.

5. פורת, עמ' 105;ספר תולדות ההגנה, חלק ב', עמ' 88

6. CZA S25 /File 7443

7. פורת, עמ' 214

8. CZA S25 /File 7621

9. ספר תולדות ההגנה, חלק ב', עמ' 93

10. CZA, KKL5 /Box 1575/ File Ein-Hai

11. שמעוני, עמ' 225

12. Interview with Joshua Palmon

13. פורת, עמ' 251

14. Oved Ben-Ami, who took part in the purchase of the land, in letter to author, 29/12/77

15. שמעוני, עמ' 223; ספר תולדות ההגנה, חלק ב', עמ' 83

16. פורת, עמ' 184

17. שמעוני, עמ' 227; ספר תולדות ההגנה, חלק ב', עמ' 459

18. CZA, KKL5 /Box 1433/ File Beit-Hanun

19. אשבל, פרשיות המפעלים, עמ' 151

20. Ibid., p.159

21. פורת, עמ' 255

22. ויץ, יומני, חלק ב', עמ' 252

23. שמעוני, עמ' 233;פורת, עמ' 105

24. CZA S25/ File 3289

25. Ibid./File 3472

26. פורת, עמ' 154; שמעוני, עמ' 234

27. Oved Ben-Ami, see note 14.

28. פפורת, עמ' 142

29. CZA S25 /File 9783

30. פורת, עמ' 60

31. CZA S25 /File 9783

32. Ibid.

33. CZA, KKL5 /Box1205/ File Idhniba

34. Ibid./Box 1337/ File Negev

35. ויץ, יומני, חלק א', עמ' 267; חלק ב' עמ' 115

36. CZA S25 /File 4022

37. פורת, עמ' 252

38. CZA S25 /File 9783

39. נחמני, עמ' 227

40. פורת, עמ' 180 ואילך

298

41. CZA S25 /File 7621/ Document No. 7247
42. אשבל, פרשיות ומפעלים, עמ' 44
43. ויץ, יומני, חלק ב', עמ' 148
44. אשבל, פרשיות ומפעלים, עמ' 46
45. CZA S25 /File 7621 / 7247
46. פורת עמ' 252
47. CZA S25 /File 7446
48. Ibis./Document 1133/4152
49. כרכור, עמ' 27
50. CZA S25 /File 6953
51. CZA A238 /File 10
52. Beit Sturman Archive /File 2, report by Haim Sturman
53. Ibid.
54. ספר תולדות ההגנה, חלק ב', עמ' 654
55. CZA S25 /File 10098
56. CZA, KKL5 /Box 1456/ File 'Iraq el-Manshiya
57. ארנון, עמ' 128
58. ויץ, יומני, חלק א', עמ' 158
Joshua Palmon, who read the manuscript, told the author that at the beginning of 1978 he met Mussa el-'Alami at his home in Jericho. When asked why he sold land to the Jews, 'Alami replied that he handed over the Power of Attorney to Dr. Cnaan, to do with his share as he saw fit, and Cnaan was the one who made the sale.
59. ויץ, יומני, חלק ב', עמ' 151
60. CZA, KKL5 /Box 1454/ File Sumsum
61. ויץ, יומני, חלק ב', עמ' 16
62. שמעוני, עמ' 226
63. פורת, עמ' 251
64. Interview with Joshua Palmon
65. CZA L18 /File 141/2/9/6/1
66. ויץ, יומני, חלק ג', עמ' 338
67. שמעוני, עמ' 226
68. CZA, KKL5 /Boxes 1575, 1758/ File Majdal
69. שמעוני, עמ' 236
70. פורת, עמ' 204
71. אשבל, פרשיות ומפעלים, עמ' 215
72. פורת, עמ' 140
73. Porath, p.164
74. CZA, KKL5 /Box 1199/ File Taiyibe
75. פורת, ע"ע 252, 255
76. CZA S25 /File 7446 / 1133/4152
77. Ibid./File 1580
78. Porath, p.38 ff.

CHAPTER TEN

1. גרנות, נתיבות ומפלסים, עמ' 36
2. ויץ, מגמדא לרווחא, עמ' 93, ניר עמ' 131

3. קדמון, עמק החולה הצפוני,עמ' 81
4. ויץ, מגמדא לרווחא, עמ' 138
5. Ibid.
6. גרנות, נתיבות ומפלסים, עמ' 37
7. Royal Commission Report, p.256
8. CZA, KKL5 /File 1570
9. ויץ, מגמדא לרווחא, עמ' 144
10. Ibid., p.75
11. Ibid., p.93
12. Royal Commission Report, p.260
13. Conder, Vol. II, p.261
14. ויץ, פירות, עמ' 78
15. ויץ, מגמדא לרווחא, עמ' 156
16. Ibid., p. 266
17. 20 שנה לקיבוץ חצרים

CHAPTER ELEVEN

1. בן-גוריון, עמ' 19
2. Ruppin pp. 63-64
3. שאיפותינו, חוברת ב', עמ' 169
4. Shaw Report, p.115
5. CZA S25 /File 6553 /K326/31
6. Ruppin, p.262
7. Ibid., p265
8. Ibid p.266
9. Memorandum on White Paper of October 1930 by Arab Executive, p.5
10. Porath, p.94
11. גרנות, נתיבות ומפלסים, עמ' 51 ואילך
12. Ibid., p.53
13. אשבל, ששים שנות הכשרת הישוב, עמ' 96 ואילך
14. CZA KKL5 /Box 1196/ File Hula
15. שרת, חלק א', עמ' 57
16. Memorandum on white Paper of October 1930 by Arab Executive, p.30

CHAPTER TWELVE

1. Notes compiled for U.N.S.C.O.P., p.12
2. Bacchi, p.398
3. Ibid., p.400
4. אטלס ישראל, ירושלים, תשט"ז מפת צפי-פות האוכלוסין 2/ ×
5. Bacchi, p.400
6. יהושע בן-אריה pp.159, 228, 304, 318 (Data for the Year 1880-1900); Government census (Data for 1922); Notes compiled for U.N.S.C.O.P. (Data for 1946).
7. Vital statistical tables 1922-1946 (for 1922 data); Notes compiled for U.N.S.C.O.P., pages 12-13, (for data for December 31, 1946).
8. The Tiberias figure refers to 1931

9. See Note 7

10. ארץ כנרות, עמ' 155

11. Royal Commission Report, p.234

12. Notes compiled for U.N.S.C.O.P., page 37

13. אברמוביץ־גלפט, עמ' 49

14. Department of Agriculture, Annual Report for the Year 1945/46. The figures in the Report refer to total production. 38,000 dunam and 54,000 tons which relate to Jewish agriculture were subtracted from these figures.

15. ואשיץ, עמ' 370

16. Survey for the Anglo-American Committee, Vol. I. p.232

17. Statistical Abstract for the Year 1943, p.73

18. See Notes 16 and 17

19. *The Jewish Plan for Palestine*, p.419

20. אברמוביץ־גלפט, ע"ע 48ֿ47

21. עלון לסטטיסטיקה ואינפורמציה מקצועית של ההסתדרות, חוברת 4, עמ' 16

22. Census of Palestine 1931, Vol.II, p.547

23. See Note 21

24. Ibid.

25. Royal Commission Report, p.318

26. See Note 21

27. Ibid.

28. Statistical Abstract for the Year 1945

29. Survey for the Anglo-American Committee, Vol. I., p.323 ff.

30. Royal Commission Report, p.126

31 Ibid.

32. Memorandum on Influence of Jewish Colonisation on Arab Development.

33. Survey for the Anglo-American Committee, Vol. I, p.532

34. אברמוביץ־גלפט, עמ' 83

35. *The Jewish Plan for Palestine*, p.434

36. Ibid., p.432

37. אסף, היחסים בין יהודים וערבים, עמ' 226

38. ואשיץ, עמ' 360

39. Survey for the Anglo-American Committee, Vol. II, p.714

40. Report to Council of League of Nations for the Year 1925, p.5

41. Survey for Anglo-American Committee, Vol. II, p.637

42. Statistical Abstract, 1943

43. Survey for the Anglo-American Committee, Vol. II, p.642

CHAPTER THIRTEEN

1. ספר תולדות ההגנה, כרך ג', עמ' 1439

2. גילברט, מפה 15

3. David Hacohen to Moshe Sharett, CZA S25 /File 10098.

4. Ibid.

5. Marie Syrkin, p.160

6. Ibid., p.167

7. Collins-Lapierre, p.386

8. ספר תולדות ההגנה, כרך ג', עמ' 1547

9. Bacchi, p.400

10. אסף, התעוררות הערבים, עמ' 331

11. בעיני אויב, עמ' 18

12. אסף, התעוררות הערבים, עמ' 334

13. בעיני אויב, עמ' 34

14. In a letter to the author, 19/3/77

15. בגליל העליון, עמ' 45

16. Survey for the Anglo-American Committee, Vol. I., p.142

17. "דבר", 19/7/77

18. Prittie and Dinnen, p.5

19. Bacchi, p.400

20. Bacchi, p.401

21. שנתון הממשלה, מס. 11: פרסומי המחלקה לסטטיסטיקה, עמ' 7

22. Ibid.

23. Ibid.

24. Bacchi, p.402

25. ממי, עמ' 9

26. ספר תולדות ההגנה, כרך ג', עמ' 98

27. Maurice M. Roumani, p.18

28. גילברט, מפה מס. 15

INDEX

302